Gender Heretics

Gender Heretics

Evangelicals, Feminists, and the Alliance Against Trans Liberation

Rebecca Jane Morgan

First published 2023 by Pluto Press
New Wing, Somerset House, Strand, London WC2R 1LA
and Pluto Press, Inc.
1930 Village Center Circle, 3-834, Las Vegas, NV 89134

www.plutobooks.com

British Library Cataloguing in Publication Data
A catalogue record for this book is available from the British Library

ISBN 978 0 7453 4901 5 Paperback
ISBN 978 0 7453 4903 9 PDF
ISBN 978 0 7453 4902 2 EPUB

This book is printed on paper suitable for recycling and made from fully
managed and sustained forest sources. Logging, pulping and manufacturing
processes are expected to conform to the environmental standards of the
country of origin.

Typeset by Stanford DTP Services, Northampton, England

Simultaneously printed in the United Kingdom and United States of America

Contents

Preface: A tower to the heavens

What do you think about when you hear the word *evangelical*? Do you think of 'good news', in line with the Greek etymology of the word? Do you think of belonging, family, and selflessness? Do you think of gentle people powered by a longing to be more like Jesus? Or are you forced into a defensive mental posture, ready to deal with whatever religiously justified bigotry might be coming your way? The latter reaction is far more common in our contemporary world. So often, *evangelical* means cultural conformity and the suppression of diversity; it means Donald Trump; it means weird televangelists, doomsday preppers, and peddlers of quack medicine; it means vaccine scepticism; it means conspiracy theories; it means ostentatiously wealthy pastors; it means lobbyists who do their damnedest to stop social justice dead in its tracks; it means unwelcome, insensitive moralising; it means patriarchy, misogyny, and homophobia; it means the very antithesis of a secular, progressive, pluralistic, multicultural, caring, open, democratic society. In short, it signals for many the worst news they could ever hear.

Today, *evangelicalism* also colloquially stands for transphobia. Scan the homepage of a mainstream news outlet during one of the media's periodic bouts of unhealthy obsession with trans people, or scroll through the records of recent government policy consultations on matters of gender identity, and you will find that the bulk of political transphobia seems to arise from two main blocs: conservative evangelicals and anti-trans feminists. What happened? How did it come to pass that so many evangelicals in the UK and across the world are now so deeply entrenched in a politicised opposition to all things gender-nonconforming, becoming in the process a major roadblock to trans liberation? How did they come to share this trait with anti-trans feminists, whose politics differ from their own on practically every other major question? And must this be the case? That is to say, is there anything essential to the evangelical worldview that leads directly to transphobic attitudes, and if not, how do we find our way out of the bog? These are the questions I explore in this book from my admittedly rather unusual vantage point as a trans evangelical feminist.

Like so many before us, we lie now in the rubble of our very own Tower of Babel. In the biblical narrative of Genesis, a poetic retelling of the creation of humanity and the birth of the nation of Israel, the first humans were instructed by their Creator to 'fill the earth and subdue it' (Genesis 1:28).* Despite millennia of pondering, we still fall well short of knowing exactly what this means, but we do know that it *does not* mean exerting sheer might over those around us, for it is the 'heroes that were of old, warriors of renown' whose actions demonstrated to God, before the Flood, that 'the wickedness of humans was great in the earth' (6:4–5). Nor does it mean the consolidation of languages and cultures beneath a single regime. At first, it is told that 'the nations spread abroad on the earth after the flood', and that each clan had its own language (10:32). As for the people of Babel, however, it was as if 'the whole earth had one language and the same words' (11:1). They consolidated in one place, in stifling uniformity, and said to each other: 'Come, let us build ourselves a city and a tower with its top in the heavens, and let us make a name for ourselves, otherwise we shall be scattered abroad upon the face of the whole earth' (11:4), and so they pierced the sky, erecting of fired bricks their Tower of vanity. As the story goes, God saw then that 'this is only the beginning of what they will do; nothing that they propose to do will now be impossible for them', so thence were they dispersed again 'over the face of all the earth', their arrogant affectations of sameness shattered, their diversity restored in beautiful, befuddling, pluriform chaos (11:6–8).

About the turn of the modern era, the Western world began to build up another Tower – a monolithic culture enforced through banal bureaucratic evil and a far-reaching monopolisation of colonial violence. In its shadow, the global bustle of languages, art forms, architectures, clothing norms, musical styles, mythologies and political systems was tamed, torn and then erased. And in

---

* Unless otherwise stated, all Bible quotations are from the New Revised Standard Version Updated Edition (NRSVUE).

this guarded Tower, just a few storeys up, there sat modern gender roles – that cocksure constitution that tells us: *this* is a woman, and *this* is a man. Nothing more. Two options. Two ways of walking, talking, dressing, working, living, loving, thinking and dying, while all else is deemed a remnant degeneracy from an uncivilised age. Two categories anachronistically projected onto the religiously mythologised past, as if those living in biblical times would have recognised the symbols and styles that mark modern manhood and womanhood.

We are only now beginning to outgrow this spiritual straitjacket. We are returning, not a moment too soon, to the knowledge that there are many more ways to *be* on this earthen plane than those synthetic simplicities etched onto the Tower's walls. As the physical environment groans beneath the Tower's influence, the invisible world that spans our souls groans too for release. Slowly, painfully, the dead weight of received wisdom is being lifted, and human life, in gusts of urgent breath, though belaboured still by global imbalances of economic and political power, is bursting free again to fill the planet with the diversity of the colours of infinity. *That* is what I invite Christians and non-Christians alike to see in the ongoing explosion of confident, proud, happy, creative and determined trans and non-binary people onto the centre stage of our cultural discourse. Not heresy, as is often claimed; nor haughtiness, nor deception, nor perversion, nor the destruction of what is real, but the antidote to such ills – the love of creation in its stunning entirety, and the muttering, sputtering, babbling embers of a defiant hope.

Acknowledgements

Thanks are due to my three PhD supervisors, Onni Gust, Laura Schwartz and Dean Blackburn, who have been a constant source of inspiration, ideas and reassurance, and to Midlands4Cities and the Arts and Humanities Research Council for funding the PhD project from which this book stems. I would like to thank David Shulman and the team at Pluto Press for their enthusiastic support throughout the writing process. I would also like to thank Tom Cordiner, my undergraduate dissertation supervisor, for giving me the passion and confidence to pursue an academic career; Lucy Delap, whose MPhil module on sexuality and gender helped me no end in identifying my research interests, and all the friends with whom I have shared ideas and frustrations during my doctoral studies. I must also extend my gratitude to my chosen family in Grace Church Nottingham and the Nottingham Meeting of the Society of Friends. Finally, my thanks go to my partner and fiancé, Leonardo Le Good, whose steadfast love imbued me with the energy to write such a book in the first place.

Acknowledgements

Introduction

God grant me the serenity to accept the things I cannot change, the courage to change the things I can, and the wisdom to know the difference.
    – The Serenity Prayer, adopted as 'A Prayer for Transsexuals' by the Self-Help Association for Transsexuals, a UK trans advocacy group, in 1980.[1]

Sunday, 13 February 2022 – In the persistent drizzle and mildly cold winds that characterise the English winter, professional anti-trans agitator and YouTuber Kellie-Jay Keen, also known as Posie Parker, assembled with a few dozen raincoat-donning supporters at Speakers' Corner, a popular spot for demonstrations in central Nottingham. Keen's muffled, meandering speech, delivered beneath a statue of the famous footballer Brian Clough, stumbled through the predictable range of anti-trans talking points – she claimed that cisgender women are no longer safe in public bathrooms because *men* might be in there; that binary sex must remain a legally codified societal dividing line in order to protect said women from cross-dressing ne'er-do-wells; that children are being turned trans by mischievous, ideologically motivated doctors; that trans activists are 'silencing' cisgender feminists who question their political demands; and so on. Apparently unsated by reciting the Golden Oldies, Keen at one point turned to one of the trans counter-protestors arrayed behind her and asked, to the audible approval of her bellicose supporters: 'How is it that you think you can call yourself a woman?' Those watching the event through Keen's YouTube livestream savoured the skirmish by adjudicating over which counter-protestors *looked* trans: 'its [sic] the hands and the necks', one viewer suggested, 'they just can't hide it. you can always tell.'[2] This was ugly trench warfare.

1

In other words, there was nothing to distinguish Keen's little Sunday gathering from any of the hundreds of micro-demonstrations organised across the United Kingdom in recent years by an obsessive subculture of cis people, primarily White women, known to their opponents as *Trans-Exclusionary Radical Feminists* (TERFs).[3] Members of this cantankerous political niche, including well-known feminist academics like Kathleen Stock and massively influential celebrities like J. K. Rowling, typically prefer to be known by the term *gender critical*. This alternative nomenclature refers to their belief that, in fighting against trans rights, they are primarily critiquing the oppressive structures undergirding gender stereotypes and, in so doing, rejecting the pretensions that 'men', meaning trans women, have a right to help shape how women-as-a-whole respond to this structural oppression.[4] The swap is also made because those in question consider TERF to be a misogynistic slur,[5] although it remains a ubiquitous signifier of transphobia in many trans communities. Ask almost any trans person to point to a specific anti-trans group, and they are more than likely to say 'TERFs'.

A sharp little acronym that rolls effortlessly off the tongue (or thumbs), the label TERF actually represents something of an inelegant mishmash of ideas, strategies, histories and political trajectories blended together mostly for linguistic convenience.[6] Viv Smythe, the Australian blogger credited with coining it in 2008, has written that it 'came about simply to save typing a longer phrase out over and over again – a shorthand to describe one cohort of feminists who self-identify as radical and are unwilling to recognise trans women as sisters, unlike those of us who do'.[7]

However, its meaning has long since departed from Smythe's original intentions. Trans historian and activist Cristan Williams identifies TERFs as 'those individuals who sympathize with and support a brand of "radical feminism" that is so rooted in sex essentialism and its resulting biologism [that] it actively campaigns against the existence, equality, and/or inclusion of trans people'.[8]

This specialised definition serves a practical purpose for trans activists, who are daily engaged in tracking and countering a highly motivated band of anti-trans feminists, and are consequently interested in what these people *do* as much as what they *believe*. On the other hand, some scholars are more interested in TERFism's utility as a general ideological classification rather than as a way of life. Sociologist Sally Hines, in this vein, defines TERFism mainly in relation to its philosophical basis in 'a rigid reading of the sex/ gender binary', as opposed to tethering it to the precise political aims that might stem from that belief.[9] In practice, however, TERF acts as little more than an us-and-them signifier – especially on social media, where some users loosely apply it to *anyone* who has knowingly expressed anti-trans views.

Much of the definitional malaise arises from the 'E' in the acronym. As Smythe explains, *exclusionary* originally referred to a refusal to see trans women as 'sisters' in the feminist cause, but this purificatory attitude often extends to a practical desire to exclude trans people from *all* women's spaces, such as bathrooms, prayer groups and rape crisis centres, not just feminist discussion groups. An exclusionary attitude can also euphemistically signal a desire to limit access to life-improving (often life-*saving*) trans healthcare, most especially for trans minors – an objective that trans scholars Ezra Horbury and Christine Yao refer to as a specialist subcat-egory of 'eugenics'.[10] The specification that a TERF is not just a feminist, but a *radical* feminist, can also cause some semantic dif-ficulty, since the label *radical feminism* is historically specific and denotes a boldly confrontational strand of feminist thought that reached maturity in the 1960s and 1970s, contemporaneous but not interchangeable with 'second-wave' feminism and the Women's Liberation Movement. Broadly speaking, radical feminists believe that patriarchal power is upheld by deep structural foundations in culture and politics that work *to the express benefit* of men, rather than simply by a web of isolated misogynistic actions *by* men. As explained by veteran American radical feminist Ellen Willis:

> We argued that male supremacy was in itself a systemic form of domination – a set of material, institutionalized relations, not just bad attitudes. Men had power and privilege and … challeng-ing that power required a revolutionary movement of women … Our model … was black power – a number of the early radical feminists had been civil rights activists.[11]

Gender theorists Robyn Rowland and Renate Klein write that the 'revolutionary intent' voiced by the likes of Willis 'is expressed first and foremost in [radical feminism's] woman-centredness'.[12] As a movement *by* women and *for* women, radical feminism is premised on ending the cycle of socialised female submission that sustains the abhorrent apparatuses of male domination. In the 1970s, this meant the formation of new campaign organisations less prone to gradualism and assimilationism than the old 'first-wave' mainstays like the Women's Institute; it meant new demands, including easier access to abortion, 24-hour childcare services free at the point of use, and the destigmatisation of lesbian relationships; it also meant louder, more visible, more irreverent public protests against the sexualisation, domestication and infantilisation of women.[13] None of these things can individually be described as the exclusive preserve of the radical feminist, but activists and scholars have nonetheless found semantic utility in historically delineating a radical feminist tradition that *combines* these characteristics.

Nothing in radical feminism's DNA leads inevitably to a greater degree of transphobia than is evident in other feminisms. Trans Marxist theorist Rosa Lee, among others, argues that its reliance on *woman* as a 'coherent and stable subject' does make it prone to hostility towards trans people if it perceives them to threaten that coherence, but Lee points out that 'mainstream contemporary liberal feminism' is not so different in this regard.[14] That there are many self-labelled radical feminists who vitriolically oppose trans rights is undeniable – we will encounter many of them in Chapter 2 – but these individuals are, despite appearances, a relatively small minority within both radical feminism and the wider world of political transphobia. Some of the most outspoken anti-trans figures either have no meaningful connection to radical feminism at all, or are influenced by, and pay lip service to, many ideologies simultaneously. If they did not self-describe as feminists of some variety, it would often be difficult to detect in them anything but a vaguely establishment-liberal reformist aesthetic with a mild feminist tinge. As we will see, this makes it exceedingly difficult to meaningfully distinguish between the TERF and non-TERF iterations of anti-trans sentiment, as 'TERFs' are just one piston in a much larger machinery of hate, and Kellie-Jay Keen is no more than a notoriously graceless, seething example of a much broader socio-political phenomenon in the age of trans people's inescapable, contentious, and often inauspicious visibility. However, while committed anti-trans feminists are not particularly numerous, they *are* zealous and willing to travel long distances to create the type of spectacle seen in Nottingham that February weekend.

An hour or so into Keen's demonstration, each side evidently satisfied with a good day's yelling and no doubt tiring of the rain, the crowd dispersed to find shelter, warmth and friendly company. After coffee with one of my academic supervisors who had also been at the protest, I too returned to my usual Sunday routine. Attempting, not very effectively, to reset my mind from the earlier excitement, I set off to church, and I was overcome at that moment by an invasive juxtaposition. Going from a queer rights counter-protest in the morning to a charismatic evangelical church in the afternoon would strike most people as an oxymoronic, even self-denying sequence of activities, giving Jesus' saying 'do not let your left hand know what your right hand is doing' (Matthew 6:3) an awkwardly sardonic twist. I was reminded as I passed over the church's threshold and into our modern-ish building of all the conversations I have had with other trans and queer people about faith and gender over the previous few months. Why, they sometimes wondered, would I willingly put myself in that kind of environment? Won't the church try to 'cure' me? Am I safe there? After all, aren't evangelicals *transphobic*? The re-emergence of *that* word, already the theme of my day up to that point, gave me pause. Am I living a contradiction?

For all intents and purposes, it might seem that I have a foot in two diametrically opposed camps. Evangelicals are obviously and manifestly to be counted among 'our' most determined oppressors, and trans activism is obviously and manifestly an affront to 'our' values. Of course, setting aside my own experiences of love, acceptance, family and growth in my faith community, this is an entirely well-founded train of thought. I cannot simply ignore the paradox, being only too aware of the shameful invective that some representatives of the evangelical movement have produced in their efforts to stall and reverse trans people's slow, agonising journey towards legal and social justice, not to mention the innumerable attempts at administering the mental horror-show that is trans-to-cis conversion 'therapy' in some evangelical churches.[15] Nor, for that matter, can I avoid the fact that, in sheer tirelessness and depth of ignorance, the anti-trans activism of certain conservative evangelical lobbyists in organisations like the Christian Institute, Christian Concern, and the Family Education Trust is rivalled only by 'TERFs' in the style of Keen, Stock and Rowling. Despite their immense cultural and philosophical differences, these lobbyists often share rhetorical space with said 'TERFs' in television segments, social media discourses and government consultations on gender-related policies including, most recently, gender recognition reform and a proposed ban on conversion 'therapy'. So complete is this overlap that journalists reporting on the so-called 'trans debate' – the network of controversies raised by trans people's existence and their demands for dignity – routinely cite the opinions of evangelicals and anti-trans feminists in conjunction, as if these are nothing more than two superficially variant expressions of the view that trans identity is invalid and that trans people should not be afforded any enhancement to their sparse, fragile legal rights.[16] The Scottish Government's 2021 analysis of the responses to its public consultation on reforming the Gender Recognition Act (2004) casually notes that 'the considerable majority of the Women's Groups and Religious or Belief Bodies that responded' took the same position – that there should be no loosening of the current mechanism for changing one's legal gender.[17]

The evangelical Christian movement is no less difficult to pin down than TERFism. The premier historian of evangelical religion in Britain, the late David W. Bebbington, placed its origins in the wave of intense, life-changing personal conversion experiences that swept parts of the British Isles in the 1730s. His quadrilateral definition, offered in his ground-breaking book *Evangelicalism in Modern Britain: A History from the 1730s to the 1980s* (1989), sees the movement as being set apart from other forms of Christianity by four basic characteristics: *conversionism*, a belief in the importance of the conversion experience as an effusively emotional and holistic reorientation of one's mind and soul towards Jesus; *activism*, a calling to evangelise proactively; *biblicism*, a belief in the Bible's divine inspiration and an affirmation of the inerrant (though not necessarily literal) truth of its contents, and *crucicentrism*, a re-centring of the victory Christ is believed to have won over death and sin on the cross, as undergirded by the doctrine of substitutionary atonement (the notion that *we* deserved to be on the cross, but that Christ chose to bear our sin for us and so set us free).[18]

Of these four ingredients, *biblicism* is perhaps the one that can most easily be associated with homophobia and transphobia, although, in practice, this depends on extra-biblical judgements concerning the applicability of some passages of the Bible to our modern circumstances, and on the extent to which one allows for metaphor, exception, nuance and mistranslation in one's reading of the text. While transphobia *is* undeniably an influential force within modern evangelical discourses, and *is* justified in evangelical spaces in a recognisably biblicist fashion, it is not an *inevitable* outcome of an evangelical approach to reading the Bible any more than is the belief, based on the biblical genealogies, that the Earth was created around 6,000 years ago. As will become apparent in later pages, evangelical transphobia stems from a selective reading of particular passages in ways that are built not upon the immovable foundations of faith, but rather upon culturally contingent anti-trans political beliefs that were absorbed (often from unexpected sources) by certain evangelical theologians over the past half-century.

Another important aspect of the modern evangelical movement is its sometimes tense relationship with broader intellectual and cultural trends. Evangelicals are often assumed to harbour resentment for all things stemming from post-Enlightenment scientific inquiry and cultural pluralism, an impression based partly on the linguistic association of *evangelicalism* as a whole with a specific type of *White*, *American* and *right-wing* evangelicalism that explicitly combines church affiliation with reactionary voting patterns and cultural insularity.[19] However, Bebbington notes that evangelicalism is in fact 'permeated by Enlightenment influences', as evident not least in its rhetorical attachment to empiricist deductive methodology.[20] Ask an evangelical why they trust in God, and you are far more likely to be answered with a series of stories and personal proofs than with metaphysical philosophising. Evangelicalism's promise is that *I experienced this, and you can too*, and evangelical belief in this sense interplays with one's personal circumstances.

There is limited data concerning the number of evangelical Christians in Britain. Twenty-seven per cent of respondents to a 2007 study on churchgoing in the UK by the Christian charity Tearfund self-described as evangelicals, which would extrapolate proportionally to around 2 million people as per the 2001 Census demographics.[21] However, as more Britons report having no religious affiliation,[22] it is likely that, if the 2 million figure was ever close to the mark, the evangelical population has declined since 2007 in line with these general demographic trends. Despite this, as is attested throughout this book, evangelical parachurch organisations and lobby groups are often highly energetic, exerting a disproportionate influence on public discourse; and, due to the power dynamics within the movement, said organisations very often cling to the most 'fundamentalist' social views.

With 'TERFism' and 'evangelicalism' defined (as best they can be), we must now turn to *transphobia*. The fact that so many feminists and evangelicals seem to be fighting on the same side in the 'trans debate' and the wider culture wars has caused trans activists, historians, philosophers, theologians and sociologists a great many headaches. Both factions are considered 'transphobic' in a purely colloquial sense, but what does that adjective signify when it is applied to so wide a dispersion of ideologies? When it describes everything from the use of incorrect pronouns and other microaggressions to housing discrimination, hostile political campaigning, media erasure, sexual violence and murder? When its effects are uneven and depend on intersecting factors like race, class and immigration status?[23] And when it might be for one trans individual an occasional annoyance, but for another a daily existential threat? What is it, specifically, that characterises a transphobic group in thought, action, or intention?

There is no denying that transphobia, not unlike homophobia, xenophobia, Islamophobia, antisemitism, ableism and other reactionary socio-political proclivities, is inherently slippery. Attempts at codifying a wieldy definition tend only to multiply the questions. The most influential attempt at codification, that offered by transfeminist* writer Julia Serano in her seminal *Whipping Girl: A Transsexual Woman on Sexism and the Scapegoating of Femininity* (2007), goes as follows:

> Transphobia is an irrational fear of, aversion to, or discrimination against people whose gendered identities, appearances, or behaviors deviate from societal norms. In much the same way that homophobic people are often driven by their own repressed homosexual tendencies, transphobia is first and foremost an expression of one's own insecurity about having to live up to cultural gender ideals.[24]

The first sentence in this passage, which is identical or similar to definitions now found in common dictionaries,[25] aims to establish *what* transphobia looks like in society, essentially incorporating any external anthropogenic force that might negatively impact upon trans people's lives as a direct result of their being trans. The second sentence purports to give us some insight into the *who* and *why*, but it offers little detail, telling us simply that transphobes are often those who themselves fall short of the strictures of gendered behaviour, which, depending on your interpretation, could refer to just about anybody. In light of its obvious definitional shortcomings, trans philosopher Talia Mae Bettcher noted in 2014 that, although it clearly exists, 'it is far from evident what transphobia *is*.'[26] The problem is twofold; first, the composition of the word implies irrationality, yet Bettcher observes that transphobia 'occurs in a broader social context that systematically disadvantages trans people and promotes and rewards antitrans sentiment. It therefore has a kind of rationality to it.' Second, while rationality surely requires some identifiable intellectual content, in real conversations *transphobia* can refer to many different attitudes, actions, or

---

* Emi Koyama defines transfeminism as a strand of feminism 'by and for trans women who view their liberation to be intrinsically linked to the liberation of all women and beyond'. See E. Koyama, 'The transfeminist manifesto' in R. Dicker and A. Piepmeier (eds.), *Catching a wave: reclaiming feminism for the 21ˢᵗ century* (Lebanon, NH: Northeastern University Press, 2003), pp. 244–59.

9

ideas, and is difficult to pin down. Bettcher therefore concludes that the word in its colloquial form is nothing more than a 'place-holder for the real intellectual work that remains to be done'.[27]

This book is, in part, an historian's attempt to do some portion of that intellectual work. It might seem a thankless task, as transphobia is popularly regarded as intellectually void, being similar in this characteristic to the way that some see the British Conservative Party, which was described in a timeless quip by the great philosopher-politician John Stuart Mill as 'the stupid party'.[28] Following in Mill's footsteps, historians long wrote as if Conservative politicians effectively served a 'non ideology'[29] – a mere feeling; an *absence* of rational thought. I hope to prove, as historians of the Conservative Party like E. H. H. Green have done in their field, that this view of transphobia is inaccurate; that anti-trans beliefs have an internally complex set of intellectual characteristics, and that these are sufficiently coherent to bind together political groupings that are, in many other political contexts, dramatically at odds.

To be sure, there are no hard-and-fast demarcation lines that tell us where one species of transphobia ends and another begins. Each magnifies the others and adds to the putrid mass of the whole. In fact, the continuing cultural pre-eminence of transphobic beliefs, and their outsized influence on the British attitudinal landscape,[30] can be attributed largely to their sheer ideological *range* – being frequently represented among feminists, traditionalist Christians, niche atheist subgroups, Eurosceptics and far-right conspiracy theorists, among other political communities – as well as to the willingness of believers to compromise on major philosophical, cultural, legislative and methodological points so long as it brings new allies to the cause. Consequently, the most fruitful approach to the subject is not a stale one-by-one typology that partitions transphobia neatly into separate boxes, but rather a comparative approach that seeks to uncover the commonalities and linkages *between* these ideologies. In the pages that follow, I will lay the groundwork for just such an approach through a close study of the relationship between anti-trans feminism and conservative evangelical Christianity.

The focus throughout will be on the United Kingdom, albeit with departures to the United States that serve primarily to illustrate how ideas and strategies that were developed there have informed, or have been informed by, feminist and evangelical discourses in the UK. Cumulatively, it is hoped that this book will help cement an understanding of transphobia as a diverse and dynamic nexus of thought; *not* because we should respect or tolerate any aspect of it, but because a) it is beneficial for activists to contemplate more precisely what it is that we are resisting, and b) a fuller knowledge of one of the key reactionary forces of our time will open up new avenues of activistic, journalistic and scholarly enquiry. As both an evangelical Christian and a feminist – who also happens to be trans – this is of course a subject of immediate significance to my life, activism and work, and though I write, naturally, with a better, brighter, less antagonistic future for evangelical Christianity very much on my mind, what I discuss in these pages should matter no less urgently to *anyone* who believes that trans people deserve respect and dignity as an innate human right, supports the decon-struction of the social and legal restraints they are currently subject to, has an interest in countering anti-trans ideologies, or simply wants to understand what trans people are up against. There is a poisonous combination at the heart of global transphobia, and we – *all of us* – need for our own sakes to know what truly makes it tick. To this end, I deliberately address this book simultaneously to two audiences that appear to be very different: secular feminists and those interested in queer politics on the one hand, and evan-gelical Christians on the other. I do so precisely because I refuse, as a matter of faith and principle, to allow these two groups to give up on each other, leaving in the lurch thousands of trans, non-binary and questioning people who attend, or are related to those who attend, 'traditional' churches.

I believe the only way to fully explain the alliance between conservative evangelicals and anti-trans feminists is to pay close attention to *both* sides of the partnership, something that many prior scholars and commentators have been unable or perhaps unwilling to do. The reasons for this hesitancy are complex, but it seems partly to be a matter of mutual incomprehension. In-depth evangelical discussions on this subject are largely contained to spe-cialist journals and publishing houses that few non-evangelicals frequent. Even when these texts *are* referenced, it often proves difficult for writers without any prior grounding in evangelical theology to recognise the key assertions that they make or to engage meaningfully with their language. This, in turn, results in evangelicalism being treated as nothing but an essentialised stooge, a pantomime villain.

Understanding that evangelical theology is in some ways just as diverse and multi-faceted as feminism allows us to trace more precisely the flow and contra-flow of transphobic ideas; how they are repackaged, reformulated and recontextualised for wider dispersion, and also how they might be challenged in both a feminist and evangelical vernacular. I certainly do not mean to downplay the harm done by evangelical transphobia by couching it in impenetrable jargon; if anything, I believe that its malignant effects are *deeper* and *more extensive* than is often acknowledged, and furthermore that it contributes in a far more substantive way to the overall discursive ecosystem of transphobia than is commonly implied. Trans activists, allies, journalists and researchers are wont to describe the contributions made by anti-trans evangelicals to this coalition primarily in financial and organisational terms, with 'dark money' sloshing from the bank accounts of wealthy evangelicals and into the buckets of anti-trans feminists, who proceed to act as paid attack-dogs. Large chunks of Shon Faye's *The Transgender Issue* (2021) and Alison Phipps's *Me, Not You: The Trouble with Mainstream Feminism* (2020) are dedicated exclusively to these links. The messaging often seems to be premised upon shaming anti-trans feminists for taking money from the wrong people in the hope that this will discredit them in the eyes of the public, but in many cases the effect is just to dilute the agency of these feminists and to shift the blame onto an ethereal pantheon of shady puppeteers.

The financial lens on its own provides a skewed impression of the nature of the coalition, a view in which the Christian Right is fully, unambiguously leading the way. On the other hand, an intellectual-historical approach adds texture and depth, informing us that primary agency in this coalition does not belong to one party alone. Evangelical groups in the UK (discounting individual theologians) almost entirely ignored trans politics until the year 2000, when the Evangelical Alliance published its booklet

Transsexuality. This came *30 years* after Germaine Greer's first expression of anti-trans sentiment in 1970 and *21 years* after Janice Raymond laid out an anti-trans feminist manifesto in *The Transsexual Empire* (1979). When conservative evangelicals did finally start paying sustained attention to trans issues, their publications relied heavily, as I detail in the chapters to come, on argumentative patterns set long ago by Greer, Raymond and company. Intellectually, then, evangelicals are not, in any meaningful sense of the phrase, running the show. Moreover, focusing on *ideas* and *rhetoric* rather than just *funding* allows us to consider the ways in which we might substantively respond to political transphobia in both its secular and religious expressions. It also allows us to diversify our strategy by refusing to accept that the evangelical world in its entirety is beyond the reach of reason and compassion.

For evangelical church leaders and individual evangelical Christians, the primary utilities of this book will be: 1) to place current theological debates surrounding trans identities in historical, cultural and political context; 2) to illustrate the profound inadequacy, erroneousness, gracelessness and harmfulness of most of the predominant evangelical preconceptions about trans people and 'gender ideology', and 3) to initiate a dialogue on how we might move forward with a renewed yearning to embody, as images of the divine, the steadfast love of God in all circumstances and for all people. I do not intend for my words to sound unnecessarily harsh, nor for them to convey a holier-than-thou attitude, but I *do* intend to emphasise the urgency of the situation and to impress upon evangelical readers the desperate need for change. We don't come out of this looking good. However, to paraphrase the common saying, we reserve our bluntest criticisms for the groups we love the most. So, to those Christians who approach this book with a sceptical predisposition, my message is simple: in spite of everything that might divide us in terms of scriptural interpretations and perhaps political views, you are my family in Christ, and we climb this slope together. I hope you would say the same to me.

This book mixes a discussion of the *theory* and *theology* of transphobia with a narrative of the *practice* and *policy* of transphobia. Part I outlines the general history and present-day nature of the 'alliance' between anti-trans evangelicals and feminists, and proposes that the alliance is rooted in a shared opposition to dualistic, or 'Gnostic', philosophies of embodiment. Part II unpacks the scriptural basis for Christian gender binarism and demonstrates how particular theological ideas have facilitated the adoption of anti-trans political beliefs. Part III asks how these two factions manage to work together despite their many philosophical and political contradictions. Finally, Part IV addresses the ways that sympathetic feminists and evangelicals might be able to work to reverse the spread of transphobic beliefs with a balanced strategy of listening, education and deradicalisation, and also emphasises the severe consequences of allowing the rot to spread further than it already has. God willing, a sea change is in the making.

PART I

An 'unlikely' alliance

1

Warzone

Trans people in Britain have not always 'enjoyed', in the loosest possible sense of the word, their present notoriety. A high political profile was for a long time neither strictly necessary nor even possible, in part because 'trans' communal consciousness was effectively vacant, but also because keeping a *low* profile could often be the best strategy for living a reasonably safe and happy life. Prior to 1970, the UK's trans population resided in a legal shadow realm; their existence was not acknowledged in any legislation, but some of them could, if they were lucky enough to meet supportive doctors and communicate with the right civil servants, change most of their official documentation (including their birth certificates) to reflect their gender identity, and could even marry a person assigned with the same sex at birth.[1] However, in the case of *Corbett v. Corbett* (1970), High Court Judge Ormrod ruled that a marriage between April and Arthur Corbett was void because April's 'true sex' had always been legally male, implying that her self-identification and medical validation as a trans woman was legally unrecognisable in *any* context, matrimonial or otherwise.[2]

In the nascent network of trans self-help groups that popped up in the 1960s and 1970s, the Corbett case was perceived as a hammer blow. Marriage, along with its financial and practical benefits, was now off the table for many, but the effects of the case did not end there. Though experiences varied, many trans people found that Ormrod had done more than just remove their chances at matrimony. For instance, civil servants at the Department for Health and Social Security began selectively deferring to Ormrod's decision in cases where trans workers wished to make pension contributions and claim state pensions in their stated gender (at a time when women retired at 60 and men at 65), arguing that the precedent set by the case meant the Department could not participate in trans people's legal 'fiction'.[3] Similar administrative practices in other government departments added up to create an uneven system that was difficult to navigate successfully, contributing to a sense of despair among sections of the trans population. In a template letter to Members of Parliament put together by the Self-Help Association for Transsexuals (SHAFT) in 1982, it was lamented that 'following Judge Ormrod's ruling ... the law treats us as if we were perverts living dishonestly on the immoral fringe of the criminal law.'[4] Sociological researcher Sally Hines, summing up the effects reported by trans interview participants in her study on gender recognition in the UK, writes that Ormrod

> disabled legal rights related to work and welfare (for example, pension and tax rights) and those related to relationships and parenting (for example, next-of-kin status, marriage, partnership recognition and parental responsibility) and impacted upon the social and cultural fabric of everyday life (for example, trans people were often required to use opposite-sex toilets and changing rooms, treated in opposite-sex hospital wards and sent to opposite-sex prisons). Legal non-recognition also brought the psychological – and very tangible – fear of disclosure (so that a trans person may be publicly outed if, for example, they were called by their original name in a public place, such as a doctor's surgery or benefit office).[5]

Throughout this period, the legal plight of trans people was effectively invisible to the average cisgender citizen or politician. Excepting sensationalised coverage of the Corbett case (April was a well-known socialite and Arthur an aristocrat) and the occasional sympathetic article about the 'legal straitjacket' imposed upon trans people in relatively progressive newspapers like *The Guardian*,[6] trans issues barely registered in Britain's mainstream political discourses. In the final decades of the twentieth century, however, a growing number of trans people sought to take matters into their own hands. The year 1979 saw the foundation of both SHAFT[7] and the Transsexual Feminist Discussion Group (which later mutated into the Transsexual Action Group),[8] helping to facilitate the political mobilisation of a nascent trans 'community' around a common sense of grievance and purpose. Starting in the 1970s, several cases were also brought to the European Commission for Human Rights (and, from the 1980s, to the European Court of Human Rights) on the grounds that the British state was failing to respect its obligations to trans people under Articles 8 and 12 (concerning privacy and marriage) of the European Convention on Human Rights.[9] Then, in the 1990s, a new wave of trans activist organisations, most prominent among them being Press for Change (founded in 1992),[10] successfully brought trans rights, particularly the issue of legal recognition for trans people's gender identities, to the attention of those at the very top of Britain's governmental pyramid. In its submission to the UK Government's Interdepartmental Working Group on Transsexual Issues in 1999, Press for Change recommended that 'there should be one single and consistent point of recognition for the official change of an individual's gender for all purposes.'[11] This would eventually be the model adopted by policymakers.

Even with this steady build-up of pressure, it took 29 years following *Corbett v. Corbett* for some aspects of the legal fallout from the case to be mitigated – although for a brief period the changes came thick and fast. First in line was the Sex Discrimination (Gender Reassignment) Regulations of 1999, instituting regulatory protections for those in employment or training who had undergone or intended to undergo 'gender reassignment'.[12] Then came the Gender Recognition Act 2004, which created a new pathway for some trans men and women to change their legal gender via the issuance of a Gender Recognition Certificate and an updated birth certificate – *if* they could provide sufficient medical evidence and satisfy a dedicated Gender Recognition Panel of the sincerity and permanence of their identity.[13] The Equality Act 2010 codified more extensive anti-discrimination protections for some trans people by including 'gender reassignment' as a protected characteristic alongside race, disability, sexual orientation, and so on.[14] And in 2013, the Marriage (Same Sex Couples) Act finally upended Judge Ormrod's core objection by enabling marriages between people of the same legal sex, although it did not offer retroactive restoration of marriages 'stolen' by the Gender

Recognition Act's requirement that existing marriages be ended as a prerequisite for changing one's legal gender.[15]

For the remainder of the 2010s, the flow of political progress in Westminster reduced to a trickle, if even that. LGBTQI+ activist groups like Stonewall have advocated for reforms to the Gender Recognition Act to replace its requirement that applicants provide medical evidence with a statutory self-identification system, and to extend legal recognition to non-binary people. They have also campaigned for a ban on the harmful practice of trans-to-cis conversion 'therapy'. The first proposal was rejected by the Johnson Government in 2020 after a public consultation, and the second was initially scrapped in 2022 before being subtly reintroduced in January 2023. That same month, the Sunak Government used powers that had never before been activated to block the Scottish Parliament's Gender Recognition Reform (Scotland) Bill, which would have implemented a statutory gender self-declaration system north of the border, and reduced the minimum age of applicants from 18 to 16.[16] While it remains possible that gender recognition reform will be realised (and not blocked) in the near future – either by a Labour government or by a less ideologically transphobic Tory government – the decade since 2013 has been a disappointing period in the journey towards trans justice throughout most of the UK.

Not that things have been standing still. On a global scale, trans issues have become embroiled in the so-called 'culture wars', as socially progressive and conservative groups grapple over the broader implications of trans acceptance, such that even the most indisposed political and religious factions have been forced to make a decision as to where they should pin their colours. In the year 2018, four years after *Orange is the New Black* star Laverne Cox and *Time Magazine* proclaimed that society had reached the 'Transgender Tipping Point',[17] and at the height of a furious political and cultural backlash against trans people's rising visibility that has been unceremoniously dubbed the 'TERF Wars',[18] Britain's largest evangelical Christian organisation published a resource booklet that aimed to help church staff understand the dizzying range of words and concepts associated with trans identity. Evangelical leaders might well have preferred to leave this can of worms unopened, but the cultural trajectory in Britain and the world dictated that this could not be so. They had to say *something*.

Founded in 1846 and now representing over 3,300 member churches in the UK (including mine), the Evangelical Alliance can best be described as doctrinally conservative, if not necessarily 'fundamentalist'. Its basis of faith affirms the triune nature of God formed of the Father, Son and Holy Spirit; the divine inspiration and accuracy of the Bible; the literal resurrection of Jesus Christ; the 'personal and visible' return of Jesus at an unknown future point, and the 'justification of sinners solely by the grace of God through faith in Christ', as opposed to justification through good works.[19] At its inception, the Alliance committed itself to upholding the Sacraments (most obviously the Eucharist/Communion), thereby drawing a line in the sand that excluded a number of anti-Sacramental Protestant denominations such as the Quakers.[20] It also placed heavy import on preaching the existence of Hell as a real place, together with the now-stereotypical fire-and-brimstone message that eternal punishment awaits the unrepentant, further distancing the Alliance from some of the less eschatologically bent Protestant denominations.[21]

While evangelicalism is, technically speaking, not a denomination in and of itself, as one can be an evangelical Methodist, evangelical Anglican, evangelical Baptist and much else besides, organisations like the Evangelical Alliance and the smaller Fellowship of Independent Evangelical Churches (FIEC) nonetheless mirror denominational leadership structures in important ways; for instance, by representing the movement in the national media, providing the space for a unified sense of identity and purpose, and distributing general statements of shared doctrine and best practice. In keeping with this quasi-denominational role, Peter Lynas, UK Director for the Alliance, responded to the burgeoning significance of questions of trans and non-binary gender identities in the late 2010s by authoring *Transformed: A Brief Biblical and Pastoral Introduction to Understanding Transgender in a Changing Culture* (2018). By and large, *Transformed* is an unmistakably evangelical document, packed as it is with Bible references, affirmations of God's goodness and love, and calls for pastors to renew their efforts to bring new people, including trans people, 'to the transformative work and power of Jesus'.[22] This is the evangelical mission in a nutshell. However, a seasoned trans reader will inevitably notice that some passages – such as the assertion that 'transgender ideology' threatens freedom of speech because it supposedly does not tolerate opposing voices,[23] or that trans identity is a 'social contagion' into which impressionable young people are being enticed for unspecified nefarious reasons[24] – are less distinctive and could easily be mistaken for the work of anti-trans feminists, who, through years of incessant agitation, have turned these very same tropes into a perverse kind of liturgy.[25] This is no coincidence. *Transformed* directly and uncritically references both Germaine Greer and the group Transgender Trend, two large-scale manufacturers of feminist-oriented transphobia in Britain,[26] offering no critique of the reasoning or (lack of) evidence behind the claims they make and providing no alternative perspectives on the issues upon which they comment.

Greer's assertion that cis women are now 'losing out everywhere' in society, in part due to the gradual rise in the acceptance of trans women as having a valid claim to womanhood, is cited by Lynas in support of the narrative that cis women's rights 'become meaningless given the concept of "womanhood" is so flexible and indeterminate in some trans and queer ideologies',[27] although the mechanisms by which this is meant to be happening are not detailed; nor is the fact that many cis feminist theorists see no contradiction between the rights of cis and trans women.[28] Transgender Trend, meanwhile, is described benignly by Lynas as 'a secular organisation concerned about the current trend to diagnose "gender nonconforming" children as transgender', and readers of *Transformed* are told that this organisation 'has produced a resource pack for schools which teachers may find useful'.[29] The resource pack in question is hardly a sober or Christ-like document. It describes trans identity in children as a 'biologically impossible situation', encourages teachers to tell questioning children that '[w]hat you think or feel can't change you from a girl [or boy]', and suggests that it will cause 'stress and anxiety' for other children if a trans peer's identity and pronouns are respected by teachers.[30] Even if one believes that children should be discouraged from exploring their gender identities, this is hardly the most graceful or effective way to go about it. Lynas appropriates these claims with astonishingly casual dexterity, leaving untouched the opinions of Greer and Transgender Trend on other matters like abortion and same-sex relationships with which he would likely disagree just as strongly as he disagrees with trans rights.

The awkward eclipse of ideologies exemplified in *Transformed* is not characterised by a one-way relationship in which conservative Christians merely find it convenient to repackage anti-trans feminist arguments. There is a risk of overstating these connections, but some anti-trans feminist groups in both the UK and the US have fostered practical links with reactionary Christian organisations and news outlets, entailing direct financial, organisational and strategic ties, shared media space, and even, in some cases, overlapping personnel.[31] The US-based Women's Liberation Front (WoLF) has a long-standing relationship with the Heritage Foundation, a staple Christian Right institution that opposes abortion access and same-sex marriage, and the similarly ultra-conservative legal defence organisation, the Alliance Defending Freedom, from whom WoLF received a $15,000 donation in 2017. Some British anti-trans feminist activists have shared platforms with the Heritage Foundation through the intermediation of WoLF, including Julia Long, one of the activists who stopped the 2018 Pride in London march in protest against trans inclusion in the LGBTQI+ community,[32] but there are others who found their way between the two camps without the help of WoLF or any other intermediary. In April 2023, anti-trans feminist Labour MP Rosie Duffield and evangelical Conservative MP Miriam Cates, the latter a co-founder of the conservative New Social Covenant Unit, announced that they were uniting 'across the political divide to make sure [women's rights] are not wiped out ... [by] a small group of extremist [trans] activists'.[33] As is customary in anti-trans material, their joint statement is extremely vague as to *how* these activists are actually threatening women's rights.

Similarly, British pro-life activist Gary Powell has a long history of working directly with the US Christian Right and appeared on a panel organised by the Heritage Foundation in 2019, sitting alongside a representative from the Alliance Defending Freedom. In September of that year, he aided the launch of the UK's LGB

Alliance, which calls from an ostensibly 'feminist' perspective for lesbian, gay and bisexual people to politically distance themselves from trans people in order to reassert their distinctive and/or mutually exclusive interests.[34] In 2021, moreover, anti-trans feminist philosopher Kathleen Stock resigned from her job at the University of Sussex amid student protests against her transphobic writings, and proceeded to take a post at the University of Austin,[35] a not-yet-realised 'free speech' college in Texas with both conceptual and organisational connections to anti-intellectual currents in the Christian Right.[36] These are neither isolated incidents nor novel manifestations of some recent, passing, or short-lived phenomenon. Some commentators, including American queer activist Patrick Califia, were already noticing in the late 1990s that anti-trans feminism

> has much in common with other fundamentalist movements, such as the New Christian Right. It is no accident that these groups, which on the surface appear to be opposed to one another, have on more than one occasion formed alliances to further their respective agendas ... And both are willing to muster the powers of the state against their enemies, even though the state is, according to their own doctrines, hopelessly corrupt.[37]

More recently, the Trans Safety Network, a research collective dedicated to tracking anti-trans political activity in the UK, has noted a 'rapid increase in the rate at which practical crossovers are happening' between these two blocs,[38] mirroring an international trend which has seen anti-trans feminists and the Christian Right work together against what they call *gender ideology*,[39] a vague and often derogatory label for systems of thought that reject 'biological sex' as a primary determinant of how one is categorised, or gendered, legally and socially. In light of this collaboration, scholars Serena Bassi and Greta LaFleur see anti-trans feminism as being part of 'a coalitional and longstanding global Far Right imagination'.[40]

Elements from within the Roman Catholic Church represent the most notorious sources of politicised religious transphobia in mainland Europe,[41] although some of the Church's early engagements with trans issues showed that an open-minded Catholic attitude towards gender diversity was possible. Reverend Richard C. Messina, a Catholic priest in Boston, Massachusetts, wrote in 1977/8 that opposition to what was then called sex reassignment surgery was as misguided as prior religious objections to organ transplants and blood transfusions. He expressed hope that 'open minded religious leaders everywhere' would in this instance wait for the publication of further research before drawing any hard conclusions, signing off: 'I, for one, feel it is not so much a moral issue as a medical-psychological one.'[42] The same non-judgemental instinct prevailed in Spain a decade later. As reported in 1989 by *The Independent*, one Susana Linares, a Spanish trans woman and 'fervent Catholic', had asked her parish priest whether it would be necessary for her to be re-baptised as a woman in order for the gender marker on her baptismal documents to be changed. The matter was elevated first to the bishop of Madrid, who seemed to 'relish the theological dimensions of the transsexual's predicament'. He remarked that 'the soul has no sex', and that anyway it would not be proper to repeat a baptism, but he reconsidered when Linares pointed out that it would be 'extremely silly' for the Church to 'marry her with her male Christian name to her bridegroom'. Linares's query was then elevated further to the archbishop, and finally to the Vatican. The matter received serious consideration from the Holy See, as Linares was informed by a counsellor to the Pope that 'only the Pope could answer' a question of such theological significance.[43]

Confusion and intrigue soon gave way to condemnation. By the start of the new century, there could be little doubt as to where the Church stood. In 2003, the Church moved to expel trans members of its religious orders 'for the good of all the souls' in these bodies.[44] Later, In 2015, Pope Francis himself likened the impact of 'gender theory' on God's creational order to that of King Herod the Great (who tried to kill the child Jesus in the Matthean birth narrative), the destructive power of nuclear weapons, and the genocidal violence of the Nazis.[45] Prolific researchers of anti-gender movements David Paternotte and Roman Kuhar trace the development of *gender ideology* as a discursive invention primarily to the internal politics of the Vatican in the 1990s, and they argue

that 'the Catholic Church as an organization appears as a fundamental discourse producer' for anti-gender activism, particularly
in Catholic strongholds like Italy and Poland.[46] However, the
influence of the Catholic Church and Catholic parachurch organisations is comparatively limited in the United Kingdom. A recent
effort to map organised transphobia in this country by the group
Global Action for Trans Equality (GATE) 'did not in general find a
strong role for Catholic groups in England or at UK Government
policy level'.[47] Instead, British transphobic feminists have been
joined more visibly in the anti-'gender ideology' space by certain
groups of conservative evangelicals.[48]

This 'toxic mix' of ideologies, as Anglican priest Jared Robinson-
Brown dubs it,[49] looks profoundly absurd at first pass. Although
gender-egalitarian currents have been present and sometimes
widely accepted in evangelical thought throughout its history,[50]
the most stubbornly intransigent elements from among today's
conservative evangelicals have acquired a deserved infamy for
being fervently hostile to feminism in any form, even that of
an evangelical flavour.[51] In direct and deliberate opposition to
prevailing ideals concerning women's liberation and gender
equality, some of them preach 'hard' versions of a gender doctrine
known as *complementarianism*. As described by British pastor
Andrew Wilson in an article for The Gospel Coalition, a global
conservative evangelical church collective, complementarianism is
fundamentally a belief in the 'beautiful difference' of creation as
represented in the 'two-isms' of the biblical creation story – earth
and seas, day and night, male and female. However, there is no
consensus among evangelicals as to what the differences between
males and females actually are in terms of behaviours, abilities,
psychologies, virtues and vices; nor is there agreement as to the
distinction (if a distinction is believed to exist) between men's and
women's respective roles in a family or in a church. Sometimes,
the distinctions are read as mild and situationally dependent;
other times, as Wilson notes, the urgent desire to put 'beautiful
difference on display' in a world that increasingly sees the sexes
and genders as more or less indistinct has led to unflattering
scenarios in which evangelicals have 'overcorrected and landed
ourselves in extrabiblical (or even unbiblical) territory: reading

postwar middle America into the New Testament, demeaning our sisters, [and] dismissing those who disagree with us as liberals'.[52] Even in its softest, most celebratory iteration, the language of complementarianism can seem absolutely dystopian to an outside reader, but in its less rosy expressions, it positively shudders the progressive mind. For example, it is hard to imagine your typical secular feminist approving of the wording of a 2016 FIEC article on complementarity that envisions a happy Christian wife is one who 'respectfully and joyfully submits to [her husband's] authority'.[53]

On a surface-level appraisal, at the very least, these ideas hardly seem compatible with feminism's foundational critiques of patriarchal marriage; nor, for that matter, do they chime with the atheism of a great many anti-trans feminists;[54] nor still, as Alison Phipps notes in her powerful book *Me, Not You: The Trouble with Mainstream Feminism* (2020), with radical feminism's ostensible aim of abolishing gender altogether.[55] It is especially difficult to explain how lesbian radical feminists justify working with a movement that is associated not just with political transphobia, but with political *homo*phobia. Conservative evangelicals are, at this stage, practically synonymous with deep homophobic bigotry, being renowned the world over for organising to prevent any advance in the rights of sexual minorities, and particularly for standing square in the way of watershed reforms like the decriminalisation of same-sex intimacy, the legalisation of same-sex unions, the protection of adoption rights for same-sex and non-cis couples, and the provision of LGBTQI+ inclusive sexual education in schools.[56] When Richard Dawkins, biology professor and author of the classic atheist polemic *The God Delusion* (2006), sought to demonstrate that faith is toxic to the toleration of homosexuality and therefore to the moral health of society at large, conservative evangelical groups were unsurprisingly among his go-to examples.[57]

Divided by so much and pulling, on the face of things, in completely different cultural and political directions, anti-trans feminists and conservative Christians were described by law professor D. C. Bradley at a 1993 Council of Europe colloquy on 'Transsexualism, Medicine, and Law' as occupying 'opposite end[s] of the political spectrum'.[58] Researchers at Open Democracy, drawing the same conclusion, have pointedly referred to feminists and evangelicals as 'unlikely allies' in the trans debate.[59] The US-based Family Policy Alliance has used the same phrase – 'unlikely allies' – to draw out the superficially unusual nature of its decision to work with WoLF in a legal effort to prevent trans girls from using girls' locker rooms in the United States. The Policy Alliance exclaims: 'How wrong does something have to be for a Christian pro-family organization and a self-described radical-feminist group to oppose it together at the Supreme Court?'[60] Samantha Schmidt of the *Washington Post* also describes WoLF as an 'unlikely ally' for the American Christian Right.[61]

Whatever words we use to describe the undeniably odd optics of these overlaps, the very existence of the transphobic collusion that we are witnessing today has prompted trans-positive feminists to voice grave misgivings concerning the sincerity and scruples of their anti-trans counterparts, who seem to be eloping with their oppressors simply because they hate trans people more than they care for the advancement of their own interests.[62] Representatives of both sides of this feminist divide have attempted, through some crafty mental gymnastics, to explain away the befuddling resonances between feminists and evangelicals on trans issues, as well as on other causes where their views overlap, such as sex work and pornography, as accidental, insubstantial, or at most a strained marriage born 'of convenience'.[63] There *must* be some sort of ulterior motive, it is often assumed, for surely there can be no question of feminists and evangelicals naturally being drawn into one another's company. After all, as historian of evangelical feminism Pamela D. H. Cochran writes, 'For most people today ... the terms *evangelical* and *feminism* are contradictory.'[64]

Until very recently, the proposed solutions to this problem have differed only slightly based on the political persuasions of the one positing the solution. One influential anti-trans journalist, Helen Joyce, argues that feminists of her persuasion sometimes choose to publish their stories – heroic tales of resisting gender ideology and being professionally and socially punished for it – in Christian Right news outlets only because they feel frozen out by mainstream media, which, we are told, is in the pocket of the trans lobby.[65] Another of Britain's most famous transphobes, Julie Bindel, acknowledges that 'dangerous' links have been forged between some feminists and the Christian Right, but she asserts that their truce runs no deeper than circumstantial agreement upon single issues,[66] and insists that her brand of radical feminism is 'more politically aligned with the left'.[67] Though we might expect them to disagree more strongly with such evasive, specious non-explanations, trans-affirming writers often describe a similarly shallow alliance, arguing, as does intersectional feminist Lola Olufemi in *Feminism, Interrupted: Disrupting Power* (2020), that anti-trans feminists cynically 'align themselves with the church and the state (who are not natural allies to feminists) … to legitimize their agenda'.[68] The explanatory emphasis is on a pattern of irrational psychological factors and cynical strategic calculations that militate to suck the two centrifugally opposed blocs into the same patch of spacetime. Ultimately, *any* explanation seems desirable over the realisation that 'opposite' ideologies really have mixed.

On the surface, the evidence for an allies-of-convenience view seems convincing. Much has been made in trans activist circles, for example, of the 2017 Values Voters Summit in Washington, DC, at which Meg Kilgannon, executive director of Concerned Parents and Educators of Fairfax County, advised her fellow religious traditionalists to adopt a 'divide and conquer' strategy against LGBTQI+ activists, which means joining up with trans-sceptical lesbian, gay and bisexual organisations in order to 'separate the T from the alphabet soup'.[69] Kilgannon's comments lend themselves only too readily to the reductive claim, commonly made on trans social media and by trans-affirming news outlets, that anti-trans feminists are 'unwitting tools' or 'useful idiots', who have been 'entirely co-opted by the anti-LGBT evangelical movement'.[70] Their work, we are told by Julian Vile on revolutionary socialist news site *Left Voice*, 'ultimately benefits the extreme Right'.[71] Meanwhile, their position in the alliance is described by Heron Greensmith of Political Research Associates, a social justice-focused research organisation in the United States, as mere 'complicity' with a more powerful bloc of religious and far-right transphobes. To such actors, anti-trans feminism is nothing more than a 'useful mouthpiece'; a 'straw-woman', that enables the Christian Right to 'access those hard to reach places' in the more progressive pockets of society and so to capitalise on the 'apparent bipartisanship of hate'.[72] Similarly, prominent left-wing YouTuber Shaun describes lesbian anti-trans feminists as 'the gay camouflage for a bunch of straight conservative homophobes',[73] and philosophy YouTuber ContraPoints says that 'useful idiots' like J. K. Rowling are being sucked into a conspiratorial whirlpool by the real 'devil', right-wing patriarchal men.[74] As thralls to shadowy religious forces, anti-trans feminists are reduced to mere spokespeople, figureheads, *promoters*. 'It is a sad day', says leading queer theorist Judith Butler, 'when some feminists promote the anti-gender ideology position of the most reactionary forces in our society'.[75]

An increased awareness of the global political influence of the 'unlikely alliance' in the first years of the 2020s has brought about a more sustained academic engagement with the question of its causation and nature. Two of the more in-depth explanations are those provided by C. Libby and C. Heike Schotten in the August 2022 edition of *Transgender Studies Quarterly*, an issue dedicated to 'Trans-Exclusionary Feminisms and the Global New Right'. Libby cogently argues that the alliance is based on a shared axiomatic belief in sexual dimorphism (i.e., the belief that there are no sex or gender realities beyond the 'male' and 'female' binary), a view that has been shared by many observers over the years. Australian trans activist Rachael Wallbank told the Eighth International Gender Dysphoria Conference in Manchester (2004) that the 'main uniting factor' that permits 'such apparently disparate folk as the radically religious and the radically feminist' to work in lockstep is 'the proposition that the biological "truth" of an individual human being's sexual identity may be discerned by only one means – the appearance of the person's genitalia at birth'.[76] Libby's argument is that the sex binarist convergence is further 'facilitated by an affective resonance of sympathy, fear, and hatred between these unlikely groups'.[77] This 'affective resonance' manifests in doomsaying predictions from both anti-trans feminists and conservative evangelicals concerning the supposed death of traditional and/or second-wave feminist values, the purported increase in the risk factors faced by cis women due to the acceptance of trans people into their spaces, and the 'seduction' of children by proponents of gender-affirming care (often implying 'grooming' for the purposes of sexual predation). Also common to both groups is the notion that granting legal recognition to trans people's gender identities would undermine their capacity to host sex-exclusive events or maintain sex-exclusive positions in their leadership structures without opening themselves to prosecution under anti-discrimination regulations. Libby thus sees the two groups as engaged in a 'politics of injury', a kind of victim complex.[78]

Schotten takes a different and less predictable approach, locating the resonance between anti-trans feminists and conservative Christians primarily in their mutual appropriation of Zionist annihilation narratives, driven by what Lynne Stahl calls 'extinction phobia'.[79] In basic form, Zionist annihilationism contends that, without a strong and independent Israeli nation-state to which they have the right to 'return' (even if this means displacing Palestinians in the process), the Jewish peoples will never be free from existential threats. In the 1970s and 1980s, Jewish-identified feminists and Zionist lesbian separatists participated in the rhetorical conflation of antisemitism with anti-Zionism, on the grounds that opposition to Israeli settlement in Palestine was tantamount to endorsing Jewish annihilation.[80] Meanwhile, anti-trans feminism, which was developing in precisely this time period, seems to have absorbed these logics in its own apocalyptic screeds. Schotten argues that Zionist lesbian separatism 'offers a strikingly clear articulation of an extinction phobia that overlaps, informs, and facilitates' what she calls 'predation TERFism'[81] – this being the belief that trans women's existence and their presence in women's spaces poses an existential threat to cis women, particularly cis lesbians, as argued by seminal American 'TERFs' like Mary Daly and Janice Raymond.[82] The same basic variety of annihilationist preconceptions is adopted by the Christian nationalist mouthpieces of American imperialism in its repackaging of Israel's ethnic cleansing of Palestinians as purely a self-defence measure.[83] Thus, Schotten believes that anti-trans feminism shares ideological genealogies with Christian Nationalism and Christian Zionism in the United States, and she concludes on these grounds that TERFism's 'overlap [with] Right-wing funders and organizations is more than just coincidence'.[84]

The work of Libby and Schotten helps point the way to a new intellectual history of transphobia that recognises anti-trans feminists and anti-trans evangelicals to be bound by a deep, genuine and time-honoured ideological compatibility, and that furthermore treats the feminists involved as full, active, equal and self-aware participants in the alliance, not 'useful idiots'. However, I find that their explanations struggle to account for prominent ideological and rhetorical features of the 'unlikely' alliance, and prove in practice to be of limited utility in mapping evangelical thought on gender identity. Libby's well-reasoned focus on biological essentialism and the 'politics of injury' strikes at the vital subconscious motivations that work to ease the processes by which particular feminists and evangelicals find themselves making roughly the same arguments, fighting roughly the same legal battles over freedom of belief, and supporting roughly the same policy agendas in this specific area. But most of Libby's time is spent on the surface-level absorption of feminist language by evangelical groups and not on the *theological basis* for evangelical transphobia, or the unique discursive material that evangelicals are bringing to the alliance. The results are epistemologically one-sided, with the evangelical component being insufficiently unpacked.

In Schotten's article, as in Libby's, the emphasis is firmly on the United States, and Schotten's view of the alliance is potently shaped by the political system and discursive landscape of that country. As a result, some of the conclusions she draws are simply not applicable to circumstances in the UK – at least, not on a macro level. Christian Zionism is deeply interwoven with the history of modern British Christianity,[85] having been a driving principle in mid-to-late nineteenth-century British evangelicalism via the influence of Ridley Haim Herschell, a convert from Judaism and a founding member of the Evangelical Alliance.[86] However, the defence and expansion of Israel does not permeate foreign policy discourses in Britain the way it does in the US, where a well-funded network of evangelical lobby groups dedicated to this issue helps to keep annihilationist language at the very forefront of the collective evangelical or 'Christian Right' imagination.[87] And while British conservative evangelicals have taken to signal-boosting cis annihilation narratives in recent years, these narratives played, at most, a minimal role in the development of evangelical doctrine as it relates to gender identity from the early 1980s to the early 2000s. There are key puzzle pieces yet missing.

My argument is that the operative locus of the alliance between conservative evangelicals and anti-trans feminists, lying far beneath the superficial embrace of 'biological reality' as the final arbiter in matters of social categorisation, and beneath even the affective expression of visceral fears of cis annihilation, is an intersecting fundamental opposition, on grounds of moral intuition rather than empirical principle, to dualistic philosophies that separate the mind or soul or spirit from the body – or, in a slightly different formulation, philosophies that separate biological *sex* from sociological *gender*. It is not simply that they both believe in an ontological sex or gender binary that drives their activism, but that they both instinctively view this as the best framework for understanding, organising and improving human relations *regardless of any ostensible scientific or philosophical justification for this idea*. It is their belief that human society in its current form *should* be structured around sex binarism, and their feeling that to abandon this structure is *morally* wrong, not their belief that sex binarism is *true* on an aetiological or taxonomic level, that motivates their campaigns and creates the common ground on which they rally.

This cluster of concepts (*biological sex, gender* and the *mind*) only makes intuitive sense if we lean heavily on our post-Enlightenment epistemology. The grounds upon which appeals to a 'scientific' view of the essential differences between men and women is based was popularised not so very long ago. As historian Thomas Laqueur explored in his book *Making Sex: Body and Gender from the Greeks to Freud* (1990), 'sex as we know it', a sharp anatomical and later chromosomal separation between males and females, was effectively invented within Western medical culture in the eighteenth and nineteenth centuries,[88] a process that Laqueur calls the 'discursive creation of difference'.[89] The advent of an endocrinological (hormonal) basis for sex differentiation is even more recent, deriving from the early twentieth century.[90] It is possible to overstate the universality of this process as it worked its way through the furrows of social and political life in the colonial homelands and out into the vast, oppressive expanses of Empire.[91]

By the mid-twentieth century, though, the binary sex model had embedded itself into the firmament of popular scientific knowledge, even while the troubling preponderance of exceptions – those bothersome people who simply do not fit the anatomical, endocrinological, or chromosomal 'norm' – threatened to knock this far-too-neat human-sorting system out of sync.

We tend to think of *gender* as a looser, thoroughly socially constructed appendage to sex that allows for a wider range of identities and ways of expressing one's self, but as Jules Gill-Peterson demonstrates in her book *Histories of the Transgender Child* (2018), mid-century White sexologists in North America and Europe – the very people who made it their business to set the boundaries of medicalised gender-nonconformity – viewed the terminology of gender not as a tool to legitimise (much less *celebrate*) diversity, but rather as a way to help *preserve* binary sex as a conceptual framework. If an individual could not easily be classified as male or female because certain sexual characteristics fell outside the normative range of variation, they could at least be made to conform as closely as possible to the *behavioural* and *presentational* gendered expectations of men and women.[92] Of course, this is not what gender theorists usually refer to when they talk of *gender* today, nor is it the interpretation that anti-trans figures use when they speak of *gender ideology*. For the latter, gender is a cheap way for an individual to deny but not override the immutable reality of sex, creating a distinction – a duality – between our socialised patterns of self-projection on the one hand, and the sexual characteristics of our bodies on the other. Mind is thus set *against* body; feelings against 'reality'.

Despite considerably pre-dating the cultural circumstances in which this particular point of contention functions, one of the most well-known forms of dualism today, and the one that looms large in this book, is *Gnosticism* – a word derived from *gnosis*, Greek for *knowledge*. 'Gnosticism' as a label was developed in Western universities in the eighteenth century and applied retroactively to a loose collection of heterodoxic Neoplatonic mystical theologies that were prevalent in the early Christian world, in large part to assert some kind of conceptual order over the messiness of distant antiquity. This might seem like a tangent. What on earth does trans identity in the Information Age have to do with systems of Christian mysticism that roamed the earth two thousand years ago, at a time when Rome still ruled in Europe? For reasons that will be explored at length in the following chapters, many seminal anti-trans writers of both a feminist and evangelical bent see Gnosticism as a direct phenomenological antecedent to trans identity, and this claim was among the very first ideas that both groups shared. To understand why they make this seemingly eccentric connection, we have to establish what Gnosticism *is* and what 'the Gnostics' are thought to have believed about the body.

Like any modern taxonomy imposed upon the far-gone past, Gnosticism is an awkward category, not least because it meshes together scriptures and traditions that seem to contradict each other on foundational cosmological questions, and because, so far as we can tell, the people now called Gnostics did not share their own sense of unitary identity, but rather were separated into local schools coagulating around a particular teacher or ideal.[93] Hence, a theological description that applies to one group of so-called 'Gnostics' might not apply to another. Nevertheless, the label has stuck, and we are able at least to guesstimate the philosophical axioms someone probably has in mind when they use Gnosticism as a shorthand. The Gnostics, who were most numerous in the rapidly expanding world of Christianity in the Eastern Mediterranean from the late first to late third centuries CE, are traditionally described as having regarded their bodies as spiritual cages that they desired to escape in pursuit of transcendent esoteric knowledge (*gnosis*) of the divine.[94] The physical world, they believed, was created by a lesser and temperamentally evil god – the Hebrew deity YHWH/Yahweh/Jehovah. The nature of this being was modelled on the ancient Greek philosopher Plato's concept of the Demiurge, an entity that acts as a sort of craftsman, taking the materials of the universe and fashioning them into their present physical form. Hence, the material is inherently negative.

The Gnostic version of Jesus is also drastically different to the Jesus of mainline Christianity. In particular, the Gnostics denied that Jesus was both fully God and fully human, as most Christian denominations believe today. Rather, their Jesus was imagined as a purely spiritual being who simply took on the *appearance* of a human for the duration of his time on earth, but did not *actually* become a human – an idea known as Docetism. This likeness of a man was an agent of the true celestial Prime Mover – the 'real' God, so to speak – and as such he could not be sullied by entrapping himself in the Demiurge's material realm, for to do this would be to subordinate himself to a lesser being. Jesus's ultimate objective, moreover, was not to defeat sin and death, in its material sense, but to show his followers the way to achieve a state of transcendent extra-materiality. His death on the cross and subsequent resurrection, then, were not literal, because the dramatic resurrection of the material body would defeat the whole point of Jesus's ministry. The human soul is entrapped, and, if awakened to its entrapment, desires to escape from a body that is entirely expendable – a body that *must* be expended if true freedom is to be attained and one's spiritual potential is to be fulfilled. Body/mind dualism, or body/soul dualism, is thus a core element of Gnosticism as we understand it.

While not necessarily viewing these ideas as part of a single philosophical whole, the Latin Church later denounced them as heretical and deemphasised many texts now categorised as Gnostic, thus limiting mainstream knowledge of Gnosti*cism*, if such a thing ever really existed, to an oversimplification of its body/mind dualism.[95] This caricature is most often represented by the salacious belief that Gnostics engaged in mass orgies and other fleshly intemperances because they held that what one did in the material realm had no bearing on one's spiritual standing[96] – the suggestion here being that they did whatever they liked with and to each other, lacking any recognisable moral code. The same reputation applies to modern philosophies that are frequently described as sharing in Gnosticism's dualistic worldview. (Mis)used in this fashion, mainly as a high-brow but semantically indeterminate insult, the label 'Gnosticism' has secured a kind of spectral afterlife in the trenches of recent theological and philosophical conflicts, being used to discredit controversial thoughts and thinkers by association with an unpopular, allegedly amoral group of heretics.

Historians and philosophers, often with less-than-honest intentions, have classified a veritable kaleidoscope of contemporary ideas and phenomena as Gnostic 'metamorphoses', including existentialism, modern mysticism, surrealism and Marxism.[97] Political theorist John Gray goes so far as to state that 'Gnosticism created the secular religions that fashioned the modern world' – referring to everything from Jacobinism to Bolshevism to Nazism.[98] Postmodernists, being those who reject modernity's empiricist claims to absolute truth and grand historical narrative, are also burdened with imputed heirship to the Gnostic tradition,[99] a fact that will become distinctly relevant in Chapter 2, as second-wave feminist critiques of Gnosticism have largely been reformulated as critiques of postmodernism in anti-trans feminist literature. These comparisons are rarely meant to be complimentary. The late, great Jewish Orthodox Rabbi Jonathan Sacks called Gnostic-style body/mind dualism a 'dangerous idea' that, in its most extreme forms, leads to the devaluation of physical human life and therefore normalises the type of systematic existential violence conducted against Jews, Slavs, homosexuals and other 'degenerate' peoples by the Nazis.[100]

Even where insinuations of rationalising violence are not involved, to be called a Gnostic is still to be accused of some grave philosophical errancy. The slightest *hint* of body/mind dualism is enough to bring down the ire of the anti-Gnostics, and they are nothing if not vigilant. In recent times, so-called 'gender ideology', another questionable categorisation of thought referring, as mentioned above, in an unfavourable manner to a branch of postmodernism that views gender roles as socially fabricated and therefore mutable, is singled out by its critics as a particularly egregious 'recapitulation' of Gnosticism's 'ancient, recurring error'.[101] This is because the assertion that the happiness of the mind is more important than the preservation of particular bodily forms is taken as a dualist, or 'Gnostic', confession of faith. This specific claim, called the *Gnostic charge* by Anglican priest Duncan Dormor,[102] has been used for decades by commentators of varied religious and political backgrounds to invalidate trans identity, either as a heresy or, in secular contexts, as a harmful, socially replicating pandemic of wilful self-deception.

The basic thrust of the Gnostic charge is that the blurring of gender boundaries propagates a schism between the soul and the body whereby the latter, having no inherent value, can be used or adjusted however the soul desires it. Trans identities are seen to be the spear-tip to this devious assault upon the real, penetrating the fabric of social norms as a precursor to the total annihilation of objective knowledge. Of course, seeing it this way depends upon an entirely subjective judgement about how we should conceptualise the worth and utility of the body, or indeed the viability of true objectivity, but either way we can see that the Gnostic charge, like many ideas that stretch credulity to its breaking point, extrapolates from some base semblance of truth.

Popular trans narratives of embodiment, particularly those found in twentieth-century trans autobiographies, *do* often hinge on a presupposition of the body's separateness from, subordination to, and potential for misalignment with an inner sense of identity; an abstraction made legible to general society by the oft-maligned yet enduring maxim that trans people are 'trapped in the wrong body', which seems to suggest the presence of a soul or 'self' that exists independently of the physical composition of a person.[103] Surgical or chemical changes to the body are justified on this model by the necessary superiority of the soul, as the true self, over the physical organism to which it is connected. Anti-trans writers, perceiving body/mind dualism of this sort to be inordinately detrimental to one's well-being, and most especially to the well-being of children (because it seems to encourage the fracturing of the self and the abandonment of stoic self-acceptance as a virtue), gravitate to this one formulation of trans embodiment precisely because it is so legible, so addictively cognisable, so readily attacked from multiple ideological directions as a straw-man substitute for more complex and diverse notions of what it means to be trans. The deceptive simplicity of the paradigm makes it vulnerable. Apparently disparate groups can thus offer similar critiques of the 'wrong body' narrative, while declining to engage with less easily abridged theories of transness that account for the enormous variations between trans people in their perceptions of themselves, including those who seek no medical intervention.[104]

What follows is not an endorsement of any particular trans philosophy on my part, but rather a selection of snippets from trans writers that, taken together, show how wrong it is to suggest that trans identity is universally premised on a simplistic 'wrong body' narrative or that it is, so defined, a precursor to dualism.

One relevant idea that has been posited by trans journalist and film-maker Juliet Jacques, among others, is that trans people are 'not trapped in the wrong body but trapped in the wrong society',[105] inviting us to perceive modern trans identities as the most recent reflection of a deep, inextricable expressive diversity within humanity that is unjustly suppressed by an artificial but brutally enforced gender binary. This is an important corrective. Placing too much emphasis on individual instances of trans people using the language of wrongness to communicate to others how they feel about their bodies can make one insensitive to the ways in which this language is necessitated by broader structural forces, particularly the societal expectation that certain body types necessarily correlate to certain gender roles. It is through these structures that we interpret what it means for a body to be 'wrong', and this does not necessarily entail conceptualising the body as 'other than' the true self in a dualistic sense. In fact, many trans people specifically memorialise their path to self-acceptance and self-love as a journey *away from*, not *towards*, body/mind dualist philosophies. Disabled trans activist and theorist Eli Clare recalls in *Brilliant Imperfection: Grappling with Cure* (2017) that he

> followed the lead of many communities and spiritual traditions that recognize body and mind not as two entities but as one, resisting the dualism built into white Western culture. Some use the word *bodymind* or *mindbody*; others choose *body/mind* or *body-and-mind*. I settled on *body-mind* in order to recognize both the inextricable relationships between our bodies and our minds and the ways in which the ideology of cure [i.e., curative approaches to disability and gender-nonconformity] operates as if the two are distinct.[106]

Talia Mae Bettcher, meanwhile, suggests that the 'wrong body' narrative is not actually dualistic at all, but rather operates on a conceptualisation of the sexed self as having *three* layers – the presentational self, the bodily self, and the hidden or inner self (identity). On the 'wrong body' model, the presentational self acts as a corrective to the perceived wrongness of the bodily self, restoring one's outward appearance to its proper relationship with the hidden self. It is rather the standard *anti*-trans view that operates on a type of dualism, since it distinguishes only between the presentational self and the 'real' body hidden beneath the deceptive veneer of femininity or masculinity.[107] Either way, Bettcher criticises the 'wrong body' approach for premising the validity of trans people primarily on the acquisition of surgeries that are often either inaccessible or not desired at all, thus excluding enormous swathes of the self-defined trans population.[108] Leveraging Deleuzean and Derridean philosophies of selfhood, Jules Gill-Peterson also rejects the idea that trans embodiment necessarily exteriorises the soul from the body or works against an immutable bodily form, arguing instead that, in the process of medical transition, 'Life reaches beyond itself and returns to itself, touches itself and the world around it, in order to grow and change, to differ from itself over time.' She continues:

> For example, sex reassignment surgery ... [is] a participation in the body's open-ended technical capacities ... The intervention of the surgeon's technologies is not opposed to the body's systems but rather informs and is informed by them. Hormone therapy, likewise, is a participation in the technical capacity of the endocrine system ... medical technologies of sex gain their relative animacy from the body's own technicity, not in opposition to or by transcending it.[109]

One does not need to agree with these theories in order to understand that they irredeemably problematise the effort to condemn all trans embodiments as dualistic. Anti-trans rhetoric leaves no space for this kind of nuance; nor does it allow for diversity. For the purposes of trans people's tormentors, it is much better, as anthropologist of trans identities David Valentine observes, to 'ride roughshod over the complex details of people's lives', as doing so makes the work of wrangling this Leviathan that much easier.[110] This is possibly the most pernicious aspect of the Gnostic charge: that it moves the intellectual conversation onto territory that very few trans people have the specialist knowledge to defend, very simply *because it is not our territory and we do not care to defend it.*

As one familiar with the morally absolutist and oft-condemnatory tone of their writings might expect, conservative evangelical purists have done most to popularise the Gnostic charge in the Anglophone Atlantic. Gripped by an 'abiding fear' of Gnosticism's return in the maelstrom of (post)modernity,[111] evangelical thinkers warn that Gnostic thought 'undercuts' and 'infects' the gospel of Jesus Christ,[112] encourages the denial of his literal resurrection,[113] leads to solipsistic disregard for the welfare of the material world and its inhabitants,[114] and is ultimately the handiwork of 'the Tempter' (Satan).[115] Evangelical writer Peter Jones warns in *The Gnostic Empire Strikes Back: An Old Heresy for the New Age* (1992) that the rising acceptance of homosexuality, feminism, abortion, environmentalism and multiculturalism are all evidences of a new wave of demonic Gnosticism.[116] The addition of trans identity to this list of neo-Gnostic transgressions in the late twentieth century was only natural, once it had been concluded in conservative religious circles that trans people were defying their God-given creational truths. Like the Fall of Adam and Eve, Gnosticism acts as a sort of cosmic rubbish bin into which one throws anything that seems out of order in the world. Hence, if you don't like something theologically, one of your first instincts as an 'orthodox' Christian is to accuse said thing of being Gnostic, thereby wrecking any chance at an intelligent conversation.

Evangelicals are not, however, wholly responsible for the Gnostic charge. A highly developed and widely circulated version of it also features in one of the founding documents of transphobic feminism, Janice Raymond's *The Transsexual Empire* (1979), pre-dating the earliest evangelical experimentations with the idea. From this text sprouts both the Gnostic charge as we now understand it, as well as the philosophical framework for the main anti-trans coalition that so doggedly harasses trans people. Accordingly, we have little choice but to begin with a long overdue re-examination of that infamous and troublesome text, for while its significance in catalysing feminist-aligned expressions of transphobia is widely recognised, its formative role in the development of 'unlikely' transphobic alliances has been peculiarly overlooked.

2

Of feminists and mystics

Born on 24 January 1943, and for twelve years of her early adulthood a member of the Sisters of Mercy, a Roman Catholic religious order for women,[1] Janice G. Raymond enjoyed an eclectic higher education in America's coastal North-East. She graduated from Salve Regina University, a private Catholic institution, with a BA in English Literature in 1965; from the Andover Newton Theological School, a Massachusetts seminary, with an MA in Religious Studies in 1971, and from the Jesuit Boston College with a PhD in Ethics and Society in 1977.[2] Her PhD thesis, the foundation for the book that would cause her to be immortalised as 'the original Terf' (Trans-Exclusionary Radical Feminist),[3] was supervised by the famous Catholic (later ex-Catholic) radical feminist theologian Mary Daly, whose works, including *The Church and the Second Sex* (1968), *Beyond God the Father: Toward a Philosophy of Women's Liberation* (1973), and *Gyn/Ecology: The Metaethics of Radical Feminism* (1978), directly and unceremoniously challenged the normative patriarchal dogmas of the Catholic Church.[4] Daly's combative approach certainly rubbed off on her soon-to-be notorious student.

Published in 1979, Raymond's legendarily caustic monograph, *The Transsexual Empire: The Making of the She-Male*, has been described by seminal trans scholars Susan Stryker and Stephen Whittle as the work that 'did more to justify and perpetuate [transphobia] than perhaps any other book ever written'. They went so far as to compare it in this regard to the *Protocols of the Elders of Zion*, an antisemitic hoax text that has fuelled genocidal attitudes towards Jews since its publication in 1903.[5] It is easy to see why this comparison felt apt. *Empire* presents the rising visibility of trans identities and the increasing availability of gender-affirming medical care as fundamentally a story of hidden intentions and

42

nefarious plots, of men working to replace 'real' women with false ones, and so make it harder for women to organise as a coherent political unit. This is the 'Empire' Raymond speaks of – an effort by the masculine to colonise the feminine using new medical technologies. As will be discussed more below, Raymond argues that this epistemic invasion constitutes the 'total rape' of the concept of womanhood, and in the face of such a threat, the best thing women can do is totally reject trans women; to expel them from women's spaces and undercut any notion that their gender identities matter.

The true extent of *Empire*'s influence in British feminism at the time of its publication is disputed, but from the contemporary perspective of trans feminists in the Beaumont Society, a trans support network, and the Transsexual Action Group (TAG), a feminist and socialist trans campaign organisation formed in London in the early 1980s, it seemed as if Raymond represented the 'general consensus of opinion among feminists'.[6] Even if Britain's Raymondites were a tiny minority in feminist spaces, they were most definitely a *loud* and *determined* minority, and given its apparently wide impact, few overviews of the trans past have been produced without at least a passing mention of *Empire*'s publication, marking the point in the narrative at which transphobia becomes a serious political force.[7] However, the exact nature of the hatred contained in its pages remains at least partially misunderstood.

A traditional trans-positive summary of *The Transsexual Empire* runs something like this: Raymond's foundational error is to rely far too heavily on information from the sexological and clinical literature that established the conventional diagnostic features, conceptual boundaries and treatment strategies of transsexuality in the mid-twentieth century. The cisgender and almost universally White and male authors behind this literature, whose ideas had a firm hold over standard medical practices in the nascent system of trans healthcare, typically sought to enforce on their trans patients strict standards of gender normativity, meaning that trans people who wanted medical intervention often had no choice but to try to dress, talk and behave in an archetypically 'masculine' or 'feminine' way.[8] From the outside, then, it was fairly easy to conclude that trans people represented a reinforcement of patriarchal gender divisions and were therefore antithetical to the gender-deconstructionist instincts of radical feminism.[9] Once that conclusion had been drawn, conflicting information, such as the existence of trans lesbian feminists – people like Hazel, a London-based trans woman with 'innate radical feminist views' who founded the Feminist Transsexual Discussion Group (later TAG) in 1979,[10] or Sandy Stone, an American activist whose engineering role in the all-women Olivia Records music collective so strongly offended Raymond that she sent an early draft of *Empire* to the group in 1976[11] – could be folded into a conspiratorial mindset that imagined these individuals as deceptive infiltrators tasked with 'invad[ing] women's space'[12] so as to sap the feminist movement's capacity to resist the patriarchy.[13] Fully imbibing this illogical and far-fetched notion, some cis radical feminists continue to insist that trans inclusion in feminism is a 'derailment' technique and that cis women are being deliberately 'taken out of the picture'.[14]

As trans historian Cristan Williams explains: 'The message TERF opinion leaders send is clear: trans women represent the wolf in sheep's clothing; an enemy that could be anywhere, especially in authenticated women's spaces.'[15] Put another way, the enemy has already breached the inner sanctum and the only option now is to proactively expel them. Assigning so high a priority to this unholy task is in large part a distraction mechanism. As Jules Joanne Gleeson and Elle O'Rourke write in the introduction to their edited volume *Transgender Marxism* (2021):

The figure of the trans woman interloper, disrupting otherwise stable and harmonious relations within the community of women, functions to relieve radical feminism of the indignity of acknowledging the incoherence of the radical feminist project as such. Conveniently, the trans woman as pest distracts from long-running doubts around radical feminism's claimed ability to speak for, represent, and defend the sanctity of women-in-general: women's rights, women's interests, women's spaces and women's knowledge.[16]

The lone phrase 'trans woman interloper' is, basically, the sum of Raymond's views on trans women in a less verbose format. As a direct result of her chronic evidentiary malnourishment, Raymond mistakenly treats prescriptive medical texts written by cis men as a window into trans people's scheming minds. Justifiably disgusted by what she saw through the glass, but unjustifiably ascribing guilt to the very people who suffered most from the gender-normativity of the medical regime, she lets fly her transphobic rage in *The Transsexual Empire*. This passage is but a sample: 'The transsexually constructed lesbian-feminist, having castrated himself, turns his whole body and behavior into a phallus that can rape in many ways, all the time. In this sense, he performs *total* rape, while also functioning totally against women's will to lesbian-feminism.'[17]

I do not aim here to dispute the standard critique of the text, but I do wish to significantly expand upon it and fill in some of its empty compartments. Principally, commentaries on *The Transsexual Empire* almost always pass over its somewhat challenging, esoteric, opaque and often quite nonsequential theological elements; this is an oversight that is irreconcilable both with Raymond's educational and cultural heritage and, more importantly, with the privileged place she gives to her discussion of Gnostic transcendentalism and androgyny in the book's final chapter, immediately foreshadowing her concluding arguments. The positioning of this discourse at the climax of Raymond's argumentative flow suggests that she saw body/mind dualism as one of the cardinal philosophical problems of trans identity and among the foremost proofs, therefore, of its illegitimacy under feminist critical analysis.

Transcendence to a higher plane of consciousness, the ostensible aim of Gnostic religious practice, is not itself the sticking point. Raymond's intellectual mentor, Daly, was not opposed to anti-materialist transcendentalism per se,[18] and neither is Raymond. In *Empire*, she makes it clear that she regards the transcendence of the self over the imposed bodily confines of patriarchal society as integral to radical feminism's mission, because, as she says, 'who we are should not be defined by exclusive reference to our bodies.'[19] However, in her idealised futurity, the soul does not transcend the body by detaching from it, nor by exploiting the body's plasticity to make it align with a particular image of the self; rather, the soul *and* body, in constructive dialogue, should together transcend the limitations of their cultural environment, because to do otherwise would be to leave either the psychical or physical aspect of societal misogynistic oppression untouched. Thus, the error of the Gnostics, as Raymond perceives it, is not their dissatisfaction with worldly constraints, for this she shares, but rather is twofold in form: first, their assumption that full spiritual freedom can only be attained extra-corporeally, and second, their propagation of misogynistic value-judgements about the female body, which male Gnostic leaders often cited to justify women's systemic subordination within their movements.[20] Raymond's reservations centre most of all on the traditionally ascribed Gnostic belief that humanity once possessed an androgynous purity which, though lost when the Demiurge divided humanity along physical, anatomical lines, we might aspire one day to recover.[21] Under scrutiny, she argues, this androgyny reveals itself to be a disguised form of purified maleness and, by extension, a technology for the stealthy annihilation of independent female subjectivities.

The creation stories in the Gnostic scriptures and traditions differ greatly, but creational androgyny – the unity of the male and female in a single *spiritual being* as originally designed by the Prime Creator, or in a single *organism* as designed by the Demiurge – is a recurring theme, representing the proper, uncorrupted human state.[22] In the *Sophia [Wisdom] of Jesus Christ*, one of a collection of texts discovered buried in pottery by an unsuspecting Egyptian farmer at Nag Hammadi in 1945, a corpus only gradually translated into English from the Coptic between 1956 and 1977,[23] the Messiah explains that when the 'self-made Father ... decided to turn his likeness into a great power, at once the strength of [his] light appeared as an immortal androgynous Human.'[24] This Human was then placed into a physical bipedal body, marking the inception of the ancestral hominid we call Adam. Only later did material sex-differentiation take place with the creation of a woman, who would be called Eve, from Adam's side – an event that took place in the earthly Garden of Eden under the self-interested (mis)direction of that most malicious sub-divinity, the Demiurge.

The imagined archetypal adherent to the Gnostic scriptures considered this partitioning to have been a tragedy, rather than a cause for celebration. That Adam now had company was beside the point; he had lost a part of himself and was condemned, so long as he remained imprisoned in physical spacetime, to a lesser, eternally incomplete existence in subordination to the Demiurge. The Gnostics wished to undo what that infernal entity had done – to become whole once again – but since Eve is a fragment of Adam, and not Adam a fragment of Eve, the barrier to the restoration of one's complete humanity tends to appear higher for women than for men. Men must recover the missing chunk taken from their side; women *are* the missing chunk, and so their journey to recompletion is not so much about 'recovering' something as it is about *becoming* the full being that they never were to begin with.

A stunningly undiplomatic expression of the view that women are innately lesser, or more aberrated, beings can be found at the conclusion of the apocryphal *Gospel of Thomas*, another of the Nag Hammadi scriptures that presents itself as a series of Christ's sayings, most of them unreported in the canonical gospels.[25] *Thomas* has amassed a mixed legacy in the history of trans and anti-trans advocacy. Some of the reported sayings lend themselves to an egalitarian gender-deconstructionist view, but others can be construed as deeply misogynistic. It is simply a matter of emphasis. Gay Christian writer Keith Sharpe, in his popular book *The Gay Gospels: Good News for Lesbian, Gay, Bisexual, and Transgendered People* (2011), cites the 22nd saying in the gospel ('When you make the two one ... and when you make the male and the female one and the same, so that the male will not be male nor the female female ... then you will enter the kingdom') as an instance of Jesus 'counselling subversion of the traditional gender roles' in a way that affirms modern trans lives; for this reason Sharpe believes the gospel to be 'very important for LGBT people'.[26] This is probably as close as any mainstream trans-affirming figure has come to utilising an explicitly Gnostic theology in service to a pro-trans message.

Raymond, on the other hand, emphasises a more challenging passage from the ending of *Thomas* in which Jesus, responding to the apostle Simon Peter's proclamation that 'females are not worthy of Life' (i.e., life in the Kingdom of Heaven), goes so far as to state that 'every female *who makes herself male* will enter heaven's kingdom'.[27] These words, if they are read as evoking a hierarchy of the sexes, naturally perturb the feminist reader, and it was in this moment of guttural recoil that Raymond found an allegory for her feelings towards modern trans people. In an argument that first appeared in *Quest: A Feminist Quarterly* in 1977, drawing particularly on this poorly aged passage from *Thomas*, she asserts that Gnosticism's 'salvific androgyny' is effectively a sham.[28] 'Although the primal Adam is written about as androgynous or hermaphroditic', she posits in *The Transsexual Empire*, 'one is still left with the impression that the original human was more male than female.'[29] While the woman must 'make herself male' to reach the Kingdom of Heaven, 'no comparable process is necessary for the man', who nonetheless has freedom to appropriate femininity as required in his mission for *gnosis*.[30] Raymond argues on the basis of this double-standard that androgyny represents a 'false foundation of liberation' from gendered oppression, because (and I would agree on this point, at least where *Thomas* is concerned) it tends to imagine femininity as the fallen aberration and masculinity as the natural default.[31] At risk of getting ahead of myself, this is fundamentally the same critique of Gnostic eschatology that is offered by evangelical theologians, whose brows scrunch in equal measure at the realisation that 'for women as least, Gnostic salvation would mean gender-bending.'[32]

This logical sequence augurs and sets up Raymond's final salvo in *Empire* – the culmination of a book's-worth of pent-up suspicion. Her relatively well-founded (if quite stale by the late 1970s) arguments against Gnosticism and other forms of dualism and idealised androgyny fly off the tracks with her characterisation of 'transsexuals', who, while apparently suffering from an 'illusion of transcendence' stemming from the transformative powers of surgery and endocrinology, are said to be 'possessed' by the desire, never fully realised, to falsify the female bodily form.[33] As Raymond puts it in her recent reprisal titled *Doublethink* (2021), trans women are engaged in a 'masculinist attempt to colonize women in the interest of appropriating the female body for one's self'.[34] Hence, trans people and Gnostics are, by Raymond's estimation, trapped within the same philosophical error, that being a dualistic, male-centric transcendental fantasy characterised by a fallacious desire to conquer the feminine. The upshot of this pained theological-sociological contortion is this: trans women are not women. They never can be. To claim otherwise is tantamount to 'total' rape.

Discounting Raymond's singularly repugnant misuse of sources and her insatiable determination to offend, this particular argument against trans identities in *The Transsexual Empire* was never very innovative. Woman's relationship with her body had been a matter of foremost intellectual significance throughout feminist history, and the notion that what we would now call *sex* and *gender* might not always be in concordance had already been troubling feminist thinkers for centuries by the time Raymond arrived at the scene. For instance, eighteenth-century Quaker feminist Pricilla Wakefield, who regarded the 'effeminate man or masculine woman' as an 'absurdity', wrote of these individuals: 'One would almost conclude, that the mind and body had been mismatched, and by some mishap had been discordantly united.'[35] The debate over where the essence of womanhood lies – the mind, the body, the society, or all three – continued into the twentieth century, although by mid-century the fashions had shifted somewhat away from material essentialism. French existentialist philosopher Simone de Beauvoir stoked the flames after the Second World War with her stark dictum: 'One is not born, but rather becomes, a woman. No biological, psychological, economic fate determines the figure that the human female presents in society; it is civilization as a whole that produces this creature.'[36] If, as de Beauvoir saw it, womanhood is more a socialised state of being than an ingrained material fact – that is, more epistemology than ontology – then perhaps the soul and the society should be the focus of feminist theory. Large numbers of second-wave feminists certainly thought so; by the early 1980s, it seemed to Elizabeth Spelman as if 'somatophobia', an instinctive belief in the soul's separateness from and supremacy over the body, had become conventional wisdom in some feminist circles. She sensed danger in this development, warning that while there was 'nothing intrinsically sexist or otherwise oppressive about dualism', it did have the potential to be used in an oppressive manner if it were assumed, as so many people do, that the female body, as raw material, lacks intrinsic worth when compared to the male body.[37]

De Beauvoir herself recognised the potential inadequacy of a purely dualist approach. The Gnostics were among the historical specimens she dissected to illustrate the point: 'Gnostic sects', she wrote, 'made Wisdom a woman, Sophia ... So woman is no longer flesh, she is glorious body ... no longer an animal creature but rather an ethereal being, a breath, a radiance.'[38] Detached from a necessary ontological connection to her flesh, woman became at once ultra-human, extra-human, and sub-human. This is a dangerous outcome, especially if one were to apply the 'radiance' model of womanhood to government policy and expected social behaviours, as the emphasis is then on the evaluated *performance* of a hegemonically developed genre of womanhood as a prerequisite to *being* a woman. For others, the dualist threat lay much closer to home: *within* mainline Christianity, not out there in some long-forgotten heretical tradition. Feminist liberation theologian Rosemary R. Ruether argued in *Sexism and God-Talk: Toward a Feminist Theology* (1983) that the canonical scriptures were themselves dangerously shot through with a patriarchal dualism that imagined womanhood as materially bound and manhood as spiritually transcendent.[39] Concerns around dualist thinking thus coloured the zeitgeist in mid-to-late twentieth-century feminism, and Raymond was merely speaking to the proclivities of her age when she listed transsexuality alongside Gnosticism and other mysticisms as a malignant, malfeasant, misogynistic manifestation of extremist dualism.

Raymond's contemporaries were also on the lookout for new dualist threats, and given that she was operating within this broader milieu, it should come as no surprise that she is neither the first nor the last feminist to attempt this logical leap. Australian-British radical feminist Germaine Greer, who is of Raymond's generation and shares some portion of her Catholic educational experience, did so five years prior. Born in Melbourne in 1939 and educated by nuns at The Star of the Sea School,[40] Greer had once expressed a backhanded and palpably disingenuous solidarity with the '[d]isgraced, unsexed' British trans socialite April Ashley after the annulment of her marriage to a peer in 1970 due to her having been assigned male at birth.[41] However, Greer made her anti-trans views much clearer in her 1974 review of Jan Morris's landmark trans autobiography, *Conundrum*. Here, she castigates Morris for extending her 'belief [in the] fundamental separateness of soul and body to fairly grotesque lengths',[42] alluding to Morris's influential description of her true self as having been 'born in the wrong body'.[43] As an accomplished academic, writer, journalist and mountaineer, Morris and her book became lightning rods for feminist-aligned versions of transphobia. Another noteworthy anti-trans feminist author, Bernice Hausman, notes with equivalent disdain in *Changing Sex: Transsexualism, Technology, and the Idea of Gender* (1995) that Morris's retelling of her bodily experience, in encouraging readers to recognise a distinction between their inner selves and their bodies, evidently 'prefers the mystical to the material',[44] and many others, such as Margrit Eichler and Leslie Lothstein, have argued that trans people like Morris, particularly those who report feeling a fundamental sense of body/mind dissonance, need therapeutic disillusionment rather than acceptance[45] – effectively an endorsement of conversion 'therapies', which I discuss more in Chapter 4.

Daly characteristically carried the feminist counter-attack on dualism in her own idiosyncratic direction, advocating what she called a *Nag-Gnostic* approach to the subject of trans identities. According to Daly, Nag-Gnostic thinkers are those who 'sense with certainty the reality of transcendental knowledge [but] never cease to Nag our Selves and others with recurrent awareness and uncertainty'.[46] Her imagined nefarious transsexual claims to have achieved transcendence by manipulating the body in accordance with spiritual whims, but the Nag-Gnostic, as mature older sibling to the over-enthused Gnostic, perceives that this corrosive 'doublethink' is among the 'Biggest Lies' invented by the patriarchy to deny women their subjective autonomy.[47] Put another way, Daly argued that, though humans should certainly seek to transcend gender boundaries as a liberatory mission, simply crossing from one side of the divide to the other (and supposedly undermining both the feminist movement and cis women's sense of embodied self in the process) is not an acceptable method of doing so.

If the emphasis on Gnosticism and mysticism in these texts strikes readers as slightly arcane, this is more by reason of a change in the way these ideas are articulated in our own time than a fundamental shift in anti-trans feminism's basic philosophical objections to trans identities. Contemporary anti-trans feminists themselves seldom recycle these arguments verbatim. Gnosticism and other forms of mysticism are simply too far removed from the knowledge base of mainstream secular feminisms to provide relatable polemical hooks; most feminists likely lack any real grasp on what Gnosticism is or why it might be viewed as harmful. Consequently, Raymond's anti-Gnostic logics have, by necessity, been repackaged for use in less esoteric contexts, with the result that, in post-*Empire* 'TERF' literature, including Raymond's own introduction to the second edition of her book (1994),[48] it is not Gnosticism, but rather the deconstruction of binary sex/gender by postmodernism (and later by its mythical subgenre, 'gender ideology') that emerges as the imagined philosophical seed of trans people's purported invocation of body/mind dualist ideas. This is not a particularly surprising development, as postmodernism is, as we saw in Chapter 1, itself thought by many of its critics to be a recent mutation of Gnosticism.

The postmodernist turn in anti-trans feminist thought has occasioned some linguistic refurbishment – *mind* or *brain* often replaces *soul*, and references to postmodernist and gender-deconstructionist texts, like Judith Butler's enormously influential *Gender Trouble: Feminism and the Subversion of Identity* (1990),[49] replace references to Gnostic gospels – but there is a clear continuity in the way anti-trans feminists position themselves in cultural meta-discourses. The Enemy still offers up hollow transcendental illusions based on the partitioning of matter and ether, and anti-trans feminists are tasked with stopping the epistemological lurch lest it collapse the whole edifice of womanhood. So, while postmodernism has superseded Gnosticism linguistically in anti-trans feminist thought, it still plays the same role conceptually and rhetorically: that is, a dualistic straw-man against which to contrast a feminist conception of *woman* in her material and ethereal fullness. So smooth has been the transition that many contemporary transphobic feminist writers, thinking solely of the evils of postmodernism, habitually use anti-dualistic rhetoric trialled in the fight against Gnosticism and mysticism without, in some cases, even displaying an awareness of that connection.

Germaine Greer's later work is typical of the secularised post-*Empire* body/mind holism that became predominant around the turn of the present century. In her aptly titled book, *The Whole Woman* (1999), published a few years after Greer tried and failed to have a trans woman academic barred from Newnham, an all-women college at the University of Cambridge,[50] she blames postmodernism, rather than a mutated remnant of Christian mysticism, for the steady annihilation of the female subject. She writes:

> Post-modernists are proud and pleased that gender now justifies fewer suppositions about an individual than ever before, but for women still wrestling with the same physical realities this new silence about their visceral experiences is the same old rapist's hand clamped across their mouths. Real women are being phased out; the first step, persuading them to deny their own existence, is almost complete.[51]

Greer sees trans identities as constituent to this overarching assault upon the inviolability of sex, which, she insists, no amount of pompous postmodernist pontification can change.[52] A man is always a man and a woman is always a woman. Hence, the glib and churlish commitment of people like Greer to biological 'fact', which so defines the 'TERF' approach to sex and gender,[53] is intricately linked to a much broader concern that postmodern systems of knowledge-production threaten to render *all* claims to absolute truth inoperable. If there is no absolute truth on which to draw in one's effort to make sense of societal dividing lines, then the questions are: Whence the woman as an identifiable, delineable, and universally communicable entity? Does she even exist ontologically? Is it a bad thing if she does not? A stereotypical second-wave feminist political imagination, structured around an oppositional (men vs women) understanding of misogyny and oppression, tends to see this questioning of the assumed essential-ness of gender categories as evidence that 'men' (including trans women) are consciously assaulting the final truth of the material *in order to* assault the feminine by proxy – and so anti-trans feminist writer Jane Clare Jones argues that 'the erasure of the feminine, the maternal, the material, and the body' is a single, unitary project.[54] The rejection of one part of queer postmodernism, the de-essentialisation of gender and the body, is thus portrayed as an act of resisting the very patriarchy itself.

This is a vital point to grasp. Political transphobia may often be expressed as a defence of scientific 'fact' as an intrinsically valuable resource – in other words, it masquerades as a *realist* philosophy based in the belief that 'binary sex' per se exists independently of human cognition (a position that does not automatically lead to transphobia) – but the deeper issue is that the decoupling of physiology from psychology is thought to be profoundly *undesirable* in the first place, irrespective of its evidentiary merits. Realism thereby gives way to *consequentialism*, the belief that the morality of actions can be judged by their consequences, and it is here that 'TERFism' shows itself to be fundamentally *pre*scriptive and not *de*scriptive.

To fully subordinate body to mind, such that the woman loses her archetypal physiology, is believed to carry with it the potential to undermine 'real' women's capacities to recognise, and thus to resist, their own oppressions. Along these lines, British philosopher Kathleen Stock has warned that '[g]etting rid of the concept WOMAN would mean we couldn't describe, explain, predict or manage' the disadvantages that women face.[55] This concern for the future of feminist politics is echoed by other notable anti-trans feminists in Britain, including Sheila Jeffreys, who complains that the visibility and political self-awareness of the lesbian feminist movement has been damaged by the relativistic de-essentialisation of 'sex' and its conflation with an inner 'gender'.[56] Children's author J. K. Rowling, perhaps the world's most famous 'TERF', also believes that trans activism is 'doing demonstrable harm in seeking to erode "woman" as a political and biological class'.[57] When arguing against this kind of rhetoric, trans activists often get bogged down in the never-ending task of disproving the idea that simplistic binary sex (let alone binary gender) is scientifically inviolable, and we sometimes lose sight of what is actually perceived to be at stake in anti-trans belief systems. Whether or not sex or gender *is* binary in the way anti-trans factions state is substantively irrelevant; the real underlying argument, whatever its merit, is that sex *ought to be* treated as such because there is believed to be greater utility in doing so than there is in developing more inclusive definitions.

Stripped like so to its bare essentials, 'TERFism' is a reflexive rejection of epistemological messiness, a reactive fear of disorder and diversity, a nostalgic pining for simpler times before trans people made everything *so damn complicated.*

It is in this context that anti-trans feminism's obsession with post-modernism, and previously with Gnosticism, starts to make sense. In fighting what they consider to be a rearguard action against post-modernist currents within feminism, these individuals are seeking to reverse the damage purported to have been wrought upon feminism's internal coherence through the (perceived) advance of dualism. They aim to do this by re-emphasising the inseverable connectedness of body and mind, bringing the (cis) woman back to an intimate awareness of, and appreciation for, her whole body (as normatively defined, with a vagina, uterus, breasts, etc.).[58] Other exceptions to the normative definitional rule beside trans women, such as cis women born without a uterus or with underdeveloped sex organs, cis women who do not experience menstrual cycles, cis women with high testosterone levels, cis women who possess Y chromosomes, or cis women who experience minimal breast growth and have deep voices, are swept aside as inconveniences to the myth that modern gender distinctions are simply unprob-lematic referents for some exclusive genetic-anatomic essence. Who women *are* is thus pinned by anti-trans feminists not to their *actual* genetic-anatomic features as they exist in our world, as these are too diverse to reliably exclude trans women, but rather to an abstract female master copy – the ur-woman. It is the interests of this essential woman, not women-as-they-are, that feminism is believed to be fighting for, and it is in light of this fact that efforts to change the body, which promise to add even more complexity to the mix, appear most threatening. Hence, even while it claims to desire the abandonment of embodied gender stereotypes, the 'TERF' ethos can be encapsulated in a pithy refrain that repeats on every page of a children's book by Rachel Rooney, published by Transgender Trend: 'I am my body, my body is me, it's a wonderful thing, I'm sure you'll agree.'[59]

3

Trans as heresy in evangelical thought

Many a conservative Christian would agree wholeheartedly with Rachel Rooney's anti-dualist ditty quoted at the end of the previous chapter, but they would differ from secular feminists in a few major respects. The first point of departure is the fact that, on the whole, their viewpoint is premised upon a more overtly scriptural-teleological base. Popular evangelical question-and-answer site *Got Questions*, for example, tells curious readers that it is because 'God does not make mistakes' that the very notion of transing gender roles, let alone of changing the body as part of that activity, is in all cases contra-biblical.[1] The second major difference is that Gnosticism *is* a meaningful point of reference within historically minded Christian communities and *can* be used in semi-casual conversation to illustrate the grievances they might bear against gender ideology, and so there has been less internal need to adapt anti-Gnostic rhetoric for use against postmodernism or another more relevant target. It is appropriate, then, that while feminists played a significant and perhaps pre-eminent role in *developing* the Gnostic charge, conservative Christians have served as its senior custodians, giving it a much wider audience and longer life than it otherwise might have enjoyed.

Traditionalist Roman Catholic theologians and lay commentators, for their part, can often be found opining that gender ideology is rooted in a 'bizarre dualism of mind and body',[2] a philosophy that 'splits the world between spirit and matter'.[3] David Cloutier, a Catholic theologian who frequently writes on subjects of sexual ethics, cautions that it is 'hard to miss the echoes of a kind of gnostic dualism' in trans life narratives, particularly those of the 'wrong body' variety.[4] His warning reflects a broader concern, still haunting the Roman Catholic Church as much as it haunts evangelicals, that postmodern individualistic liberalism heralds the return of that millennia-old heresy known today as Gnosticism. A 2018 letter to Catholic bishops from the Congregation for the Doctrine of the Faith, the highest doctrinal council in the Church, makes precisely this claim, arguing that 'recent cultural changes', particularly the reification in some Christian theologies of journeys of individualistic self-discovery as pathways to salvation, rely on a 'neo-Gnostic disregard of the body [that] deface[s] the confession of faith in Christ'.[5] In plainer terms, postmodernism and individualism are considered antithetical to the Catholic doctrine of salvation, Christ's incarnation, and human existence as a soul-*and-body* reality.

However, as I mentioned in Chapter 1, it has typically been conservative evangelical Protestants, rather than Catholics, who have done most to popularise this line of reasoning in Britain and the United States. The man usually credited with kickstarting the trend in both evangelical and Catholic thought is English evangelical theologian and Christian ethicist Oliver O'Donovan.[6] Since being ordained as a deacon in the Church of England in 1972, O'Donovan has held a number of prestigious clerical and academic positions, including a brief period of service on the General Synod from 2005 to 2006 and a longer stint as Regius Professor of Moral and Pastoral Theology at the University of Oxford from 1982 to 2006.[7] His intervention in the field of trans theology in the early 1980s, arising in response to a report from an Anglican bishop in Canada who was asked to permit a trans parishioner to marry in their 'new sex-role', was brief and somewhat perfunctory, but his influence was enormous. In a 1982 booklet titled 'Transsexualism and Christian Marriage',[8] republished the following year in the *Journal of Religious Ethics*, O'Donovan wrote:

Any attempt to bypass the sexuality of the body ... runs counter to the close integration of the physical and the spiritual in the human person ... If I claim to have a 'real sex', which may be at war with the sex of my body ... I am shrinking from the glad acceptance of myself as a physical as well as a spiritual being, and seeking self-knowledge in a kind of Gnostic withdrawal from material creation.[9]

Though quoted many times as the foundation for the Gnostic charge through the years, this is the first of only two instances of the word *Gnostic* in O'Donovan's essay. The second, following closely on the same page, comes when O'Donovan concedes:

> But of course it will be argued that this conception [the wrong body paradigm] never really did justice even to the self-consciousness of the believing transsexual. Transsexuals do not retreat from their bodies into a Gnostic spirituality; if anything, they are preoccupied with them. Their very insistence in pursuing the hope of surgical intervention shows with what anguish they experience the dividedness of physical sexuality from gender identity.

This seems a fairly definitive wrapping-up of the Gnostic issue. It has been raised and then discarded with no real need for further elaboration – at least to the extent that it cannot, on its own, account for the complexity of trans people's embodied experiences. After all, the purpose of O'Donovan's essay is not primarily to adjudicate between different modes of understanding trans identity, but rather to ask how (or if) the Church can maintain an 'authentic' doctrinal position on male-female marriage and binary creational sex while 'conceding a certain autonomy to the public realm of appearances', that is, the realm of ever-evolving social norms as detached from Christian ontology.[10] As such, his discussion of the Gnostic charge sits unjustified, ephemeral, and seemingly random, like a passing nod to an established notion, leaving curious readers with the residual question: just where did he get the idea to compare trans identity and Gnosticism in the first place?

O'Donovan provides no citation to accompany this passage. In one sense, his musings are simply reflective of general trends in conservative religious philosophy at this time, when the staggered release of English translations of the Nag Hammadi texts kept interest in Gnosticism high. Additionally, whether linked with Gnosticism or not, the dualism argument has always served as the low-hanging fruit for lazy critics of trans people, particularly because it *seems* philosophically sophisticated but actually requires very little effort. If trans identity implies a distinction between bodily and spiritual selfhood, as any casual observer might be inclined to believe, then it follows that it can be partially blamed for the breakdown of sturdy societal norms and, by extension, for the slow death of objective truth. Therefore, trans is bad. Job done. Along these lines, conservative philosopher Roger Scruton argued in an article for *The Times* in March 1983 that, in trans-affirming belief systems, 'a person's sexuality is no longer regarded as part of his essence' and becomes instead a swappable attribute 'which he might change as he changes his clothes'. Scruton went on to assert that the decoupling of selfhood from the body (or 'our destiny', as he puts it) has negative consequences that are felt 'not by the [trans] patient only, but by the whole community'.[11] In other words, personal dualism breeds societal dualism. As Scruton later suggested in his book *Sexual Desire* (1986), 'it is precisely the existence of gender that serves to unite our sexual nature to the moral life that grows from it'.[12] Without traditional gender, traditional sexual morality becomes unworkable. This argument is only differentiated from the Gnostic charge by a few passing allusions to 'the Gnostics'.

The question of where O'Donovan 'got' the Gnostic charge is thus more a matter of style than of substance, but it is still a fruitful line of inquiry. Tellingly, he references *The Transsexual Empire* repeatedly and glowingly elsewhere in his essay, saying, for instance, that Raymond 'perceived with perfect clarity' the apparent conflicts between transsexualism and gay liberation, referring here to Raymond's unsubstantiated belief that trans people would reinforce the prescriptive behavioural bipolarity of gender and would therefore undo the gay liberation movement's de-essentialisation of gendered expression.[13] We know with certainty, then, that O'Donovan read Raymond and was influenced by her perspectives on trans politics, and it is likely that her book was also the source of his playful suggestion that trans embodiment could be seen as a form of Gnosticism. In gleaning this idea from Raymond and choosing not to challenge her, he made a choice between two evils, since it was entirely possible, as so many other evangelical writers have done, to depict feminism itself as a Gnostic heresy.[14] Prolific evangelical theologian Donald Bloesch, for example, labelled feminism the 'rebirth of a Gnostic mentality' in 1989, predicting that it 'can only end in a dilution of the Father symbol and the subversion of the Trinitarian name for God – Father, Son, and Spirit'.[15] O'Donovan, conversely, judged that transsexualism posed a more fundamental challenge to Christian orthodoxy than did Raymond's style of feminism, and so was more worthy of being lumped in with heretical traditions. He may not have been entirely convinced by the Gnostic charge, but he at least felt it informative enough to warrant mention; as food for thought if nothing else. Most of his evangelical readers failed to make that distinction, however, and the seed was thus planted for a future rhetorical alliance between them and the direct inheritors of Raymond's ostensibly feminist transphobic logics.

Whatever the genealogy of his arguments or his intentions in making them, O'Donovan hooked transphobia up to existing evangelical frameworks and made it intuitively readable to Christian traditionalists by positing a particular scriptural exegesis (interpretation, explanation, and unpacking of the biblical text) on trans identity that has remained almost entirely undiluted down to the present day. He equated surgical transition, for example, with the apostle Paul's concept of sinning against one's own body (1 Corinthians 6:18), rendering medical intervention for the purpose of reducing gender dysphoria immediately antithetical to Christian living. The alluring neatness of the paradigm ensured its recurrence in subsequent evangelical expositions, being revitalised in the year 2000 by an Evangelical Alliance Policy Commission report titled *Transsexuality*, wherein the 'reconciliation and peace' of Christ's gospel was contrasted with the 'sex/gender alienation of the self' that the Commission argued was intrinsic to the Gnostic outlook on the terrestrial and corporeal world.[16] David Horton, an evangelical Church of England clergyman who served as honorary chaplain to the Gendys Network and Sibyls (both trans support groups, the latter for trans Christians) and who produced a sympathetic booklet on trans issues in 1994,[17] complained that 'neither I nor the 3 or 4 other ministers I know who are working in this area' were being consulted by representatives of the Alliance, who seemed instead to be following 'some of the American [i.e., conservative] material put out'.[18] Horton nonetheless maintained contact with the Alliance, and he bemoaningly reported to the Gendys Conference in 2000 that they were working with 'unsustainable assumptions about transsexual life', by which he seems to be referring to an over-reliance on the 'born in the wrong body' narrative of trans embodiment to the exclusion of a more nuanced (and more mentally taxing) understanding of trans identities.[19]

The Alliance's report was cited eleven times, more than any other source, in a chapter on 'Transsexualism' in *Some Issues in Human Sexuality*, a book produced by a (partly evangelical) working group within the Church of England's House of Bishops (2003). In this chapter, the authors explicitly describe trans identity as 'a new form of gnostic dualism',[20] and argue that its rise represents the fulfilment of Christian ethicist Robert Song's warning that the powers of modern medical technology may prompt a hubristic desire to 'transcend the proper limits of our creatureliness by attempting to escape the body given by God'.[21] These arguments acquired heightened political pertinence when the UK Houses of Parliament at Westminster deliberated over the possible creation of a pathway for those diagnosed with gender dysphoria to change their legal gender in 2003–04, a process that ultimately yielded the Gender Recognition Act of 2004. Conservative evangelicals, fearing that the total legal decoupling of the body from the soul was about to be effected, offered the only organised resistance to this proposal – much to the bemusement of trans activists, who found them to be 'staggeringly inept' and unable to present arguments that would appeal to a wider secular audience.[22] During a House of Lords Grand Committee session on the Gender Recognition Bill, Baroness O'Cathain, a long-time associate of the evangelical Christian Institute, argued that '[u]ndergoing a sex change represents a desecration of the image of God ... and a rejection of God's providence', that is, the placement of the whims of the mind over the hard 'facts' evident in one's ordained bodily reality.[23] In 2007, in the wake of the Gender Recognition Act's implementation (and with interest in Gnosticism at an all-time high due to its role in Dan Brown's 2003 novel *The Da Vinci Code*), O'Donovan's original booklet was reissued under the new title 'Transsexualism: Issues and Argument'.[24]

More recently, the rise of *gender ideology* as an us-and-them signifier in traditionalist religious communities has further cemented the socio-political utility of the Gnostic charge. Much like the atrophied Gnosticism of modern Western imagination, *gender ideology* is thought by conservative evangelicals to be, at base, an un-nuanced belief that the body is separate from the soul, and that, where conflict arises, precedent should go to the latter.[25] The notion that one might make physical bodily adjustments (or at least present differently to how one is culturally coded) on the basis of gender dysphoria therefore seems, from an orthodox perspective, eerily Gnostic. British evangelical lobbyist Sharon James, who serves as the Social Policy Analyst at the Christian Institute, specifically characterises trans identity as 'a new form of an old heresy called Gnosticism' in an *Evangelical Times* article,[26] while the prolific evangelical theologian N. T. Wright, in a 2017 letter to *The Times*, calls the 'confusion' of gender identity a 'modern, and now internet-fuelled' rendition of that indomitable, inextinguishable ancient creed.[27] Moreover, in the aforementioned resource for affiliated church staff, *Transformed*, Peter Lynas of the Evangelical Alliance has restated the belief that:

> Any form of Christianity that devalues the body and the physical creation in general is deeply problematic. These ideas have more to do with Gnosticism, or ancient Greek Platonism, than following Jesus. While we must all wrestle with the resurgence of these ancient ideas in contemporary culture, they will raise particular issues for those seeking to live biblically with gender dysphoria.[28]

Despite being nearly two-score years removed, the flow of reasoning in this passage is practically identical to that in O'Donovan's 1982/3 essay – at least, the first half of O'Donovan's train of thought. In its sheer obstinacy, mitigated only slightly by a softening of language, *Transformed* is symptomatic of conservative evangelicalism's chronic failure to keep up with the moral and cultural knowledge-base of a changing world; its failure to assemble *new* and culturally responsive justifications for its strict gender dimorphism. Is this the hill we evangelicals want to die on, in defiance to an ever-mounting body of evidence showing that our preconceptions are flat-out wrong?

It seems, at a glance, that the answer is affirmative. Those few conservative evangelical writers who make some effort to move beyond the Gnostic charge, including Preston Sprinkle of the US Center for Faith, Sexuality & Gender, struggle to conceptualise trans identity as anything other than a biblically incompatible philosophy of dualism. In *Embodied: Transgender Identities, The Church, & What The Bible Has To Say* (2021), a book that, like *Transformed*, is aimed primarily at evangelical church leaders, Sprinkle at first appears to tackle the Gnostic charge head-on. He admits to having previously been convinced by the assertion that 'the "soul sexed differently from the body" view is straight-up Gnosticism and not a serious Christian option', but he now professes to believe that it is 'lazy and unthoughtful to simply write off every trans* claim as Gnostic and anti-body'. However, Sprinkle seems to be more concerned with developing effective messaging strategies than with acknowledging the factual inaccuracy of the association. Rather than resolving to topple the Gnostic charge from its slippery perch, Sprinkle observes simply that he has 'never met a trans* person who immediately *changed their view of human nature* after being called a Gnostic', strongly hinting that trans embodiment is at odds with Christian orthodoxy all the same, even if it is strategically counter-productive to *call* it Gnosticism.[29]

With his mind set on civility, Sprinkle goes on to spend considerable time making the case for a gentler, kinder conveyance of evangelical beliefs on sex and gender – even addressing trans readers directly with assurances of love and respect – but he still does not recognise the urgent need for a humble reconsideration of the very beliefs that have sowed hate and disrespect for decades. Elsewhere in the book, he reaffirms with minimal discussion the essentialist viewpoint that 'our biological sex determines who we are.' He further underpins this idea with the claim that part of Christian discipleship is 'learning to embrace our bodies as important aspects of identity' – a sentiment that many trans

Christians would fully agree with, but which, as Sprinkle expresses it, unfairly implies that they hold their bodies in contempt. He even argues, in no uncertain terms, that 'a strong ethical case can be made that transitioning is not just unwise but also morally wrong', because, as any proponent of the Gnostic charge will concur, it goes against 'God's creative intention'.[30]

Nor, despite Sprinkle's self-described scepticism, is Gnosticism itself entirely decoupled from trans identity in *Embodied*. Sprinkle's proposed route forward is not to grow beyond circular discussions of dualism but merely to distinguish between *soft dualism*, the belief that 'the soul is ontologically distinct from the body', and *strong dualism*, the belief that 'if there's incongruence, then the immaterial soul obviously overrules the body'.[31] He does not say into which category he believes most trans people's identities should fall. It is not even clear if this matters, for while *soft* and *strong* dualism are semantically differentiated by Sprinkle, they are functionally identical in this context in that both are judged to be out of step with Christian orthodoxy, and it is difficult therefore to avoid the conclusion that Sprinkle – though I believe him to be sincere in his desire for more constructive dialogue and for this issue to be humanised – has created less distance between himself and the Gnostic charge than he claims. After all, he still comments, without fully unpacking his words, that 'when I read statements from some gender-affirming writers, it sounds like they're quoting from an ancient Gnostic hymn'.[32] Which statements? Which hymn? What are the similarities?

Sam Allberry's *What God Has to Say About Our Bodies: How the Gospel is Good News for Our Physical Selves* (2021) follows a similar formula. Allberry actually manages to avoid the words *Gnosticism* and *dualism* entirely, but his conformity to the broad strokes of the Gnostic charge is unmistakable. The book opens with the argument that being pro-body 'is part of what makes Christianity stand out'. Allberry elaborates: 'It has been common among other religious (and nonreligious) belief systems to demean the body, along with our physicality – to see it as something unspiritual or in need of escaping.'[33] Because the body is 'intrinsically good, not bad', it does not need to be 'abandoned or changed into some completely different form'.[34] In fact, according to Allberry, Christianity holds that our very identity 'is something we find in our body',[35] and this view, we are reminded, stands in sharp contrast to the prevailing cultural perception that 'the "real me" is my soul or spirit' while the body is 'simply the lump of matter I am connected to'.[36] As usual, nothing is said about trans people's experiences of feeling the euphoria of wholeness as a result of their social or medical transitions, and indeed one has to wonder if disavowing the inherent plasticity of the created body is really a pro-body stance.

In any case, the fruit of this strange inability to move beyond accusations of destructive dualism is an astonishing disconnect between the rich diversity of today's trans lives and the unvarying enemy that the most immovable conservative evangelicals seem to think they are combating; the latter represented by a warped, sun-bleached Polaroid image of the 1970s trans stereotype that they borrowed from Janice Raymond. To argue, as they do, that 'gender ideology' is wrong *because* it superficially resembles a peculiarly anti-materialist form of heresy is a comically ineffective method of persuading all but the most predisposed audiences. Indeed, if the goal is to guide societal attitudes back to the mores of 'traditional' morality (as the writing of popular books and the submission of letters to national newspapers would suggest), then one might as well claim that trans people are Sabellians or Tondrakians for all the good it will do. However, all this presupposes that changing societal attitudes *is* actually the goal. It may well be that the Gnostic charge's chief rhetorical purpose is interior to the evangelical movement, where the more traditionalist factions tend to be dismissive of *all* forms of purportedly (post)modern individual or communal identity regardless of its philosophical underpinnings.[37]

As trans people's public visibility grows, and as pastors and churchgoers alike experience ever more frequent contact with trans people in their day-to-day lives, an appetite for doctrinal modernisation has developed in some sectors of the evangelical grassroots, ranging from quiet acceptance of trans churchgoers[38] to an open and sometimes angry refusal to tolerate anti-trans teachings.[39] Katie Pope, a UK mother of a trans child, wrote in to the evangelical outlet *Premier Christianity* in November 2019 to publicly challenge the 'scaremongering' anti-trans advice for parents distributed by groups like the Christian Institute.[40] Meanwhile, a few evangelical thought leaders, such as Methodist pastor and self-described progressive evangelical Morgan Guyton, have laid bare the logical inconsistencies of the Gnostic charge, pointing out that the Gnostics 'would criticize transgender identity for the same reason that [N. T.] Wright criticizes it: because they believed that what our bodies tell us is a lie'.[41] Christian ethicist and former progressive evangelical David P. Gushee (writing when he still openly identified with evangelicalism) sensed a paradigm shift on LGBTQI+ acceptance in 2015: 'The landscape is changing dramatically. And if even part of the vast evangelical community softens its stance, it could presage (even more) dramatic cultural and legal changes in the United States and other lands where evangelicals are a large part of the population'.[42] David Horton, a trans-affirming evangelical reverend, even knew of three (presumably closeted) trans ministers who were active in Evangelical Alliance churches in the year 2000.[43]

This gradual but unmistakable shift has not gone unnoticed by the sticklers for doctrinal gender binarism. The aforementioned Sharon James has warned that 'many professing evangelicals now believe that personal experience is an authority alongside Scripture', which, she says, has created 'intense pressure to "accommodate" transsexuality'.[44] It seems unlikely that James and others like her will be able to reverse this momentum. Data collected in the United States has detected a sharp decline in anti-trans opinions among self-described evangelicals in recent years[45] – a trend that is probably also applicable to the UK. A 2017 quantitative psychological study also found that American evangelicals, though they mostly view gender as binary, fixed and immutable, are at the same time almost as likely as nonreligious persons to affirm the intrinsic value of trans people, leading the authors of the study to suggest that 'there may be substantial support within evangelical Christian memberships to reduce discrimination toward transgender persons', and moreover that there could, despite appearances, be scope for a 'constructive approach' to LGBTQI+ acceptance based on 'shared values'.[46]

The erosion of anti-gay and anti-trans values among young Christians has been a particular cause for reactionary panic,[47] raising as it does the prospect that conservative purism will one day in the not-so-distant future be swept aside by a more interpersonally attuned, compassionate and gracious approach. Put simply, the homogeneity of the evangelical movement's gender doctrine, never as solid or time-honoured as it seemed, is in a state of slow-motion collapse. For those conservative evangelical leaders who have pinned their colours most determinedly to the mast of 'tradition', countering that collapse has become a matter of first-order moral gravity, a do-or-die moment in the history of the movement. Anti-Gnosticism serves as a convenient touchstone in this feverish reactionary effort against accommodation, distilling a complex cluster of phenomena into a reassuringly simplistic battle between God's revealed will and ancient heresy. The opportunity to develop more nuanced and relevant, not to mention gentler and more Christ-like, theological responses to trans people's lived experiences – or, even better, to *rejoice* in the gifts manifested in trans lives, prayers and testimonies – is eternally and tragically missed.

4

The alliance goes to war

Recent political developments have expedited the process by which anti-trans groups have abandoned any pretence of moderation and nuance. The rush of trans-positive legislation from 1999 to 2013 helped create the impression that the stability of the gender categories these groups once knew was about to be legally nullified, and the subsequent push by trans advocacy groups towards legal gender self-declaration or even the abolition of legal gender as a concept has set the claxons blaring in the halls of traditionalist thought. From their perspective, this is an all-hands-on-deck situation. So, as might be expected, the coordinated efforts of the 'unlikely' alliance have played no small role in facilitating both the slowdown in legislative progress and the raised volume of anti-trans sentiment in our society.

We have already seen that many conservative evangelicals and anti-trans feminists share a common opposition to dualistic attitudes to the body. Sometimes, particularly in secular feminist contexts, that opposition is aimed at 'postmodernism' rather than Gnosticism per se, but the two are almost interchangeable in trans-phobic literature. Both are believed to entail a damaging separation between the material and the ethereal and to promise a false path to transcendence. It is evident, also, that the two blocs, possessing this deep intellectual connection, are comfortable with (and rather well-practised in) the routine exchange of ideas and rhetoric. It has already been observed that Oliver O'Donovan cited Janice Raymond repeatedly in his work, but this point can be extended, for she is also quoted at length in a great many subsequent evangelical tracts on the subject, including *The Rise and Triumph of the Modern Self* by British evangelical Presbyterian theologian Carl R. Trueman, where her arguments go largely uncontested.[1] Sharon James of the Christian Institute often references Germaine Greer and the group Transgender Trend in her writings,[2] as does the Evangelical Alliance.[3] The New Social Covenant Unit, a campaign group founded in 2021 by evangelical Conservative MPs, has cited Transgender Trend articles to support its baseless claims that healthcare practices and school sex education classes are being hijacked by a post-truth leftist ideology.[4] As C. Libby writes, 'it is almost impossible to find an evangelical opinion paper or book on transgender issues that doesn't make use of such writing.'[5]

Years of citing feminist texts has left a perceptible imprint on the evangelical political vocabulary. Evangelical groups often mimic the emotive portrayal of trans women as sexual 'predators' who, if allowed into the corresponding bathrooms, prisons, sports, or other spaces, pose a 'danger to women',[6] all the while downplaying the dangers faced by trans women in men's spaces. They also share in the celebrations when a prominent anti-trans feminist is seen to have struck a blow against 'gender ideology',[7] and they helped popularise the bad-faith suggestion of like-for-like equivalency between transgender and transracial identities following the 2015 media coverage of Rachel Dolezal, a former chapter president in the National Association for the Advancement of Colored People (NAACP) in the United States, whose White ancestry was revealed, to great fanfare, by her parents.[8] There *are* interesting conversations to be had on this topic, but anti-trans voices are more interested in stoking public outrage against trans people by associating them with Dolezal's toxic reputation than they are in genuine dialogue.

Evangelicals have also played a part in legitimising the idea that the rising numbers of young people and adolescents seeking gender-related medical support is attributable to something called Rapid-Onset Gender Dysphoria (ROGD), an entirely unsubstantiated hypothetical subcategory of the clinical diagnosis 'gender dysphoria'. ROGD was popularised by social scientist Lisa Littman in a 2018 study that relied on survey data gathered from parents on three exclusively anti-trans hate websites, including Transgender Trend, concerning the parents' perceptions of the timing and causation of their children's expressions of having experienced dysphoria.[9] Although Littman's methodology and conclusions have been roundly discredited in the clinical[10] and sociological[11] communities, anti-trans feminists, including Abigail Shrier – the author behind an infamous transphobic screed, published by Christian Right-aligned Regnery Publishing, titled *Irreversible Damage: The Transgender Craze Seducing Our Daughters* (2020) – have leveraged ROGD to claim that trans influencers online are convincing healthy young girls to fool themselves and their peers into believing that they are experiencing gender dysphoria.[12] Aforementioned evangelical author Preston Sprinkle dedicated an entire chapter of his book *Embodied* (2021) to this conspiratorial ROGD narrative, suggesting that Christians must be aware of it and be able to identify the signs so as to stem the tide.[13] Additionally, the Evangelical Alliance's *Transformed* resource references an earlier article, published by Littman in 2017 in the *Journal of Adolescent Health*,[14] as evidence for ROGD, misleadingly placing this study alongside more reputable sources and failing to identify its obvious methodological shortcomings.[15]

Nothing is necessarily new here. The Christian Right has a long-standing propensity to 'appropriate' feminist language,[16] as feminist literary scholar Ellen Flournoy observes, and it is very experienced at using this adopted language to create the illusion of progressive credentials for quintessentially conservative campaigns on things like sex work and reproductive issues.[17] That this same strategy should be wheeled out and weaponised against trans rights is, on its own, nothing novel. But this is not the whole story. Less commonly noted, but no less real, is the transmission of argumentative material *from* conservative evangelicalism *to* anti-trans feminism, a contraflow that became especially visible during a UK Government consultation initiated in 2018 on reforming the Gender Recognition Act and a 2020 Women and Equalities Committee consultation on the same subject, both of which considered the removal of some of the more onerous barriers to changing one's legal gender, such as the requirement for a diagnosis of gender dysphoria. Hitting the ground at exactly the moment that political transphobia was embedding itself as a serious cultural force, these consultations 'trigger[ed] a powder keg of transphobia', as feminist writer V. S. Wells puts it.[18] Anti-trans feminist groups immediately mobilised to prevent any widening of the gates, and their publicity campaign appeared so effective that, before the publication of the 2018 consultation's findings, trans legal scholars Stephen Whittle and Fiona Simkiss prophesied that '[m]ost responses will be from women influenced by the myths perpetrated by organisations like Fair Play for Women', an anti-trans feminist group.[19] However, we must recognise that such groups are *importers* as well as *exporters* of language and ideas.

Most prominent among their imports is the 'religious freedom' trope, which has been used for decades by the Christian Right to discredit socially progressive legislation covering issues like same-sex marriage and anti-LGBTQI+ discrimination on the grounds that it might criminalise the practices of traditional-ist religious communities whose perceptions of morality and divine will preclude LGBTQI+ affirmation.[20] To a great extent, Christian Right voices in the 'trans debate' have resorted to a fairly unremarkable and unimaginative reprisal of this theme. The Scottish Government's analysis of the responses to its own consultation noted that religious groups expressed 'disappoint-ment that fuller consideration has not been given to the effect of a declaration-based system on communities of faith, including the evangelical community who, it was reported, would not recognise the term "gender identity"'. It was suggested by these groups that a self-declaration system as proposed in Scotland might override 'existing religious exemptions' in the original Gender Recognition Act, under which certain religious groups do not have to permit trans people to adopt sex-specific roles or enter sex-specific spaces if this is in conflict with the group's religious beliefs.[21]

In response to the UK-wide consultations, conservative evan-gelical groups like Christian Concern professed a belief that some of the suggested adjustments to the gender recognition process, such as the mooted abolition of a provision colloquially called the 'spousal veto', would 'violate religious freedom'.[22] The 'spousal veto' in this context refers to the formal capacity of a spouse to delay a married trans person's change of legal gender by refusing to give their necessary statutory consent to the change, thus stalling the process until the marriage is ended and restricting the applicant in the meantime to an Interim Gender Recognition Certificate, which can only be used to effect said annulment within a six-month period of receiving it. This sub-optimal system took its current form in an amendment to the Gender Recognition Act under

Schedule 5 of the Marriage (Same Sex Couples) Act 2013,[23] prior to which *all* existing marriages had to be ended as a prerequisite step towards obtaining a full Gender Recognition Certificate.[24] In certain conservative religious contexts (these, of course, being the only contexts alluded to by Christian Concern), statutory consent might be withheld by the spouse in order to prevent the creation of a same-sex marriage; or as an expression of their belief in the immutability of sex/gender; or as a way to avoid exposing their children to the putative 'confusion' supposedly created by their having an openly trans co-parent; or to facilitate annulment as an alternative to seeking a divorce, which is itself forbidden in various religious traditions. In these cases, the trans partner must either change their mind or annul the marriage.

One of the key problems under the current system is that the Interim Certificate's annulment utility cannot be activated if the other spouse starts divorce proceedings before this is done, which in some cases can be drawn out over long periods by vindictive partners. In other words, applying for a Gender Recognition Certificate as a married person can be absurdly risky if one's partner is remotely apprehensive or indecisive. Of course, trans activists do not disagree with the basic premise that a spouse should be able to exercise autonomy over their relationship status if they are unwilling to continue the marriage under these conditions. Instead, they point out that the spousal veto is an unacceptably damaging method of trying to uphold the objecting party's legal and moral rights.[25] Both parties to a marriage will naturally undergo changes as the years progress – one partner might leave the religion upon which the marriage was originally premised, for example – and sometimes there will be no mutually agreeable solution. Still, such considerations are not sufficient justification for the continuation of a system that puts married trans people in so precarious a position. This is undoubtedly a complicated matter which cannot be equitably and holistically resolved unless due consideration is given to a diversity of religious beliefs, but it is not insurmountable if all parties engage in good faith to find the best legal formula. To say that the protection of 'religious freedom' *requires* the maintenance of the spousal veto and all the anxiety and indignity that it entails is indicative of a catastrophic failure of imagination.

That Christian Concern would prioritise the defence of the spousal veto on grounds of 'religious freedom' is no great surprise, but few might have expected that many feminist groups and individuals would adopt the same narrative with alacrity in their own consultation submissions. The Authentic Equity Alliance, for instance, argued in relation to the veto clause in its own response to the 2020 Women and Equalities Committee consultation:

The consent provision should be retained … The ability to annul a marriage should not be taken away from women of religious communities in which divorce and homosexuality is forbidden. Indeed, it could be argued that to do so would be discriminatory toward the protected characteristic 'Religion or belief' [as established by the Equality Act 2010].[26]

Miranda Yardley, a transsexual woman who tends to side with anti-trans voices against the perceived excesses of trans rights activism, also advocated for the Government to retain the spousal veto on the grounds that 'nobody should be forced into being part of a same-sex marriage where they may have religious or other objections,'[27] a sentiment echoed by the anti-trans feminist group Sex Matters.[28]

Other feminists have extended their affectation of support for 'religious freedom' to their discussion of clause 9(1) of the Gender Recognition Act, which states that the holder of a Gender Recognition Certificate should be regarded for 'all legal purposes' as the gender legally bestowed by that certificate. They levy the language of the Act to stoke fears that a statutory gender self-identification system would render religiously ordained gender distinctions in churches or other places of worship unworkable – although *how* this would happen, given that religious exception clauses are baked into the Act as it currently exists and are also included in most proposed models for reforming it, is not elucidated. In an October 2018 article posted to *The Conversation*, an online magazine platform for pieces written by and for employed academics and postgraduate students, feminist legal scholars Rosa Freedman and Rosemary Auchmuty suggested that liberalising the gender recognition process might 'conflict with the rights … of religious groups that require segregation of the sexes in some contexts'.[29] Freedman elaborated on this supposed 'conflict of rights' in a Women and Equalities Committee hearing, during which she noted that some religions 'have sex-based roles, whether it is in terms of spiritual leaders or roles within a church, a synagogue or a mosque'.[30] Hitting a similar note, Transgender Trend has invoked the importance of preserving religious freedom in one of its transphobic resource packs for educators, using the hypothetical conservative religious traditions of pupils' families as grounds for arguing that it would be better for teachers to refuse to make adjustments for trans children, such as the use of preferred pronouns or the teaching of trans-inclusive sex education, in their schools.[31]

In addition to planting seeds of doubt about the legality and ethicality of trans-affirming policies, this shallow performance of concern for the rights of religious traditionalists has a more immediate pragmatic function for the feminists involved. Paranoid that they are being 'silenced' by trans activists, anti-trans feminists are, as described at greater length in Chapter 8, increasingly joining religious reactionaries in seeking anti-discrimination relief from the Equality Act 2010, under which 'religion or belief' is a protected characteristic. This is because transphobic statements and behaviours at work (or on social media) have put some anti-trans feminists in the same rickety boat as conservative Christians, some of whom occasionally face threats of dismissal from their places of employment for refusing to treat trans clients or colleagues with due respect. As such, 'religious freedom' has become an important vector through which anti-trans feminists are, in a calculated and intentional manner, pursuing their own interests, as they recognise that the verdicts in anti-discrimination cases involving Christians will impact upon their own ability to discriminate without consequence.

Another UK Government consultation run in 2021–22 brought into plain view an altogether more sinister convergence – a shared desire to close the cultural space in which trans people are permitted to exist. This time, the matter under consideration was the prospect of banning anti-LGBTQI+ conversion 'therapies', referring loosely to a set of practices which aim to make gay people straight or trans people cis. These 'therapies' are widely considered by medical professionals to be harmful and dangerous, often leading to increased risk of self-harm and suicide,[32] but anti-trans activists continue to cling to the morbid hope that trans people, having exploded onto the cultural mainstream, can feasibly be forced back into a state of repression and self-denial. Janice Raymond, in one of her most-quoted passages, argued that cis women should respond to trans identity by 'morally mandating it out of existence',[33] and Helen Joyce has stated that the function of anti-trans feminism amounts to 'reducing or keeping down the number of people who transition [because] every one of those people is ... damaged [and poses] a huge problem to a sane world'.[34] A large number of conservative evangelical groups, meanwhile, believe that trans people must reclaim their 'creational' and 'God-given' identity by laying aside the serpentine deceptions of 'gender ideology' and finding true freedom in obedience to Jesus.[35] Being so driven, anti-trans feminists and many conservative evangelicals passionately oppose the banning of conversion practices.

Both projects are ultimately rooted in a misguided desire to reverse the effects of Gnostic/postmodernist dualism by repairing the wounds that, so the argument goes, are created by the brutal separation of the mind/soul from its body. However, there is one major point of dissonance evident in the consultation responses of anti-trans feminists and conservative evangelicals. Whereas the former group pursues trans-to-cis conversion as a way to rescue what they see as repressed lesbian, gay and bisexual children from the alleged coercion of gender-affirming medicine, which they insist is 'itself a form of conversion therapy',[36] the latter group typically entertains no such reinforcement of non-normative sexualities. The end-goal of most Christian conversion 'therapies' is not to make a person *cis and gay* but to make them *cis and straight*. In theory, this should present a barrier to cooperation, but anti-trans feminist groups, perhaps seeing faith-based conversion practices as the devil they know, are meticulously conscientious to avoid breaking ranks with their Christian allies.

One leading group, Sex Matters, argues in its consultation response that, because 'the UK is an increasingly secular country' and conversion practices in religious settings are now contained to 'small pockets', targeting religious conversion therapy would be 'fighting yesterday's battles'.[37] The Welsh group Merched Cymru and the Scottish group For Women Scotland similarly cast doubt on the idea that 'additional legislation' to stop 'largely historic' conversion practices is necessary.[38] The LGB Alliance describes religious attempts to 'cure' queer sexualities as 'abhorrent', but denies that it is 'the role of the state to say some forms of religious belief are valid and others are invalid, or that some religious rituals are acceptable and others are unacceptable'. To rally support during the consultation period, the Alliance used a campaign slogan that evokes the common homophobic religious exhortation 'pray the gay away', but diverts the blame onto gender-affirming medicine – 'Stop Transing The Gay Away'.[39] Meanwhile, the submissions of some other feminist groups, including those of the Women's Human Rights Campaign (now Women's Declaration) and the Bayswater Support Group, simply neglect to mention faith-based practices at all, conspicuously glossing over the integral role that anti-trans Christian institutions play in the perpetuation of these acts.[40]

With so many anti-trans feminists quite deliberately leaving the way clear, hard-line religious groups have been at liberty to defend their damaging 'reparative' rituals with minimal interference. 'Religious freedom', which is also commonly used as an argument against banning conversion practices in the United States,[41] is once again the issue at hand. The UK Government's consultation document promised that any new provisions to ban efforts at conversion would 'not impact everyday religious practice',[42] but anti-trans evangelicals were not convinced. A letter signed by over 2,500 evangelical ministers and church staff expressed concern that 'our duty ... of proclaiming the Lordship of Jesus Christ ... which includes living by his laws, will be criminalised.'[43] The Family Education Trust, an evangelical lobbying group which has actively sought to bring conservative evangelicals and 'gender critical' feminists into contact,[44] notes: 'Since talking conversion therapies frequently take place in a religious context, this proposal [to ban them] has serious implications for freedom of speech and religion.'[45] Meanwhile, John Stevens, National Director of the Fellowship of Independent Evangelical Churches, warns that a ban could pose 'a real threat to ordinary gospel ministry',[46] and the Let Us Pray campaign, founded by the Christian Institute, suggests in a fit of hyperbole that it might soon be 'illegal for Christians ... to pray for their friends'.[47]

The Evangelical Alliance, while encouraging its members to support the ban in general terms, also insists that 'common ministry practices could be caught by these proposals' and urged for the ban to be watered down.[48] In April 2021, then-Prime Minister Boris Johnson wrote to the Alliance to reassure them that, under the proposed law, adults would still be able to 'receive appropriate pastoral support (including prayer), in churches ... in the exploration of their sexual orientation or gender identity'[49] – an innocuous way of saying that some forms of prayer-based conversion 'therapy' could continue unabated. The cumulative effect has been to erode, via a series of tenuous whataboutisms, the notion that conversion 'therapy' is a recognisable phenomenon that can be made subject to law without far-reaching unintended consequences. What about 'ordinary' Bible ministry? What about prayer? What about 'successful' conversions? What about Christian or 'gender critical' parents trying to dissuade their trans children? Anti-trans feminist organisations, many of which ostensibly exist to protect lesbian, gay and bisexual people from coercive abuse, elected not to undercut this diversion.

At first, this approach seemed to prove itself tactically sound. After a series of leaks and hurried public statements on 31 March and 1 April 2022, the UK Government announced that it would ban gay-to-straight, but not trans-to-cis, conversion 'therapies',[50] thus threatening to act against the clear advice of leading medical experts.[51] This came less than two years after the same Government announced that it would not pursue reform of the Gender Recognition Act,[52] despite the great majority of respondents to its consultation having endorsed legislative change to loosen the current system.[53] A meagre morsel of relief for trans campaigners came on 17 January 2023, when the UK Government about-turned on its prior decision and declared that anti-trans practices *would* be included in the ban on conversion practices,[54] although the very same day it also declared its intent to activate never-before-used powers under Section 35 of the Scotland Act 1998 to prevent the Gender Recognition Reform (Scotland) Bill from attaining Royal Assent.[55]

Its rationale for the latter move contained three points. First, that it would be disadvantageous and overly complicated for the UK to have two 'parallel and very different regimes' for obtaining a Gender Recognition Certificate within its borders, especially if it meant that a citizen of the UK could 'have a different gender, and legal sex ... depending upon where they happen to be within the UK' (this would not have been a problem had the UK Government carried through on its stated intentions under the premiership of Theresa May to modernise the system along similar lines via legislation in Westminster).[56] Second, that the loosening of requirements and definitions under the Bill would lead to an increase in 'fraudulent applications' (this is unavoidable if the overall number of applications rises, but to suggest that this would constitute a prohibitive problem is far-fetched) and would potentially effectuate 'a substantive change to what a "man" or "woman" is for the purposes of the 2010 [Equality] Act'.[57] Third, that protections for women under the Equality Act 2010 would be diluted if a larger 'cohort' of people could obtain a Certificate and thus be entitled to be treated according to their new legal gender 'for all purposes'. As regards single-sex spaces, the Government claimed that the Bill would lead to the 'self-exclusion of [cis] women who, for religious, philosophical belief or other reasons, may only feel able to attend an association if they understand them to be segregated by biological sex'. Such people, it is stated, 'are more likely to believe, given the increase and expansion of the cohort [of Certificate holders] if the Bill is enacted, that [complete segregation based on biological sex] is unlikely'.[58] The evidence detailed for these claims is scant-to-absent.

The arguments concerning overcomplication are agonisingly close to getting the point. As the legal, cultural and civil distinctions between genders become fewer in number and lesser in significance, greater attention is being paid by policy experts to the question of whether the Government needs to record a person's 'official' gender in the first place. The Future of Legal Gender Project, led by researchers at King's College London, considered various ways that gender might be legally 'decertified', and concluded, contrary to the Government's opinion, that such a move would not undermine gender-based protections in anti-discrimination law. 'The current grounds of "sex" and "gender reassignment" in the Equality Act 2010', reads the project's final report, 'would be merged to form the ground of "gender" as a "protected characteristic" for discrimination, harassment etc. and the public sector equality duty.' Gender identity would not cease to exist as a legally 'real' phenomenon; rather, it would begin to operate on a similar legal plane to sexual orientation and other characteristics that do not appear on one's identity documents: 'Recognising gender as a "ground" of inequality and discrimination, i.e. the basis on which inequality and discrimination take place, does not require individuals to be legally assigned to specific gender categories.'[59] Unfortunately, as with the spousal veto, some interest groups refuse to entertain the possibility that the balance struck in our current system is unjust, let alone set their imaginations loose to consider how we might create a better system that works for everyone.

In each of its main points, the rationality behind the January intervention closely conforms to the argumentative tropes modelled by both anti-trans feminists and conservative Christian groups; that is, a poorly substantiated web of speculation concerning the purported 'adverse effects' of law reform, coupled with a total disregard for the safety and well-being of the very community – trans people – for whom the legislation is of most relevance. Fears that male sexual predators will use self-identification *en masse* to enhance their access to women's spaces (or *are* doing so in countries that already have such a system) are presented as beyond reasonable question; the *fear* or *concern* alone outweighs any empirical evidence. In this way, the Government's rationale relies on the fact that the rhetorical groundwork has already been laid for such assertions to be made without the proper enumeration of proof. And so it would seem, at the time of writing, that a far-reaching intellectual, rhetorical and strategic pact premised on resisting the exaggerated and misconceived evils of body/mind and sex/gender dualism has played a significant role in scuppering, or at least stalling, the progression of key trans rights objectives in the UK. That is to say, an ideological eclipse that started as a steady agglutination of anti-dualist sentiments in the 1970s and 1980s has matured into an actualised collaboration with considerable, if under-reported, political clout.

What are we to make of all this? In what way are we to account for the calculated and deliberate nature of feminist involvement with extremist conservative evangelicals in UK politics? In her own effort to explain how Christian fundamentalists in Britain have managed to attract so many secular feminist allies to their various reactionary causes, including the public demonisation of sex workers, scholar Sukhwant Dhaliwal suggests that progressives are being fooled by 'the fact that [the Christian Right's] ideological commitment to creating God's law on earth is often obscured from view'.[60] In the case of anti-trans Christians, however, their theocratic tendencies have remained fairly self-evident, *and yet* significant numbers of feminists seem to regard them as apposite associates. There is more to this than a simplistic 'enemy of my enemy' calculation. These belief systems have been crossing paths for nearly half a century. Gender ideology serves as the mutual receptacle for each group's gripes about contemporary society, and resistance to its dissemination acts as the 'symbolic glue' that holds a wide array of factions together.[61] But that does not mean the anti-gender movement is, as Stefanie Mayer and Birgit Sauer put it, merely an 'empty signifier [that] allows for the ongoing addition of further ... threats ... that can in some way be constructed in relation to the denaturalization of gender and/or sexuality'.[62]

Rather, membership of this movement is defined by an authentic (if sometimes inauthentically expressed) belief that the mind or soul cannot be 'other' or 'opposite' to the biological organism of which it is a part. Mind informs body; body informs mind; mind *is* body. Transcendence over the here and now is thus achieved not by leaving the corporeal behind, for that way lies self-atomisation and/or alienation from God's plan, but by accepting the body as it is, as it was designed, and by carefully repairing any cracks that open between psyche and physiology. This is both a negative and a positive statement; a rejection of 'gender ideology' and, more fundamentally, a declaration of intent, a sort of socio-political manifesto. Understood in this way, as a body-holistic movement at its core, the entente between transphobic feminists and some conservative evangelicals ceases to appear 'unlikely', and reveals itself instead to be entirely natural. Certainly, their drive to work together is strong enough to justify the careful redirection of attention away from those matters on which the two sides remain irreconcilable. This being the case, activists, researchers and journalists alike must resist the misleading, if cathartic, belief that anti-trans feminists are 'useful idiots' being directed by nondescript Christian Right puppet-masters. The feminists in question are often entirely conscious of their involvement with conservative religious groups, and in fact are frequently the ones doing the 'using' – by affecting concern for 'religious freedom' as a vector for protecting their own legal interests, for example.

By and large, however, this is not a user-and-used relationship. The sense that body/mind dualism, whether Gnostic or postmodernist, is damaging to one's well-being is felt passionately and sincerely by both groups. Nor can this affinity be dismantled or discredited simply by pointing to it in scandalised indignation. While some casual participants in anti-trans feminism might be discomfited to discover that the movement's leaders have links to the Christian Right, others will conclude, as those leaders have done, that there is nothing untoward about collaborations between people who substantively agree. That is why, in all likelihood, the discursive, strategic and organisational integration of anti-trans feminism and the more purist, unbending iterations of conservative evangelicalism will continue into the foreseeable future. Indeed, the task of telling them apart, already difficult in some cases, promises to become ever more laborious.

PART II

The theological bit
(and why it matters)

5

Gender orthodoxy

There is a pervasive perception in trans spaces that anti-trans religious doctrines are really just a front for an irrational disgust response towards trans people, and for many readers it probably feels as if attempting to analyse the theology of transphobia on its own terms is already to give it too much credit. I agree, at least to the extent that it would be wrong to create a false equivalency between the belief that trans people have an innate human right to live dignified lives and the belief that they, ideally, should not exist. We cannot detach the latter belief from its detestable real-world effects, but *this is precisely why understanding it and being able to counter it matters so much*. Christian organisations are among the most energetic and well-funded progenitors of anti-trans activism in the UK and around the world. As the previous chapter attests, they are expert at portraying their beliefs as unproblematically reflective of Christians-in-general, as if there is a unitary 'Christian view' that policymakers should feel obliged to take into account. Whether or not you are yourself a Christian, it is important that we (by which I mean anyone who is unwilling to accept dangerous bigotry as doctrine) know what lies behind these ideas. So, let's dig a little deeper into anti-trans theology.

Anti-trans beliefs are widespread in evangelicalism, but they are not intrinsic to it and they *can* be challenged – *if* one knows how they work. One important reason for the Gnostic charge's extraordinary longevity and undeserved fortitude in evangelical religious communities is its reliance on intuitive theological truisms to which most evangelicals would subscribe in one form or another. These truisms are very easy to parse on a semantic level, being communicable to anyone with a basic knowledge of mainline Christianity, yet at the same time are near-impossible to fully unpack on a conceptual level. Take, for instance, the statement *God does not make mistakes.* This assertion seems inarguable if one believes in an omnipotent and omniscient Creator-God – I believe it, in the round – but much like the statement *God created Adam and Eve, not Adam and Steve,* which intuits the apparent ungodliness of homosexuality from the fact that God did not create two men in the Bible's creation story, the statement *God does not make mistakes* in this context elides a long list of contestable assumptions.

Among these are: 1) that divine command dictates that human social interrelations must remain as they are described in the Genesis creation story; 2) that God grants humans no agency to define their own modes of embodiment or societal roles; 3) that trans and intersex people, so clearly a part of observable reality, have no place in God's creational order or providence, and 4) that trans Christians see the material conditions of their existence as a divine 'mistake'. Packed so tightly with questionable truth claims, the statement is like a super-condensed Gish gallop – a rhetorical technique in which one fires an unmanageable number of ideas at an interlocutor in order to confuse and distract. Given that the Gnostic charge gestures towards these larger questions, even while not actively engaging with them, it is worth attempting to map out its theological genealogies. To do this, we first have to understand the essentials of theological and ethical thought in modern evangelicalism, as well as the biblical methodology behind evangelical argumentation. The two main ingredients here are *systematic theology* and *Christian ethics.*

In its most conservative and 'orthodox' guise, *systematic theology* is fundamentally nothing more than a gameplan for reading the Bible. I will refer here mainly to the work of prolific American Southern Baptist scholar, translator and theologian Wayne Grudem, one of the world's most influential anti-trans evangelicals. He co-founded the Council on Biblical Manhood and Womanhood in 1987 and was a key contributor to the Council's 2017 Nashville Statement, a meticulous reaffirmation of the biblical illegitimacy of LGBTQI+ identities, including trans identities, that has been signed by thousands of Christian leaders.[1] In his widely distributed textbook for seminary students and churches, *Systematic Theology: An Introduction to Biblical Doctrine* (1994, 2020), Grudem describes the methodology behind this theological school as a process of 'collecting and understanding all the relevant passages in the Bible on various topics and then summarizing their teachings clearly so that we know what to believe about each topic'.[2] Because it affirms that each book of the Bible relates to the rest as part of a joined-up story, systematic biblical argumentation often takes the form of quoting a series of passages that might be construed as relating to the theological topic of interest – say, the Trinity – and finding the through-lines that can be put together to tell a consistent narrative. These snippets are sometimes referred to as 'proof texts', and the act of quoting them as 'proof texting'. This often comes with an uncharitable overtone of intellectual condescension from theologians of other schools, in large part because systematic theology is thought to abuse the passages it relies upon by decontextualising them and drawing inferences that may not be justified.

Christian ethics in this context is effectively an outgrowth of systematic theology. In another of his mammoth textbooks, *Christian Ethics: An Introduction to Biblical Moral Reasoning* (2018), Grudem defines this ethical framework as 'any study that answers the question, "What does the whole Bible teach us about which acts, attitudes, and personal character traits receive God's approval, and which do not."'[3] Though it does not assert that all ethical questions are equally significant before the eyes of God, evangelical Christian ethics does tend towards the view that the Bible offers *some* instruction on every question that matters to the Creator. A section on 'The Transgender Question' in Grudem's *Christian Ethics* offers a fairly representative example of ethical exegesis as it plays out in conservative evangelical contexts. Near the beginning of the section, Grudem presents readers with a wall of text comprising 13 Bible passages in which distinctions between men and women are discussed, and from these he draws the conclusion that a person's gender identity 'should be the same as that person's biological sex' and, by extension, that it should be intuitively recognisable to other people from an individual's physical characteristics and aesthetic presentation.[4] These passages include Leviticus 18:22 ('You shall not lie with a male as with a woman; it is an abomination') and Deuteronomy 22:5 ('A woman shall not wear a man's apparel, nor shall a man put on a woman's garment, for whoever does such things is abhorrent to the Lord your God'). The contention is that this type of gendered instruction breaks down if 'man' and 'woman' are taken to be anything other than strict, biologically determined classes.

Grudem's belief that these passages can be applied directly to modern trans people reflects wider conservative Christian opinion.[5] In a 2016 article titled 'Confronting the Transgender Storm', another evangelical ethicist, Jason DeRouchie, places particular emphasis on Deuteronomy 22:5. In order to make the passage seem relevant to the issue of trans identities in the modern world, DeRouchie evades discussion of the Christian doctrine that the letter of the Law of Moses (of which Deuteronomy is a part) is not binding on Christians. He also slides past the constant changes in cultural norms that preclude any stable distinction between men's and women's clothing across time. He wholly rejects alternative interpretations of the passage as an injunction against pagan ritual or as a culturally specific measure to protect the distinctiveness, stability and fertility of post-Exodus Israel, and argues instead that the verse provides a 'corrective to gender confusion and transgender identity' because it tells us to 'celebrate men being masculine and women being feminine'. His prescription, based on this painfully extrapolative exegesis, is for trans people to 'realize that [their] sin is a direct affront against God and to repent'.[6] Most anti-trans evangelical texts rely on similar logical leaps and strategic occlusions to arrive at an ostensibly Bible-centred point of view, the aim being to present anti-trans theology as an intuitive, back-to-basics form of Christian faith. However, as another systematic theologian, Jamin Hübner, argues, this is deliberately misleading, and anti-LGBTQI+ theology in actuality 'emerges out of a particular ideology and cultural ethos. It is not religiously, ideologically, or culturally neutral. It is not "mere Christianity."'[7] This can be seen most clearly if we recall that Deuteronomy 22:5 was once used to argue that women should not wear trousers – something that few evangelicals believe today. The only thing that has changed is our *culture*, which no longer views trousers as masculine per se.

Despite the common use of systematics to undermine the acceptance of trans people, a trans-affirming exegesis does not in any way have to abandon the systematic methods of biblical reasoning upon which modern evangelical theology rests; nor are these theologians justified in declining to accept exegetic conclusions on this subject that differ from their own. Though he believes that the weight of scripture supports a gender-binarist view, Grudem himself leaves significant room in his *Systematic Theology* for honest disagreements between Christians – even concerning some fairly major matters. He stresses, first, that the conclusions drawn from one person's collation and interpretation of passages 'does not have to take the exact form of anyone else's conclusions on the subject, because we each may see things in Scripture that others have missed, or we may organize the subject differently or emphasize different things'.[8] He offers by way of example the variance of opinion among some evangelicals as to the age of the earth: whether old (billions of years) or young (thousands of years). At the conclusion of a long chapter evaluating the scriptural basis for each position, Grudem insists that 'both old earth and young earth viewpoints should be acceptable' to evangelical church leaders. He continues: 'It is not ... a question of believing biblical authority versus believing scientific authority. It is simply a question of *interpreting* the Bible that both sides firmly believe to be entirely true.'[9]

Another example of systematic theology leading to contrasting conclusions might be found in the different ways that trans Christians like me and socially conservative cis Christians like Grudem go about finding passages that could relate to trans identities. Grudem, with a largely medicalised understanding of trans epistemology and a long-standing belief that gender is immutably binary, would ask what the whole Bible has to say about the morality of wearing certain clothes, or of surgically and hormonally adjusting the body to address gender dysphoria. This leads him to passages like Genesis 1:27 (in which it is stated that God created humanity 'male and female', as discussed at greater length in the next chapter) and Deuteronomy 22:5 (the injunction against mixing male and female clothing). On the other hand, a trans Christian, particularly one who believes that their experience of gender and embodiment is part of God's good plan for them, would tend to ask what the Bible has to say about issues like free will, diversity, inclusivity, marginalisation, gentleness, charity, God's love, self-love, loving thy neighbour, loving God, personal growth, and life events such as coming out or changing one's name. The latter believer's engagement with the Bible is entirely consistent with the basic praxis of systematic theology, and is arguably *more so* than anti-trans biblical theology in that it is more holistically concerned with how the passages that touch on sex and gender *relate to* the Bible's overarching messages on God, creation and the godly treatment of self and others, especially the marginalised. The take-away is that the questions we ask of the Bible must themselves be subject to prayerful consideration, because we might otherwise ask poorly considered questions rooted in inaccurate and oppressive preconceptions.

Relatedly, Grudem also acknowledges that the Bible does not tell us 'every fact there is to know about any one subject', leaving many things open to human reasoning.[10] Our senses come into play here, as what information we do find in scripture ideally 'corresponds closely to the information we have gained from our own sense-experiences of the world around us'.[11] Our investigations into observable reality *should* cause us to question accepted doctrine that does not account for new information – say, the prior cosmological doctrine that the sun revolves around the earth, or that it rises and falls over a flat plane – because to do otherwise is to suggest that the Spirit-breathed words of God contradict every datapoint we now have available in our present scientific age. Maintaining a dialogue between exegesis and other forms of historical or scientific study is not, therefore, contrary to faith, but is *a necessary part of how faithful discipleship is practised*. For this reason, notes Grudem, Christians 'should eagerly anticipate the publication of [new historical and scientific] data with the absolute confidence that if it is correctly understood it will all be consistent with Scripture and will all confirm the accuracy of Scripture'.[12] The rapid emergence of intriguing new historical, archaeological, sociological, anthropological, biological and medical information concerning various aspects of gender-nonconformity and human sexuality *does* directly challenge our traditional understandings of certain passages of the Bible, but this need not be a cause for concern. Systematic theology is theoretically equipped for a thoughtful reconsideration and synthesisation process in which a thorough about-turn in exegetic norms *must*, as a non-negotiable aspect of faithful discussion, remain on the table.

It follows also that we should exercise considerable caution when drawing conclusions from observations of the world, as our somatic comprehension of our surroundings is limited by the fact that 'in a fallen world knowledge gained by observation ... is always imperfect and always liable to error or misinterpretation.'[13] Like any enthusiastic humanities student, I am reminded of French philosopher-historian Michel Foucault's preface to *The Order of Things* (first published in English in 1970), in which he quotes from a fictionalised ancient Chinese encyclopaedia that breaks down the animal kingdom into the most curious categories, including those that belong to the Emperor, fabled ones, stray dogs, those drawn with a very fine camel hair brush, and those that from afar look like flies. From the perspective of a society versed in modern scientific speciation, we are, upon encountering such an eccentric taxonomy, taken aback by 'the stark impossibility of thinking *that*'.[14] Indeed, it can be difficult to accept that another person's cognition of the world is as overwhelmingly real to them as mine is to me. Grudem recognises that, in at least some cases, 'the possibility must be left open that God has chosen not to give us enough information to come to a clear decision' about how something came to be, and in such contexts 'the real test of faithfulness to him may be the degree to which we can act charitably toward those who in good conscience and full belief in God's Word hold to a different position.'[15] Just as Grudem can tolerate young-earth creationists because he does not believe that 'the Bible tells us or intends to tell us the age of the earth or the age of the universe,'[16] I do not believe that the Bible tells us or intends to tell us the finer details of human biology or the full sociological diversity of human gender. If such had been the will of God, then such would be the case.

As the example of young- and old-earth creationism demonstrates, there *is* precedent in conservative systematic theology for the practice of epistemic humility and for the accommodation of a wide range of beliefs on subjects upon which the Bible does not offer a single, exhaustive and unambiguous message. This flexibility, furthermore, is commonly applied to ethical questions as much as to scientific or historical questions. Grudem's *Christian Ethics* encourages the incorporation of subjective factors, including one's inner sense of right and wrong, one's heartfelt desires, and one's perception of the urgings of the Spirit, in ethical decision-making. He acknowledges also that 'wisdom from God might lead Christians to different conclusions in these areas according to their different circumstances, preferences, stages in life, and sense of calling from God.'[17] It is believed in evangelical Christianity that God actively participates in the formation of at least some of these subjective experience-factors, such that 'the desires of a person who loves God and takes delight in him will often be the very desires that God wants that person to have.'[18] Only the individual in question can speak authoritatively to the truthfulness of their desires – although there are guide-rails in that these desires can never contradict the clear instruction of scripture, where that is available. No murder, for example.

The perceived weight of an ethical conundrum can also vary. It is not always easy to determine whether one is faced with a major or minor ethical issue, how much time and energy one should dedicate to resolving it, or whether intervention from other parties, such as members of church leadership, is proportional. Deliberately hurting another human being is obviously a major ethical issue and clearly justifies outside interference, whereas violating one's New Year's resolutions is not and does not. Where exactly an individual will draw the line between these two extremes will differ from scenario to scenario, historical moment to historical moment, and, for Christians, church to church. 'Christians', says Grudem, 'will need to ask God to give them mature wisdom and sound judgment as they try to determine to what extent an ethical issue should be considered "major" in their particular circumstances.'[19] Consequently, there is always a need for Christians to be careful when expressing their ethical opinions concerning another person's behaviour, and they should try, where possible, to avoid 'being picky and judgmental about minor details that might even be wrong but that should be overlooked because they are none of any other person's business'.[20]

In sum, Grudem details at least five integral components to his version of systematic theology that militate for the tolerance of differing epistemic and ethical conclusions as drawn from scripture. 1) The Bible passages one sees as being relevant to a particular topic will differ from person to person. 2) The Bible does not tell us everything about every topic, meaning that we must cross-reference some of the more indeterminate passages with scientific, historical, or other data. 3) Our senses and judgement can be mistaken in a fallen world. 4) Wisdom from God, while it will not contradict scripture, can nevertheless inform one's heartfelt desires and sense of calling in unpredictable ways. 5) For all of the above reasons, we can come to different conclusions about the relative biblical weight of an ethical issue and so pay it more or less attention than another person might. Ultimately, concludes Grudem, 'unless Scripture clearly requires or prohibits something, Christians would do well to allow for a considerable variety of personal preferences and individual choices.'[21] The price of doing otherwise – of artificially adding to the list of things considered sinful by the church – is to foster 'a false sense of guilt and a resulting alienation from God' in the minds and souls of those who, as a result of church-led ostracism, mistakenly seek God's help in repenting from these manufactured sins.[22]

The point of my explaining all this is to show that anti-trans beliefs are not a necessary downstream result of evangelical theology or evangelical ethics. If anything, anti-trans dogma is enabled only by the *selective suspension* of the principles of systematic theology – that is, by failing to acknowledge that some Christians might organise and interpret biblical passages that touch on gender differently, or might emphasise a whole other set of passages due to a different understanding of what it means to be trans. It requires one to assume that trans Christians do not experience a prayerfully tested heartfelt calling that is consistent with their gender identity. And it requires the flattening of all trans existence along a singular plane, characterised first and foremost by bodily alterations, in order to justify its universal treatment as an issue of 'major' ethical significance (i.e., something of such weight that it justifies commenting on and even openly denouncing the actions of another). This is despite the fact that many trans people's gender identities actually form a fairly minor part of their lives, do not entail any physical alterations to the body, and are outwardly manifested only in language (such as changed names, for which there is ample biblical precedent) and in the alteration of clothing and presentational styles.

Even within an evangelical theological analysis, then, anti-trans beliefs fall short of the minimum standards for reasonable argumentation as Grudem himself defines them. That their proliferation continues nonetheless is rendered only more absurd when one considers how Grudem goes about dissecting a separate issue (concerning safety railings, of all things) that is addressed a mere three verses after the infamous biblical injunction against mixing clothing styles in Deuteronomy 22:5. In verse 8, Moses instructs the Israelites: 'When you build a new house, you shall make a parapet for your roof; otherwise you might have bloodguilt on your house, if anyone should fall from it.' Grudem fully recognises that the context in which this law makes literal sense – a society where socialising commonly takes place on top of flat-roofed houses – no longer applies to most Western communities or housing, including Grudem's own house. Consequently, he reassures himself, he cannot be impugned for failing to install railings, and in any case, the Law of Moses is no longer believed to be directly relevant in our new covenant age, in which God's law is said to be more powerfully imprinted on our *hearts*. As commonly expressed, this belief holds that we may gain wisdom from the old laws – being reminded, for example, that it is wise to take steps to protect other people's safety on our property – but that we are 'no longer under any part of the Mosaic covenant as a binding law'.[23] Contrast the rational coolness of this exegesis with Grudem's simultaneous insistence that Deuteronomy 22:5 is 'a passage of special importance in the transgender debate' and that it clearly shows the fundamental ungodliness of adopting other-gendered presentational styles, irrespective of reason or context.[24] At a certain point, it is difficult not to conclude that this jarring inconsistency of tone has more to do with extra-biblical prejudices than with prayerful analysis. If our culture placed greater moral capital on the issue of railings and less on the issue of gender, perhaps this dynamic would be reversed, and perhaps Deuteronomy 22:8 would be held aloft as 'a passage of special importance in the railings debate'.

The importance of reappraising the functional dynamics of systematic theology in the evangelical discussion on trans identities is also heightened by the relative absence of alternative theological justifications for anti-trans beliefs. Not all evangelical theologians who follow O'Donovan's assertion that trans identity recapitulates Gnosticism are systematicians of Grudem's school. N. T. Wright is a notable example, having criticised systematic theologians for 'going round and round in circles' as they seek meaning in the Bible without sufficient grounding in the study of the text's historical context and with 'minimal reference' to the wider authorial intent behind each of its constituent books.[25] However, Wright's endorsement of the Gnostic charge, having come in the form of a brief letter to *The Times*, offers no alternative justification for this belief; so, while Wright may not be a classic systematician, his anti-trans intervention failed to distinguish itself from the typical patterns of conservative systematic reasoning. The fact is that, in almost every respect, including its use of proof texts to contrast biblical sex and gender with (post)modern trans identity, and also its trust in the basic timeless truthfulness of the Bible's message on gender (as *traditionally* interpreted, to be specific), the evangelical version of the Gnostic charge is an intractably systematist critique. It is in the genetic code of systematics, too, that the key to its dismantlement rests.

6

Rebellion

Biblical proof texts form the outer shell of conservative evangelicalism's answer to the challenges it faces in the trans cultural
moment, but a simple run-through of these passages, complete
with the obligatory translation notes and historical contextualis-
ation, would tell us little about the motivations of those who collate
and quote them today. The fact that an 'answer' to trans identities
is felt necessary is itself far more revelatory. Systematic theological
arguments can be constructed for any number of things, from capital punishment to godly protocol for herding sheep, but it is only
when something is felt to carry heavy implications for the moral
and spiritual health of a whole community that evangelical thought
leaders rush to clarify right doctrine in book after book, article after
article, and sermon after sermon. In line with the now-standard
perception of gender ideology's heretical resonances, it is generally implied in both academic and popular writings by evangelical
thinkers that trans approaches to gender do more than just contravene the technicalities of biblical instruction; rather, it is said that
they clearly and severely violate core aspects of Christian orthodoxy.[1] Vaughan Roberts, an evangelical Anglican rector in Oxford,
argues that there seems to be something *especially* unbiblical about
trans identity that sets it apart from other objects of popular ethical
discussion and makes it fertile ground for doctrinal controversy.
Roberts writes, 'We show our rebellion against God in a *particularly obvious way* when we refuse to go along with the way in which
he has made the world, such as in the division of the sexes.'[2] Referring to the description of mixing gender-coded clothing as an
abomination to the Lord in Deuteronomy 22:5, Owen Strachan,
Research Professor of Theology at Grace Bible Theological Seminary in Arkansas, makes a stronger version of the same claim in
his book *Reenchanting Humanity: A Theology of Mankind* (2019):

All sin dishonors the Lord in full, but abominable behavior offends God in a special way. The implication is clear: the man or woman who wears the clothing of the opposite sex makes a conscious decision to contravene the design of God. The circumstances behind this choice do not matter ... [T]his practice is part of a complex of behaviors that are wrong through and through, and no explanation can change this truth or erase God's law.[3]

Because the stakes are set so high, systematic theologians and evangelical Christian ethicists reflexively flit in their writings between rearticulating standard conservative readings of the aforementioned proof texts and tangentially defending the fundamental tenets that permeate every crevice of modern evangelical discourse – the elemental doctrines of God, creation, scripture and divine providence – as if these are what their intellectual opponents are *really* attacking. In this chapter, I will disambiguate two of these tenets, as well as the objections to trans identity to which they give rise, and I will examine a range of possible theological responses to these objections. I do so not in an effort to dictate 'correct' beliefs, but simply to demonstrate, first, that the received wisdom of the evangelical movement is not as axiomatic as it seems, and second, that, should we desire it, a more sophisticated, considered and constructive conversation is well within our reach.

As is so often the case in Jewish and Christian theology, everything eventually loops back to the Book of Genesis, the source of so many of the Bible's most culturally ingrained stories, including the global Flood and Joseph's unlikely journey from incarceration to princedom in Egypt. Preceding these, both textually and in reputation, is the creation narrative in chapters 1 through 3. Whether taken literally or allegorically (contrary to popular perception, outright rejection of evolutionary biology is a minority opinion in British evangelicalism),[4] the story of Adam's and Eve's creation and ultimate expulsion from the Garden of Eden for eating of the forbidden fruit is believed by millions of evangelical Christians, myself included, to be a timeless contemplation on the brokenness of humanity's present condition – how, having been made in God's image, we became, in the words of Bible teacher and Gospel Coalition contributor Nancy Guthrie, 'corrupt, defiled, and foolish'.[5] However, as the story is so brief (around 2,000 words in most English translations), a great deal of interpretive work has to be done to draw out workable theological and ethical significances.

Typically, as trans lawyer and clergywoman Victoria Kolakowski observes, the operative assumption in conservative exegesis has been that the biblical creation story is 'paradigmatic for God's intention' across space and time in a very particular, inflexible way.[6] The Southern Baptist Convention's 2014 Resolution on Transgender Identity states that 'God's design was the creation of two distinct and complementary sexes, male and female ... which designate the fundamental distinction that God has embedded in the very biology of the human race', and moreover insists that '[d]istinctions in masculine and feminine roles as ordained by God are part of the created order and should find expression in every human heart'.[7] The practical implications of this understanding depend entirely on what paradigms, or 'roles', one recognises in the story, leaving significant space for a range of creative interpretations – some more life-giving than others. Literary historian Stephen Greenblatt explains that the story elicits a wide variety of cultural, moral and political responses which have been, over the course of millennia, 'both liberating and destructive, a hymn to human responsibility and a dark fable about human wretchedness, a celebration of daring and an incitement to misogyny'.[8] Evangelical responses to the increasingly unavoidable fact of trans people's existence have unfortunately evidenced in nauseating abundance the story's capacity to elicit pure wretchedness, and have modelled in depressing scarcity its liberatory potential.

The first and most obvious tenet of Christian orthodoxy that so many evangelical thought leaders hold to be violated by trans identity is the belief that humans are created male *or* female, permanently, as distinct and complementary genres of God's image. This is based on a straightforward reading of Genesis 1:27, which states: 'So God created humankind in his image, in the image of God he created them; male and female he created them.' Jesus paraphrases this passage in Matthew 19:4, where he says that 'the one who made them at the beginning "made them male and female".' Laid down so emphatically at the dawn of God's story and stressed by Jesus in his brief ministry on earth, the male/female binary would seem to be unassailable as a pillar of Abrahamic doctrine. R. Albert Mohler Jr., president of the Southern Baptist Theological Seminary in Louisville, Kentucky, writes:

> Scripture clearly defines human beings as male and female, here not by accident but by divine purpose. Furthermore, this purpose, along with every other aspect of God's creation, is declared by the Creator to be "good." This means that human flourishing and happiness will take place only when the goodness of God's creation is honored as God intended. An evangelical theology of the body affirms the goodness behind male being male and female being female.[9]

Although there has been a movement in queer theologies away from engagement with apologetics (the use of historical, anthropological and scientific argumentation to rationalise scripture and religious tradition in light of new information),[10] the danger here is that trans-affirming theologies will make themselves impotent in the very religious communities where they are most needed, all because they detach themselves too readily from any investment in the truth or applicability of scripture. In any case, there fortunately remains a strong interest among trans theologians in asking how the verses commonly used against trans people, including Genesis 1:27, might be read as compatible with the known realities of trans life. Their arguments generally gravitate towards two points: first, that, if the other binaries described in the creation narrative (day and night; earth and seas) are inherently fuzzy, describing things that morph into and complicate each other in infinite potential combinations, then 'male and female' cannot be read as an exhaustive list of clearly delineable options; and second, that recognising *sex* binarism in Genesis does not necessarily precipitate recognising *gender* binarism in the same verses.

At the outset, creation-centred proscriptive arguments only function if we unify the biblical *is* with the biblical *ought*, something we do selectively by default. Thus, when we read in Genesis that God created *Day* and *Night*, we recognise that the immediate problematisation of these categories by the mention of *evening* and *morning* is essentially irrelevant to the gist of the text; we know and are not troubled by the fact that Day and Night blend into each other and are anywise simply terrestrial referents for the circumstantial results of cosmic activity. Equally, when we read that God gathered the waters together and called them Seas, as apart from the land, which he called Earth, it is of no particular concern to us where lakes, marshes, rivers, puddles, reefs, volcanic islands and traversable ice caps might fit into the creational blueprint. No tight moral *oughts* follow: our spiritual health is not endangered when our choropleth maps misleadingly display Greenland as a solid mass of Earth. We allow the Bible's poetic aetiology of nature to stand on its own terms, *as* divine poetry, and no less true for its being so.

But when Genesis 1:27 tells of the creation of humanity as 'male and female', some readers propel themselves down a path of teleological extrapolation that leads to a place where any mixing, blending, or deconstruction of these categories is outright blasphemous – an insult to God born of the same insubordination that got Adam and Eve kicked out of the Garden in the first place. Never mind that woman (not yet named Eve) is described in Genesis 2:23 as being created *from the side of Adam*, who calls her 'bone of my bones and flesh of my flesh', implying that sexual bimodality is itself to be imagined as the result of one thing transmutating into another – either the flesh and bone of the male becoming female, or the androgyne becoming both male and female.[11] Never mind also that the New Testament emphasises God's intention to 'make all things new', our bodies included, in the 'new heaven and new earth' of which it foretells (e.g., 1 Corinthians 15: 35–58; Philippians 3:21; Revelation 21:1–5). Never mind, then, that transitional trajectories are as important to the Bible's story as the implied virtue of permanence – the latter being a characteristic that is reserved for the divine *in contrast to* the transience of earthly humanity (e.g., Psalms 102:25–27; Malachi 3:6; Hebrews 1:10–12).

The first chapter of Joy Ladin's tear-jerking masterpiece of emotive theology, *The Soul of the Stranger: Reading God and Torah from a Transgender Perspective* (2018), is arguably the most influential meditation on Genesis 1–3 by a trans person – in Ladin's case, a Jewish Orthodox trans woman. Ladin argues that while the raw material for phenotypical *sex* differentiation is clearly described in Genesis as being created by God, *gender* differentiation, meaning the canonisation of stereotypical roles and behaviours loosely associated with sex, is actually initiated by Adam, who announces upon the creation of his female companion that 'this one shall be called Woman, for out of Man this one was taken' (2:23). At this point, before the expulsion from Eden, it seems to be the *commonalities* between the two humans that define their relationship. Ladin writes:

> That recognition of common humanity inspires Adam to invent gender, that is, to interpret the differences between male and female bodies as implying different but intimately related identities ... This moment, when Adam begins to give human meaning to divinely created (but thus far not divinely interpreted) maleness and femaleness, represents the biblical genesis of gender, and the first budding of the gender binary.[12]

Ladin concedes that the humans who inhabited the Garden of Eden were divided (or, more accurately, *united*) both by a male/female (sex) and man/woman (gender) distinction, but she refutes the notion that 'the version of gender we see in the Garden of Eden [represents] God's idea of what human beings are and should be.' Their relationship was binary only in the very purest sense of the word: 'a gender binary built for two'. Ladin continues:

> Adam and Eve seem to have been created as adults and they have not yet had children, so there are no sisters or brothers, best male or female friends, grandmothers or grandfathers, or, for that matter, girls or boys. Clearly, this version of the gender binary is not meant to define all, or even most, of humanity.[13]

The conditions in which societal gender distinctions as we know them are nurtured have not yet come into being. Behavioural prescriptions cannot pass from one man to another, or one woman to another; systemic material inequalities, clothing distinctions, and the organs of religious and state power that enforce cultural norms are unimaginable from the perspective of two naked hominids, alone together, dwelling with their God in a garden where they are plentifully fed and know no death. Gender is here a love language, or a tool for self-exploration, not a means of hierarchically distinguishing roles. But this Edenic euphoria does not last forever.

Even as a system designed for two people, gender relations between the man and the woman are soon reconstituted in the third chapter of Genesis. Having eaten of the fruit of the tree of the knowledge of good and evil, the man and the woman are afflicted with different (but interlocking) curses by God on their way out of Eden. The woman is cursed to endure great pain (or strife – *itsavon*) in reproduction; the man to struggle by the sweat of his brow to extract sustenance from the earth. Their interests will be contrary, and the man will 'rule over' the woman (Genesis 3:16–19). It is only now, (re)defined in reference to her physiology, that the woman is named Eve, 'because she was the mother of all living' (3:20). Ladin notes that the gender roles have here 'change[d] radically, in a single generation',[14] with the definitional locus having shifted from sameness to differentness, from the joy of kinship to the pains of labour. This rapid evolution of signification highlights the changeability of anthropogenic categories. We might still use the words *man* and *woman* like previous generations, but the range of meanings imparted by those words has changed in the past thousand, the past hundred, and even the past ten years, and will change further. As for Adam and Eve, so for us.

Trans literary scholar M. W. Bychowski expands on Ladin's points by reading God's instruction to humans in Genesis 1:28 – that they should 'be fruitful and multiply' – as an indication that, in time, there will be 'more and more varied [images of God] than … in the beginning', including 'more varied forms of sexual embodiment'.[15] Read in this way, the text seems not only to leave room for sex and gender diversity, but actually to *assign goodness* to it, as the fulfilment of God's intentions for his children. Even the troubling airs of what appears to be the beginnings of misogynistic oppression in Genesis 3 become less insurmountable if the text is released from the bounds set by received wisdom. As Bychowski states: 'We created (or subcreated) this cage [gender] and so we can uncreate it', if not by abandoning gendered labels altogether, then perhaps by imaginatively and compassionately redefining them in ways that atone for the fallen-ness of misogyny.[16] At the very least, we can say with confidence that our current accursed gender system is not God's ideal, and that it is within our capacity as free beings to travel back in the direction of harmonious social relations.

On a closely related point, the problems created by inflexibly interpreting Genesis 1:27 as establishing a timeless idyllic gender system only multiply if we zoom out, as good systematicians should, to consider the whole Bible. In particular, its numerous and complex mentions of *eunuchs* – sometimes referring to surgically castrated individuals and sometimes to celibate men[17] – are difficult to interpret without inferring that *some* level of qualification must be applied to the notion of a simple male/female or man/woman binary in God's creational order. Many of these references are morally neutral. In the Book of Esther, eunuchs feature as both malicious conspirators and as key players in the effort to stop an anti-Jewish genocide in the Achaemenid Empire. Other passages are outright celebratory. In Isaiah 56:4–5, the Lord directly assigns unique value to a gender-liminal group by promising that he will give to faithful eunuchs 'in my house and within my walls, a monument and a name better than sons and daughters; I will give them an everlasting name that shall not be cut off'. In Jeremiah 38:7–18, an Ethiopian eunuch heroically rescues the prophet Jeremiah from death at the hands of King Zedekiah's officials, following which God sends word that the eunuch will also be rescued from the swords of the Babylonian invaders 'because you have trusted in me'. In Matthew 19:12, Jesus explains, alluding to celibacy and infertility as well as to surgical castration, that eunuchs can be born so, made so by others, or can choose to be so 'for the sake of the kingdom of heaven' (i.e., celibacy). And in Acts 8:26–40, another Ethiopian eunuch becomes the first Gentile (non-Jew) to be baptised in the New Testament.

These passages are sometimes invoked to prove that diversity and liminality is fully a part of God's creation,[18] or even to claim that intersex or trans people are themselves represented in the Bible.[19] Katherine Apostolacus describes this as an example of *self-insertion* – the act of deliberately or passively interpolating oneself into the biblical narrative, as is common to all readers of religious texts.[20] However, many conservative Christians, including evangelical Anglican theologian Martin Davie, dismiss this argument with the semantic and hardly insightful point that 'the eunuchs referred to in the Bible were not transgendered [sic]'[21] as if it is necessary for the Bible to prefigure cultural, taxonomic and linguistic developments by thousands of years in order for it to speak to the conditions of our present time – a criterion that would invalidate *most* applied theology. That a distinction must be drawn between modern trans identities and ancient eunuch traditions is incontrovertible, but this distinction alone is not sufficient as a response to trans theological claims relating to biblical eunuchs. It leaves unanswered the broader point that the Bible clearly *accounts for, fails to unequivocally condemn*, and even *rejoices in* manifestations of what we might now call gender diversity, in clear contrast to large subsectors of modern Christianity. No satisfactory explanation has yet been given as to why this discrepancy exists.

The second tenet of Christian orthodoxy supposedly violated by 'gender ideology' is the supremacy and permanence of divine authority over our natural bodily anatomy. Because we humans are said by David in Psalm 139 to be 'fearfully and wonderfully made' – lovingly woven together in the womb as image-carriers of the perfect God – we should recognise therefore that our bodies ultimately belong to our Creator (1 Corinthians 6:19–20), and that we accordingly have no right to reformulate those bodies in line with our own whims. All biblical exegesis is selective to some extent, but this point is aggressively so, extrapolating situational theology from a biblical poem and applying a highly subjective interpretation of its meaning to one specific category of body-modification – gender-affirming surgeries and hormone replacement therapy – while ignoring others, such as routine operations to deal with chronic conditions or hormone replacement therapy to relieve menopausal symptoms in cis women. It also paints a deceptively unrefined picture of the biblical discourses on embodiment.

The bounds of our imaginations as evangelicals are on this point severely hamstrung by the spectre of Gnosticism as an imagined theological enemy, which facilitates the faulty presumption that our role as 'orthodox' Christians is to take the equal and opposite view to that of 'the Gnostics' in all instances, even if the Gnostic opinion in question has mostly been imputed by centuries of modern critique, or if the modern belief system being attacked is connected to Gnosticism in only the most tangential, inconsequential way. On the 'orthodox' view, Gnostic cosmology mistakenly interprets the fallout from humanity's first catastrophe in the Garden of Eden, including our propensity towards bodily dissociation and dysmorphia, as stemming from the very placement of our souls in these prison-bodies by the sub-divine Demiurge, not from human sin. Blame goes thence to this Demiurge, loosing Adam and Eve from the deadweight guilt of their indiscretion and handing to their offspring the licence to ignore what 'the LORD your God' – *that impostor* – cast firm in the Hebrew scriptures.

To say that gender ideology is heresy is thus an absolutely proportional response within the context of a reactionary evangelical mindset. According to this view, reshaping and reinterpreting God's anatomical creations in service to a neo-Gnostic 'inner self' would appear, on the face of it, to precede the total rejection of monotheistic divine authority as communicated through scripture. Owen Strachan writes that, in God's original design for humanity, there was 'no tension or ranking between body and soul', and so Christians simply 'cannot adopt any gnostic vision that renders corporeality bad and the soul good'.[22] Christianity *precludes* dualism. If we take this assertion to its logical conclusion, the price paid by those who fall into this trap is, as in Strachan's reckoning, 'eternal damnation',[23] because, as orthodox Christianity has it, one cannot have faith in the biblical Jesus if one simultaneously believes that the Hebrew prophecies fulfilled through Christ in the gospels are sub-divine forgeries. The issue of surgical or hormonal transition is thus attached to a much larger theological controversy, leading to esoteric accusations of heresy that, to the average trans person, would seem utterly bizarre.

If it is accepted that the material conditions of our world are causally linked to the Fall, the question must arise as to how we can distinguish between the created and the fallen in our surroundings – that is, how we can identify what God *made* and what humanity *broke*. To be sure, modern evangelicals are not alone in interpreting the discordant aspects of the human condition as deriving from the Fall. As I have already touched upon, Genesis itself attributes the shame of nakedness, the pain of labour, and the difficulty of extracting sustenance from the earth to that pivotal event, and later writers expanded the list through creative hermeneutics and artistic interpretation. Seventeenth-century English poet John Milton tells in his epic *Paradise Lost* of the moment at which the internal harmony of the self that Adam and Eve once enjoyed was shattered as they partook in the first great transgression. At that ruinous juncture

> high winds worse within / Began to rise, high passions – anger, hate, / Mistrust, suspicion, discord – and shook sore / Their inward state of mind, calm region once / And full of peace, now tossed and turbulent: / For understanding ruled not, and the will / Heard not her lore, both in subjection now / To sensual appetite, who from beneath / Usurping over sovereign reason, claimed / Superior sway. (Book 4, lines 1122–31)[24]

For Christian traditionalist theologians, gender-nonconformity is, like lust and mistrust in Milton's retelling, a disturbance injected directly into our thought-stream through our collective fallen-ness. Christian psychologist Mark Yarhouse tells us that Adam and Eve 'delight[ed] in their physical existence as gendered persons' in the Garden, but goes on to explain that the Fall 'corrupted all of existence, including human sexuality and experiences of our gendered selves'.[25] The so-called 'Gnostic' approach to gender – that is, the view that the body and soul are different entities – must therefore be attributed, as Stephen McQuoid, director of the missionary organisation Gospel Literature Outreach, writes, to the 'confusion' endemic to our morally degraded state.[26] Or, as Strachan and English footballer turned evangelical pastor Gavin Peacock put it, it appears that 'gender dysphoria is as old as the fall' – [27] that is, not created per se but rather crudely formed from the twisted fragments of creation and accordingly misaligned with God's model for human living. However, a closer look at discussions of human embodiment in the Bible reveals this Gnostic-versus-Christian dichotomy to be at best one-dimensional, and at worst disingenuous. It also shows that, if we read certain passages of the Bible with the same bent towards oversimplification that many conservative evangelicals display when reading trans writings, it is fairly easy to claim that Christian orthodoxy itself promotes body/mind dualism. In both cases, the dualism lies primarily in the reader's preconceptions.

Drawing on language and scenarios that would have been immediately relevant to his first-century Israelite audience, Jesus himself makes it an important part of his ministry to articulate a perceptive observation that the body and soul, as colloquial subdivisions of the human being, are not always in harmony, and that sometimes the soul, or conscious will, must assert its dominance for the greater good of both. This is precisely why Jesus uses amputative imagery in the Sermon on the Mount to drive home his provocative, escalatory message about the origin of sin and the fulfilment of the Law of Moses:

> If your right eye causes you to sin, tear it out and throw it away … And if your right hand causes you to sin, cut it off and throw it away. For it is better that you lose one of your members than that your whole body go into hell. (Matthew 5:29–30)

This passage is not an endorsement of 'dualism'; nor, in its situational specificity and obvious hyperbole, is its imagery exactly analogous to the removal or reshaping of dysphoria-inducing anatomies in gender-affirming medical care – even if some trans readers have hopefully interpreted it this way.[28] However, it *does* problematise the effort to render the canonical scriptures doctrinally antithetical to our straw-man conception of 'Gnosticism' in all cases, regardless of context, because one cannot entirely excise the underlying assumption that the somatic aspect of the self *can* cause problems that the soul or Spirit, exercising senior agency, must rectify.

The rhetorical distinction between flesh and soul, or the inner and outer being, as expressed by Jesus himself, also features prominently in the letters of the apostle Paul to the early churches. In the English Standard Version (ESV) translation of the Bible, overseen by Wayne Grudem, Paul distinguishes between the ways and desires of a person's 'inner being' (Romans 7:22; Ephesians 3:16) and the ways and desires of a person's 'members' – that is, their body parts (Romans 7:23). Paul's letters also opine upon the possibility that we, as embodied beings, can be overtaken by our material impulses to the detriment of the whole self (e.g., Romans 6:12–13, 8:6–8; 1 Thessalonians 4:3–5). To the Galatians (5:17), Paul goes so far as to say that 'the desires of the flesh are against the Spirit, and the desires of the Spirit are against the flesh, for these are opposed to each other, to keep you from doing the things you want to do.' Paul is here pointing to scenarios in which individual human consciousnesses, living as part of a Christian church community, are unable to act according to their moral principles without a disciplined approach that prayerfully filters the 'desires of the flesh' through the 'desires of the Spirit'. Again, if we engage only with the plain sense of the text and refuse to engage with deeper meanings, these words could very easily be described as dualistic or even Gnostic. Conservative Christians, while often being unwilling to look beyond the text's surface when faced with trans texts, are more than happy to do so to dispel such a misreading of the Bible. It is not that they *lack* critical thinking skills, but that they seem to be disinclined to *apply* those skills to afford trans people a respectful, unprejudiced hearing.

My aim here is not to develop a fully tested scriptural framework for trans embodiment – that is beyond my ability – but simply to highlight the extent to which the prevailing evangelical attitude of open hostility to the slightest hint of dualism is clouding our theological judgement. We have to be able to talk about and work through experiences of internal dissonance without our choice of language, which as a matter of utility can only ever be an approximation of our complex thoughts and feelings, being used as grounds for others to accuse us of engaging in Gnosticism; for, if this is the case, we will lose our ability to faithfully consider large chunks of the New Testament. It has also been my aim to demonstrate, first, that evangelical texts on gender identity suffer from scriptural tunnel-vision, and second, that the building blocks are there for a more nuanced and biblically intelligent exegesis, should that be willed. In all this, my overarching point is that conservative evangelicals who fall back on the Gnostic charge to justify anti-trans teachings are making an interpretive *choice*, not guarding a sacrosanct, inexpungible truth from the pages of scripture. The real question, then, is not whether trans identity is compatible with a biblically inspired life, but how some religious leaders could be so arrogant as to intercede into the deeply personal discernment of trans people when a reversal of roles – say, a trans person citing scripture to a cisgender pastor to prove that having their appendix removed is a violation of God's creational covenant – would certainly be considered a hateful and scripturally unjustified imposition.[29] Whence this self-righteous surety? Whence this extraordinary abrogation of humility?

As Paul wrote to the Romans (14:4–5) concerning differences in religious observance between Jewish and non-Jewish members of the Jesus movement: 'Who are you to pass judgement on servants of another? It is before their own lord that they stand or fall. And they will be upheld, for the Lord is able to make them stand … Let all be fully convinced in their own minds.' Or, as he wrote in his first surviving letter to the Corinthians (7:17): '[L]et each of you lead the life that the Lord has assigned, to which God called you.' That Paul was here operating on a contextually specific plane is reinforced several verses later by his offering a mere 'opinion' on the subject of celibacy (7:25).

Sadly, these letters are just about the *last* place in the Bible that trans Christians would usually turn to find spiritual guidance and affirmation. Paul is in fact roundly detested by many progressive and marginalised readers, who, as Karen Armstrong notes, are wont to castigate him as 'a misogynist, a supporter of slavery, a virulent authoritarian, and bitterly hostile to Jews and Judaism'.[30] John M. G. Barclay explains in *The New Cambridge Companion to St. Paul* (2020) that one of the major reasons for this revulsion is that Paul 'is still deployed in support of gender inequalities, by means of an over-simple transfer of Pauline statements to the modern world, and, in reaction, his gender remarks are obvious targets for hefty criticism'.[31] However, I believe that faith in the divine inspiration of Paul's words is not at odds with a trans-affirming pastoral (or political) stance. At the very least, the use of Paul to buttress anti-trans doctrine is unjustifiable from a systematic perspective, because a surface-level reading of the passages that are interpreted as reinforcing gender binarism and the immutability of sexual distinctions leads to ethical conclusions that are wholly incompatible with the plain-sense meaning of many other passages, even elsewhere in Paul's own writings. With little thought seemingly given to the complicated role of sex and gender liminality in the Bible, nor to Paul's repeatedly stated directive for distinctions to be drawn between personal, communal and societal morality – nor to the inbuilt flexibility of systematic theology – conservative evangelicals still often make it our business to meddle in matters we do not understand.

I want to conclude this chapter by recentring our minds on what is actually at stake in all these abstract conversations – the very *viability* and *dignity* of trans life in our communities, and also the ability of trans Christians to talk about their own experiences without becoming embroiled in some never-ending 'debate' about long-forgotten mystical sects. The overuse of the Gnostic charge by conservative cis Christians has directly shaped trans theology, such that the unambiguous disavowal of body/mind dualism often takes precedence over all else. For many writers, the solution to trans people's characterisation as heretics has been to counter the Gnostic charge with an equal-and-opposite reaction. Their argument is that trans people, being viscerally aware of their bodies, in fact represent the very apotheosis of Christian body-mind holism, and that trans Christians can help bring the wider Christian communion back from the quagmire of individualistic dualism to which our atomised consumerist culture binds it. Once thought to be theologically venomous, trans people instead become the antidote.

As early as 1997, trans Catholic Karen F. Kroll made a point of rejecting Gnosticism in her chapter 'Transsexuality and Religion: A Personal Journey' in the edited volume *Gender Blending*. Gnosticism, she tells us, was one of the 'first major heresies', and it held that pure knowledge 'could only come from the soul since it could not be corrupted like the body'. Although it is ostensibly at odds with orthodox Christianity, Kroll argues that Gnosticism and its inbuilt mistrust of the body 'continued to exist underground, and sprang up over the course of history with a variety of different names', including as an explanation for the bubonic plague in the Middle Ages, as 'one of the reasons given for the plague was that people had refused to control their bodies'. Dogmatic anti-Gnosticism also survived through the epochs, including in Christian opposition to dissection of the human body in the Middle Ages and opposition to organ transplants in the modern era on the grounds that the body is an inviolable creation of God that ought not be reconfigured. This very same argument was then transferred onto gender-affirming medicine with minimal theological effort. In Kroll's experience, however, the decision to change her body was ultimately a decision to embrace, not deny, the spiritual and material wholeness of her being: 'Sexual reassignment surgery was for me a rebirth, because it gave me my life; I was finally in union with my world.'[32]

More recent trans-affirming Christian writers echo Kroll's view of the matter. Queer cis theologian Mary Elise Lowe, for example, *contrasts* trans people's efforts to bring their bodies into harmony with the cognitive resonance of the soul with 'damaging beliefs about mind and body [that] have their roots in Greek philosophy and Gnosticism'. Lowe goes on to observe that 'the lived experiences of many transgender Christians lead them to reject these false assumptions, reclaim the biblical testimony, and witness to others that humans are an inseparable unity of … body-mind.'[33] Meanwhile, Christian ethicist Scott Bader-Saye, also cis, argues that bodily transition 'is not best seen as Gnosticism but rather as a mending of the self that allows for human participation in God's redemption of the whole person'.[34] For both Lowe and Bader-Saye, the psychological-physiological wholeness of trans embodiment as they imagine it is something that cis Christians can learn from.

Moving the conversation onto the spiritual gifts that trans Christians bring to their siblings in Christ injects some crucial positivity into the conversation. However, I would hazard that this ascription of redemptive virtue to trans people as champions of human wholeness lays precarious foundations for the future, as it potentially encourages an unrealistic expectation that the self-stories of trans Christians will necessarily conform to a strictly anti-dualist testimony. This is not and cannot be so in all cases, for there are indeed trans mystics, posthumanists, transhumanists, spiritualists, pagans and so on whose beliefs concerning the body's relationship to the soul cannot be neatly pigeonholed. And, though I have yet to encounter them, there are also no doubt avowed trans Gnostics somewhere out there in the world. In the final analysis, trans people are probably about as likely as cis people to interpret their embodiment either holistically or dualistically (or in some other way entirely), albeit with a slightly different set of available justifications for each philosophy.

One way or another, trying to paint trans Christians or trans people in general with too broad a brush can only store up inaccurate preconceptions that will need to be dispelled later. As the Evangelical Alliance itself rightly acknowledges in *Transformed*, there are as many different ways of being trans as there are trans people.[35] That is certainly not to say that there are no life experiences or theological insights that trans people tend to share; simply that any attempt at forming an accepted philosophical stereotype of trans people for ministerial or pastoral purposes will not survive first contact with a trans individual. So, rather than demonising them as heretics or elevating them as couriers of salvific essence, churches that currently lack visible LGBTQI+ communities would best be served, before anything else, by recommitting themselves to the rules of positive engagement. This means constructive listening, educating church staff on proper terminology, using correct names and pronouns for trans people, reading beyond the evangelical Christian bubble, and exercising caution when talking about gender identity in sermons/preaches. I will elaborate on these themes in Chapter 10.

PART III

Covering the cracks

7

'God is bullshit, and so is gender.'

While evangelicals like Roberts, O'Cathain, James, Sprinkle and Wright posit a similar set of philosophical objections to trans identity to those offered by Raymond, Daly and Greer, questions must still be asked as to how anti-trans feminism and conservative evangelicalism can possibly be paired up when they seem to be divided on two of the most intractable theological and sociological questions of all: the very existence of God and the social value of religious belief. While it is important to note that there is ideological overlap between the groups of interest, as indeed is the premise of this book, this does not, on its own, counterbalance the immense differences that exist between them on other basic points of principle and outlook. For instance, there remains a foundational incompatibility between the scriptural, even theocratic, groundings of conservative evangelical transphobia on the one hand, and the fact that many of Britain's defining anti-trans feminists are alumni of the anti-religion (or at least anti-*organised*-religion) Sceptic movement on the other. Looking askance at the severity of the contrast between the devout and the un-devout, we have to wonder: are the atheist feminists in question aware of the problem? Does the width of the chasm matter to them? And can this formidable gap, despite the appearance of unassailability, be bridged?

Best described as a loose conglomeration of people who publicly dispute the veracity of deities, 'alternative' medicines and other 'irrational' holdovers from a pre-Enlightenment past, Scepticism, along with its more specialised anti-theistic corollary, New Atheism, reached the apogee of its cultural relevance in the late 2000s and early 2010s.[1] At its best, Scepticism is effectively a social justice movement that takes aim at spiritual confidence tricksters who prey on the vulnerable, quack medicines that endanger the sick by discouraging the pursuit of genuine medical help, theocrats who encourage the encroachment of faith-based truth claims on school science classes, and the like.[2] At its worst, however, it fetishises an abstract, decontextualised concept of empirical objectivity that sees all matters, including those of a purely social or cultural nature, as subordinate to the probity of scientific rigour. In sum, it *can* (though not *must*) suffer from an intoxicating epistemic haughtiness – a refusal to see its own internal biases, because to do so would be to surrender to relativistic indeterminacy and relinquish the authority to identify and shame 'irrational' groups.

These words written by Christopher Hitchens in his classic anti-religious manifesto, *God Is Not Great* (2007), poignantly capture the tone of the movement:

> Our belief is not a belief. Our principles are not a faith. We do not rely solely upon science and reason, because these are necessary rather than sufficient factors, but we distrust anything that contradicts science or outrages reason. We may differ on many things, but what we respect is free inquiry, openmindedness, and the pursuit of ideas for their own sake.[3]

When confronted with unfamiliar subjective identities that challenge long-held assumptions about society and human nature, fundamentalist Sceptics often default to a pseudo-scientific approach that seeks to deduce the empirical validity of those identities, with one eye always fixating on the construction of a perfectly 'rational' future via the delegitimisation of 'religious' or 'magical' thinking. Journalist Edie Miller, writing for *The Outline*, has observed that some Sceptics seem to 'think they can "debunk" a person's claim to their gender identity' in much the same way that they would debunk the claims of the astrologer, the young-earth creationist, or the homeopath. Though it seemingly caters to a niche audience, Miller believes that Sceptic transphobia has an 'outsized legacy' in that 'both the ideological basis and some of the specific proponents of U.K. scepticism in the noughties are implicated in the spread of transphobic thinking.'[4] She cites the fact that anti-trans feminist journalists like Helen Lewis, former deputy editor of *The New Statesman*, were previously visible participants in the British Sceptic ecosystem, and that some events lauded in anti-trans circles, including a 2013 debate between trans and anti-trans activists in Soho, London, have been hosted by Sceptic organisations, helping thereby to kickstart the 'TERF' phenomenon as we know it.[5]

One could point to much else besides. British Scepticism's greatest prophet, English biologist Richard Dawkins, has intervened on social media platform Twitter on multiple occasions to pronounce the finality of chromosomes in determining sex,[6] rally support for anti-trans advocacy groups,[7] and condemn students who try to 'no-platform' anti-trans speakers.[8] Nor is Dawkins an outlier. Religious Studies professor Kathryn Lofton has pointed out that 'atheist voices are loud, expert at public battle, and engaged with both trans-exclusionary radical feminists and gender critical feminists.'[9] Meanwhile, trans-affirming Sceptics have described with dismay the proliferation of 'science'-derived transphobia within the movement.[10] Zinnia Jones, a transfeminist atheist YouTuber, described in 2014 being bombarded with transphobic comments on her videos from self-declared Sceptics and atheists. Working up from the core assumption that the body and mind must be treated as one because they together form a mammalian organism like any other, some particularly zealous Sceptics told Jones that her identifying as trans (by which they are typically referring to some version of the 'wrong body' paradigm) is no better than believing in spirits, ghosts, spectres and gods, since there is apparently no empirical basis for Jones believing herself a woman. As this type of comment indicates, Sceptic transphobia stems from a perverted refraction of the underlying principles of empiricism and scientific methodology. In an affectation of expertise, Sceptic transphobes play word games to give the impression that they have, in some way, simulated a repeatable scientific experiment that demonstrates trans identity's counter-factuality. Accordingly, Jones writes that the hostile commenters who targeted her 'aren't transphobic in spite of their atheism ... [but] *because* of their atheism', which is to say that their atheism 'actively *made their transphobia worse*' in that a synthetic reverence for 'the values of science, observation, and reality', absent any genuine specialist knowledge, works to power a pseudo-rationalist crusader mentality.[11]

Transphobic attitudes rooted in some form of Scepticism have proved sufficiently prevalent and distinctive to warrant the coining of a unique label – *gender atheism* – to describe a specifically athe- istic formulation of anti-trans ideas,[12] although it is currently the preserve of marginal and idiosyncratic online figures. The impli- cation behind the label is that gender, as apart from sex, is just as empirically unfounded as deities, and that belief in either is equally wrong-headed. Canadian market anarchist and Sceptic author Francois Tremblay sums up the gender atheist view of trans people in a punchy little couplet: 'God is bullshit, and so is gender.'[13] Both have to be left in the past if society is truly to embrace the inquisitive values of the Enlightenment. Sierra Weir, a linguist and feminist who previously identified as a trans man and now disputes the reality of trans identities, offers a more expansive defi- nition of her belief system in an article published by *The American Mind*, a publication of the anti-LGBTQI+ Christian Right-aligned Claremont Institute:[14]

Gender atheists judge gender to be an undemonstrated asser- tion that can't be proven by observable reality. We consider such concepts to share the status of religious beliefs, dependent on the existence of a spiritually created consciousness separate from and superior to the body.[15]

Note the distinctly anti-dualist nature of Weir's worldview. She believes that consciousness is contiguous with the body; so do many conservative evangelicals. She believes that it is morally wrong and philosophically erroneous to try to separate these two components; so do many conservative evangelicals. The point of departure between gender atheism and anti-trans evangelicalism comes fairly late in the logical sequence, when Weir concludes that, *because* consciousness and body are contiguous and inseparable, it makes no sense to talk of one's conscious soul as being 'spirit- ually created'. So, whereas a conservative evangelical will usually say that spirit and matter are intentionally conjoined in the human, Weir says that *there is no spirit*. When gender atheists and conserv- ative evangelicals look to form a united rhetorical front to combat a common enemy – trans activism – their ability to do so hinges on an unspoken agreement to focus on the earlier parts of the logical sequence and avoid too much public discussion of the later parts, because doing so would muddle the messaging and invite difficult questions. How they go about achieving this sleight of hand will be explored more fully in the following chapter, but it is worth noting here that the publication of Weir's article in *The American Mind* signals an eagerness on the Christian Right to compare notes and build alliances with secular transphobic spokespeople *despite* the fact that, in this case, Weir's anti-religious tone clashes with the broader messaging of the Claremont Institute.

Typically, trans identity is linked by gender atheists not to mainstream religious practice as found in your typical Catholic, Anglican, Jewish, or Hindu place of worship, but rather to high-control religions, colloquially called cults, the leaders of which regularly take it upon themselves to exercise authority over the minutiae of members' life choices and to violently enforce conformity of thought. US Army veteran and gender atheist Matt Osborne, for instance, compares trans activism to Scientology, a famously invasive religion, heavily influenced by Gnosticism,[16] which practices shunning of so-called 'suppressive persons' (i.e., those who are not to be associated with because they failed to follow accepted doctrine).[17] Sierra Weir herself opts for a comparison with the Society of Jesus, or Jesuits, a Catholic order with a controversial history, not least in relation to its prominent role in the murderous Inquisitions of the sixteenth century,[18] and Dan Fisher, founder of think-piece platform *Uncommon Ground*, borrows from the universe of the *Dune* books to label the advancement of Judith Butler-inspired queer postmodernist ideology in universities the 'Butlerian Jihad' – a phrase that also evokes an irrational Islamist fervour.[19] Meanwhile, Miranda Yardley and Jenn Smith, two transsexual women who have made a side hustle out of siding with anti-trans forces in Britain's 'trans debate', accuse trans activists of being 'fanatics',[20] of suffering from 'mass delusion',[21] and of belonging to a 'bizarre religious cult' similar to the abusive self-improvement and drug-rehabilitation scheme Synanon, in which participants had to endure excruciating verbal humiliation sessions called 'The Game'.

Ostensibly 'rational' anti-superstitious sentiment has made its way into the every-day linguistic praxis of anti-trans feminism. On

Mumsnet, a parenting resource website that serves as a key locale for anti-trans radicalisation and agitation in Britain,[22] particularly that of a 'TERF' variety,[23] anti-religious sentiment born of an incomprehension of religious mindsets routinely rubs shoulders with transphobia, and indeed religious 'delusions' and gender 'delusions' are commonly conflated. During one of the first prolonged discussions of trans politics on Mumsnet's message boards in 2015, a user set the tone by complaining that some trans activists possess 'a zeal which is practically religious in nature'.[24] In 2016, another user described 'trans activists and Islamists' as 'together the two biggest contemporary threats to feminism',[25] and in January 2018, in a thread misleadingly titled 'How can we work towards a constructive debate about all things transgender', it was argued that 'radical feminist theory is rooted in science' while trans identity is akin to 'spiritual belief'.[26]

These posts position anti-trans views as an evidentially sound theory like gravity and evolution, quite unlike trans identities, which are judged to be about as valid as other Sceptic bugbears like homeopathy, faith healing and young-earth creationism. The notion that trans identity is incompatible with an abstracted and lionised conception of 'science' is also put forth by former Canadian athlete Linda Blade and Canadian journalist Barbara Kay in their book *Unsporting: How Trans Activism and Science Denial are Destroying Sport* (2020), published by the right-wing Rebel News. Blade and Kay erroneously assert that followers of 'gender ideology' do not recognise differences in physical sex characteristics.* They claim on this basis that, should sporting authorities capitulate to activist demands, the Olympic Games will eventually

---

* Few, if any, trans activists claim that bimodal sex characteristics do not exist, nor that the law, healthcare practices, public facilities, and so on should not cater for specific needs – say, specialist health requirements related to different reproductive organs. Rather, the issue is more about the significations assigned to these characteristics, such as the presumption that a person with a vagina must necessarily conform to the *social* classification 'woman' for all time. As regards sports, the overarching question is not whether certain physical characteristics produce certain advantages in certain scenarios, but whether the simple distinction between 'male' and 'female' categories is justifiable when a great many other biological, medical, social and environmental factors also codetermine average performance levels. See C. R. Torres, F. J. L. Frias and M. J. M. Patiño, 'Beyond physiology: embodied experience, embodied advantage, and 'wither and die, all because of a pseudoscientific theory of human biology held by a tiny minority of the world's 7.8 billion people'.[27] Neuroscientist turned anti-trans activist Deborah Soh, another Canadian, similarly describes trans activism as a 'battle against biology' in *The End of Gender: Debunking the Myths about Sex and Identity in Our Society* (2020).[28] Another anti-trans feminist activist, Isidora Sanger, claims that, as a philosophy rooted in 'metaphysics' as opposed to empiricism, trans-affirming ideologies are waging 'war on reality'.[29]

Helen Joyce, Britain editor at *The Economist*, also recapitulates this imagined *trans v. science* dichotomy in her recent book, *Trans: When Ideology Meets Reality* (2021), which ends with the anticipatory claim that 'gender-identity ideology … would crumble before a renewed societal commitment to the Enlightenment values of open inquiry and robust debate'.[30] If only 'Enlightenment values' could be restored and 'robust debate' freed from its tethers, Joyce argues, the whole trans phenomenon would evaporate. Nothing fundamentally distinguishes this forbidding expectation from a standard Sceptic prospectus for the future of religion as a whole. To reformulate a famous Bill Maher quote that casts religion as a threat to human survival, the mantra of gender atheism could be rendered: 'Gender ideology must die for reason to live.' With the stakes again set so high, cultural issues that are primarily about subjective human socialisation and societal categorisation are dragged into the dehumanised realm of data and experimentation, leaving the average trans person, for whom scientific theories about the 'cause' of their gendered reality are at most a matter of tangential academic interest, gasping for air.

Some readers will immediately recognise an authoritarian streak in the ideas and objectives described above. 'Enlightenment values' are desirable only because unfiltered 'debate' (read: unimpeded abuse of trans people) would have a restraining influence on trans activism, thus taking society one step closer to an empirically faultless end-state. Implied in this imaginary is the idea that some social groups, often including trans people, feminists and

the inclusion of transgender athletes in competitive sport', *Sport, Ethics and Philosophy*, vol. 16, no. 1, 2022, pp. 33–49.

Muslims, are expendable, since 'rationality' as a cultural resource is poorly defined and must inevitably rely to some extent on arbitrary criteria to define in- and out-groups – not so unlike nationalism. Indeed, scholars have noted a strong rightward tendency in the politics of some subsectors of Scepticism, with the gender 'debate' being a key battleground on which the reactionary implications of dogmatic ultra-empiricism are potently exhibited, even among those whose political positioning is expressly left-of-centre.[31]

Rationality Rules, for one, is a popular atheist YouTuber with a subscriber count of 317,000 at the time of writing. His signature video format sees him forefronting something that he considers to be irrational, and then 'debunking' it in a less-than-charitable tone (one video thumbnail reads 'Islamic Feminism Debunked', for example). He has also dabbled in the 'trans debate' on a few occasions, usually from the perspective of someone who supports trans rights but sees problems with the ways in which certain aspects of trans advocacy are carried out, as seen in his video criticising the American Humanist Association's April 2021 decision to strip Richard Dawkins of his 1996 Humanist of the Year award in response to his anti-trans comments.[32] He has also been accused of transphobia as a result of his videos arguing that trans women have an unfair advantage in women's sports.[33] These videos are not usually hostile per se, but the privileging of ossified 'scientific' data over and above ethical and cultural factors does tend to favour anti-trans conclusions, if for no other reason than that it is easier to quantify the pros and cons of the status quo than it is to imagine and empirically account for other possibilities. In a more extreme case, Thunderfoot, another YouTuber with over a million subscribers and 325 million video views, has made the routine mockery of social justice movements, most of all feminism, a core part of his messaging. He has published numerous videos dedicated solely to attacking online feminist figures like Anita Sarkeesian, whose cultural and political assertions he proceeds to 'debunk' in snide intonations.[34]

Although there is a significant and probably more numerous contingent of Sceptics whose drive for social justice, including trans rights, overrides any sense of loyalty to 'atheism' (assuming any such loyalty existed in the first place),[35] there remains a sizeable group for whom suspicion of trans people and other minority groups seems to have dislodged suspicion of religion or quackery as the prime motivator.[36] Andrew Bidmead, in this vein, notes in his 2015 PhD thesis on the politics of New Atheism that the movement 'is *not principally about atheism*'.[37] The words 'atheist' and 'Sceptic' have undergone a mutation, now referring in some cases to communities whose common denominator is neither atheism nor Scepticism per se, but social conservatism, resistance to 'political correctness' or 'wokeness', deliberate offensiveness for the sake of shock value, and a politicised commitment to 'Enlightenment values'. This slippage has carried the language of Scepticism and atheism straight to the heart of political transphobia, and it has also eased the process by which the many atheists who swell the ranks of anti-trans feminism can conclude that working with the Christian Right is not a betrayal of their principles but rather a necessary, justifiable collaboration for the furtherance of a far greater cause: a free speech rescue operation and the restoration of the human being to its natural fullness, in defiance to the ever-building pressures of postmodernity.

8

Masking strategies

Every group with transphobic tendencies – conservative evangelicals, anti-trans feminists, populist Eurosceptics, even some socialists[1] – brings its own distinct frame of reference to the table. Feminist texts are placed beside the Bible; trade union praxis beside right-wing traditionalism. Not all aspects of political transphobia are so serendipitously compatible as the common opposition to dualism; some aspects are simply beyond reconciliation, and each camp's ambassadors often resort to masking strategies designed to obfuscate the fault lines. If all these parties were to make known the diversity of their views within the context of the 'trans debate', the cracks in anti-trans activism would be exposed and its coherence as a movement would be jeopardised. To avoid that eventuality, representatives of the anti-gender movement will often try to reduce their activism to a fuzzy, deceptively innocuous point of democratic principle: the right to the free expression of political opinions as an end in and of itself. Freed from the immediate expectation of offering detailed arguments or rebuttals, the factions then unite in the intellectually vacant complaint that they are being silenced, thus (temporarily) resolving the problems presented by the intermixture of otherwise competing vernaculars.[2]

The British national press has served as the primary testing ground and landing vehicle for the 'free speech' masking strategy. It was not without reason that Christine Burns, a leading light in the 1990s wave of UK trans activists and one of the driving forces behind the campaign that culminated with the Gender Recognition Act, described the British press as 'the single most terrifying force in the lives of the average transsexual person'.[3] Journalists writing for major British news outlets have called trans people a 'Monstrous Regiment of the Thin-Skinned',[4] 'gender fascists',[5] 'thought police',[6] 'easily offended',[7] 'snowflakes',[8] the 'trans-Taliban',[9] 'enemies of liberty',[10] and much else besides. The justification given for these heavy-handed insults is a pervasive belief that trans activists are trying to 'advance their cause by stealth'.[11] Debate is said to be anathema to trans campaigners, who would much rather gag their opponents with social media bans and punitive new censorship laws that prohibit the utterance of anti-trans opinions than actually discuss the merits and demerits of their proposed changes to the law, culture and medical practice. The average consumer of mainstream news could be forgiven for thinking this assertion well-established, as barely a week passes without a new opinion piece decrying the erosion of free speech in the name of trans people's rights.

Nigella Lawson (yes, *that* Nigella Lawson) was among the earliest authors to level this charge in the pages of a national newspaper. In 1996, she penned an article for *The Times* that complained of the 'sheer vitriol and threatening aggression' of trans rights advocates who, Lawson believed, were incapable of accepting any other narrative than their own. '[E]ven while transsexuals complain about the intolerance that the rest of us have for them and their condition', she wrote, 'it is they who are so intolerant.'[12] The article was titled 'Sex change operations don't work' and purported to present more reasonable alternatives to gender-affirming procedures. Then, as now, cis people's freedom of speech as it relates to trans people was characterised mainly as the freedom to circulate uneducated, dangerous misconceptions about their personal lives and medical decisions. (Lawson has since apologised for her comments in the 1990s and has moved significantly in a trans-affirming direction.)[13]

It was not until the 2010s that the supposed trans threat to free speech came to be ubiquitous in British media coverage. This came about as a consequence of the fallout from two articles published in December 2012 and January 2013. The first, by *Daily Mail* columnist Richard Littlejohn, was an ugly personal attack on a trans schoolteacher on the basis that teaching children was the 'wrong job' for a trans individual,[14] thus playing into the popular portrayal of trans people as mentally damaged would-be predators. The teacher, Lucy Meadows, took her own life a few months later.[15] Littlejohn was predictably subject to calls for the *Daily Mail* to fire him,[16] causing a number of cis journalists of different politi-cal persuasions to jump to his defence. Feminist broadcaster Libby Purves, for example, wrote in *The Times* that 'even foaming dino-saurs deserve free speech.' She warned that Littlejohn's firing would play 'right into the hands of those who want a legally enforced code preventing any criticism of personal lives and professional choices'.[17] The outline of a narrative was beginning to emerge.

The second article, by feminist journalist Suzanne Moore, con-tained a throwaway line about the impossibility of attaining the beauty standards hoisted upon women by the idolisation of 'Bra-zilian transsexuals'.[18] Many trans readers condemned the comment as ignorant and potentially dangerous given the stratospheric trans murder rate in Brazil.[19] At the same time, however, Moore reported receiving obscene messages from some trans people on social media, including death and rape threats.[20] Responsibility for this vile behaviour was generalised to trans activists as a whole, leading to ominous, slur-laden communal counter-threats such as that issued by Julie Burchill:

> Shims, shemales, whatever you're calling yourselves these days – don't threaten or bully we lowly natural-born women, I warn you … we've experienced a lifetime of PMT [pre-menstrual tension] and sexual harassment, and many of us are now staring HRT and the menopause straight in the face – and still not flinch-ing. Trust me, you ain't seen nothing yet. You *really* won't like us when we're angry.[21]

The mainstreaming of the *trans activists vs free speech* dyad accel-erated significantly in 2015 when Germaine Greer was subject to no-platforming campaigns at a number of universities where she was due to speak, including Cardiff and Cambridge, prompting a new obsession in the anti-trans press: left-wing students and their use of safe spaces and content warnings.[22] With almost no reference to the substance of Greer's beliefs and with little explanation as to *why* they were so controversial, national news outlets portrayed progressive students as simultaneously fragile and tyrannical, pathetic and terrifying, weak and powerful.[23] They uncritically sided with academics who complained of a 'culture of fear' allegedly created by trans activism on campus.[24] In the years since 2015, they have also identified social media platforms like Twitter as Orwellian hellscapes dominated by university-educated 'social justice warriors' (SJWs), 'woke' ideology, and 'cancel culture.'[25]

Meanwhile, Gender Identity Development Service (GIDS) clinics are portrayed as places where the slightest intimation of discomfort with the terminology or current medical practices associated with gender dysphoria brings down spurious accusations of transphobia.[26] In her book *Time to Think: The Inside Story of the Collapse of the Tavistock's Gender Service for Children* (2023), *Newsnight* journalist Hannah Barnes details one scenario in which a doctor at Tavistock said in a team meeting: 'I don't have a gender identity, I'm just female.' She was told by colleagues that this was a transphobic statement. Barnes describes this as an instance of 'shutting down thinking,'[27] but while it is certainly the case that the word 'transphobia' can be unhelpful in one-to-one conversation, this instant ascription of thought-stopping intent drastically, and perhaps deliberately, misses the point. Look again at the statement: 'I don't have a gender identity, I'm just female.' Now compare it with this statement: 'I don't have an accent, I just speak English.' In both cases, the statement does two things that render it illogical: it conflates one concept with another (gender and sex; accent and language), and it makes the claim that the speaker's identity or accent *isn't actually an identity or an accent, but is just normal.* And if the speaker is *normal*, what about other people – those exotic trans people or those Liverpudlians? It turns them into deviations from the ideal. In that sense, yes, the doctor's statement is transphobic, or at least betrays a severe lack of thought given to its broader implications. Her colleagues were not trying to stop her from thinking, but were, in an admittedly inelegant way, *inviting her to think a little more* about what it means to have or not have a gender identity – to get her to recognise that she, too, possesses a culturally contingent set of assumptions about what being 'female' *means* on both the personal and interpersonal levels. In any case, she said it. She was not professionally penalised for saying it. Other people do not have an obligation to agree with or continue to listen to people who say such things.

Because the free speech argument is so vague as to be asinine, and because it can be used to defend the purveyor of any transphobic belief regardless of its derivation, anti-feminist journalists like Piers Morgan have had little trouble jumping on the bandwagon.[28] Some of them even uphold, with an affectation of reluctance, prominent feminists like Greer as free speech martyrs.[29] Anti-trans figures on the Christian Right have also made a point of issuing repetitive prophesies of a dystopian future devoid of dissenting viewpoints due to the advances of trans activism – for example, the Catholic Church, the Free Church of Scotland and the Evangelical Alliance wrote a joint letter to the then Scottish Justice Secretary Humza Yousaf in February 2021 to claim that proposed changes to hate crime legislation would stifle free discussion of trans issues.[30] We thus arrive at a point of empathy and shared interest between feminists and evangelicals that circumnavigates their substantive political differences. Each argues in perpetuity that the other should be able to state their opinions in public fora, even if that right is not actually threatened, because it is more convenient to do this than it is to *explain* to the undecided why other transphobes have such divergent opinions about the ideal societal end-state. Despite its resultant shallowness, this strategy seems to be working.

Baroness Kishwer Falkner, Chair of the Equality and Human Rights Commission and a noteworthy public ally of transphobic feminists, has argued that anti-trans ideologies should be shielded by the 'religion or belief' protections of the Equality Act 2010.[31] More concretely, a number of Employment Tribunal cases have been brought concerning employment discrimination against both transphobic Christians and 'gender critical' feminists on the basis of their 'religion or belief' as it relates to gender identity.[32] One such case, that of Maya Forstater, a tax expert whose annual work contract at the Centre for Global Development was not renewed after she posted Tweets delegitimising trans women and deadnaming* multiple trans users in 2018, was ultimately resolved in Forstater's favour on appeal in July 2022, although the original

---

* Deadnaming refers to the use of a person's prior name, usually one coded to a gender that does not correspond with a person's current gender identity. This is often done with the intention to offend.

judge had described her views as not 'worthy of respect in a democratic society'.[33] In recognition of their reliance on the same legal mechanisms, conservative evangelical lobbyists at the Christian Institute hailed Forstater's efforts,[34] while a number of individuals associated with the 'gender critical' movement helped raise £314,000 for conservative evangelical lawyer and former church director Paul Conrathe from early 2019 to early 2021.[35]

The paradox in all this is that, in spending so much time defending expressive liberty while clearly having no trouble finding a platform on which to do it, anti-trans commentators are undermining their own narrative. Indeed, given that national news outlets almost never provide space for trans authors to issue rebuttals to their large audiences, one could argue that, if anything, it is anti-trans activists who are doing the silencing. Open Democracy researcher Natacha Kennedy associates this hypocrisy with 'mirror propaganda', a technique often deployed by fascist groups to accuse their opponents of doing the very thing that they themselves do systematically.[36] One has to ask: if trans people are shutting down debate, why can transphobic journalists publish article after article with impunity? Why are Government organs like the Equality and Human Rights Commission publicly declaring support for them? The answer is self-evident. The threat exists primarily in their overstimulated imaginations.

How do we explain the popularity of this most uncritical of critiques? The panic over freedom of speech in the trans rights debate has taken on an essentially memetic quality, meaning that it does not require factual sustenance to reproduce. That the trans rights movement is a mortal danger to free speech is taken as axiomatic and therefore, ironically, beyond debate, leaving the door wide open for the unthinking duplication of a simplistic narrative that resonates with a broader distrust of 'political correctness'. This also acts as a cop-out for anti-trans authors. By focusing solely on the narrative that trans people are 'shutting down debate', they shift attention *away from* the immense volume of trans advocacy material that is already in public circulation. Again, this is deeply paradoxical. Anti-trans public figures use the pretext of championing the virtues of 'open debate' as a foil to *avoid* anything beyond the most cursory, shallow discussion. They lament from their platforms that they have no platform, but it is not entirely clear what they would actually *say* if even the whole world stopped to listen.

By creating the impression that the trans rights movement is a totalitarian ideology doing its damnedest to surreptitiously destroy its opposition, transphobes have successfully elided the requirement to provide any specific verifiable or falsifiable claims – the very pivot on which constructive debate turns. Generalisations are deemed sufficient. Transphobic viewpoints, no matter how far removed from reality, are therefore valued by news outlets as a counterweight to trans activism, even if they fall well short of journalistic standards. In October 2021, *BBC News* journalist Caroline Lowbridge published a piece promoting the conspiracy theory that trans activists are systematically forcing cis lesbians to have sex with trans women.[37] After receiving thousands of complaints, the BBC's Executive Complaints Unit found that the article, 'though a legitimate piece of journalism overall, fell below the BBC's standards of accuracy', pointing in particular to the failure to properly vet sources and the questionable use of a statistically invalid survey conducted by the anti-trans hate group Get the L Out.[38] However, the BBC refused to take the article down, contending that it had a duty to 'ensure debate and make sure a wide range of voices are heard'.[39] In other words, the value of the article did not lie in the evidentiary foundation of its core argument, but simply in the fact of its existence.

For all the obvious empirical failings of the appeal to 'free speech', the strategy makes a lot of sense for a reactionary movement that is so riven with internal contradictions. Throwing thousands of vague falsehoods at the wall, and then wailing in unison when trans people suggest that there must be some kind of reckoning with journalistic accountability, is a convenient way to avoid difficult questions concerning the internal ideological cohesion of anti-trans campaigns. Transphobic groups might all claim to value free and open discussion in equal degree, but they *do not* necessarily agree on where they want that discussion to lead politically and culturally – say, in relation to reproductive rights. Much easier, then, to avoid these thorny questions altogether and rally around a hyper-distilled memetic chant – *trans activists want to take away our right to speak.*

Whatever its purpose, the empty appeal to freedom has made its way into the halls of power. Politicians in the Houses of Parliament have parroted the belief that university students lack 'the spirit of liberty'[40] and that progressive discourses are exerting a 'chilling effect' on the personal liberties of both students and academics.[41] In February 2021, the UK Department for Education published a report on 'Free Speech and Academic Freedom' in which it declared that 'even one no-platforming incident is too many',[42] continuing a general anti-woke trend in the May, Johnson, Truss and Sunak premierships.[43] By seeking to remove the right of students to rescind speaking invitations, even in cases where the full extent of the speaker's bigotry was not publicly known beforehand or where the inviting party was simply not aware of that bigotry, a blanket ban on no-platforming would effectively represent a government subsidy for a set of ideologies that are losing badly in the open marketplace of ideas. That no-platforming is itself a vibrant form of political expression with a long history as a tool of the anti-fascist, anti-apartheid and radical feminist movements is, of course, completely overlooked.[44] Facts are irrelevant anyway. As trans activist Shon Faye notes, so long as trans liberation is stalled and the 'debate' remains trapped in an infinite loop from which no positive cultural or legislative change can emerge,[45] transphobia's priests and prophets will be more than happy to stay the indeterminate course.

Another masking strategy approaches the problem from a different angle. Instead of filling the airwaves with a meaningless distraction, this one tries to shift ownership of transphobic sentiment onto a nonspecific, 'ordinary' demographic of socially conservative, no-nonsense, 'common-sense' working- or middle-class people. What ultimately forms from this process is a circular system of passing-the-buck. When an evangelical group cites the conspiratorial 'concerns' of anti-trans feminists as if they represent ordinary cis women, they are often trying to resign ultimate responsibility for the transphobic beliefs and policies being advocated to those feminists, who, in turn, will inevitably try to offload responsibility in the opposite direction by appealing to the protection of religious liberty as a universal value. This back-and-forth game was most obviously displayed in Chapter 4, where the responses of anti-trans feminist and evangelical groups to recent UK and Scottish Government policy consultations on gender recognition and conversion 'therapy' exemplify an effort to reify each other's 'concerns' as authentic.

Joe Kennedy's concept of 'authentocracy' offers an instructive lens through which to view this phenomenon. In *Authentocrats: Culture, Politics and the New Seriousness* (2018), Kennedy defines authentocracy as 'a laundered, centrist populism that seeks to wield power with reference to an authenticity that is always "just over there"'.[46] It fetishises an imagined provincial English working class that is socially conservative, poorly educated, allergic to Bohemian lifestyles, and far too preoccupied by the grind of work to concern itself with anything that smacks of metropolitan liberalism. 'Imputation', Kennedy continues, 'is central to [authentocracy's] workings: it's rarely the commentator themselves that wants less immigration, or, let's face it, more racism, but someone more allegedly authentic who is, we're told, not being given the opportunity to speak for themselves.'[47] The practitioner of authentocratic imputation will claim to be acting as a conduit through which the silent majority can finally speak, but in practice this amounts to the laundering of ideas, a way to frame one's unsavoury beliefs as those of authentic others, who are a population of innocent ordinaries that is thought to be beyond serious scrutiny.

A particularly striking example of how this works can be found if we step outside the evangelical and feminist circles for a moment. David T. C. Davies MP (Conservative Party, Monmouth), is a Eurosceptic and socially reactionary politician who, despite patently not being a feminist (he has consistently voted against reproductive and sexual rights), very publicly aligns himself with transphobic feminists, having repeatedly urged UK Government ministers to consult leading anti-trans groups Fair Play for Women, Woman's Place UK and Transgender Trend before pursuing trans law reform.[48] In 2018, in collaboration with the group We Need to Talk UK, he hosted an event in the House of Commons building titled 'Transgenderism and the War on Women', at which Sheila Jeffreys, a leading anti-trans feminist academic, described trans people as having a 'parasitic' link to cis women.[49] Davies has also entered an assortment of transphobic tropes into the official parliamentary record: He asked Prime Minster Theresa May why children were being supplied with 'potentially life-altering sex change drugs' (presumably referring to puberty blockers, which are also used in cases of precocious puberty) on the National Health Service.[50] He has suggested that female prisoners are at higher risk of assault by 'male prisoners who claim to be transgender' despite having no data to support that assertion.[51] And he has warned that Gender Recognition Act reform on the basis of statutory gender self-declaration would let a '15-stone bearded man' enter women's lavatories (he already can).[52] All of this is delivered with an airy, 'common-sense' tone that purports to represent what 'ordinary' people think.

We can clearly see the mechanism of imputation in operation in Davies's speeches. In November 2018, for instance, he expressed his hope that 'the Government will stop listening to some of the [trans] activist organisations and start listening to people, very often outside the M25 [i.e., outside London], who have a different opinion.'[53] This statement glosses over the fact that the organisations Davies tells the Government to consult are themselves metropolitan. Fair Play for Women, Woman's Place UK and Transgender Trend are all registered with Companies House under London or Home Counties addresses.[54] In fact, Davies does not cite a single provincial individual or organisation, but, in the absence of truly 'ordinary' points of reference, he dresses up London-based radical feminists as his authentocratic muse. It is *their* dislike of trans people, not his own, that he claims to represent, creating a buffer of plausible deniability between himself and the transphobic beliefs he actively propagates.

In addition to these nondescript individuals from 'outside the M25', Davies even makes a claim to represent authentic trans people. He says that he has 'met many trans women who share my concerns about this and want nothing to do with the kind of activism that seems to be going on and shutting down debate.'[55] He is not alone in trying to hide behind authentocratic realism with regards to the beliefs and political desires of the trans population. J. K. Rowling also tried her hand at imputation in her infamously bilious June 2020 article on trans politics by ceding that 'the majority of trans-identified people … pose zero threat to others.' In light of her claim in the same article that trans activists are 'offering cover to [sexual] predators', this would seem to imply that the 'majority' she speaks of has no ambitions to improve the legal conditions of trans people,[56] because if they did, they too would presumably be guilty of enabling predators.

This specific form of passing-the-buck works because, just like the Gnostic charge, it builds on a foundational truth: Queerphobia and assimilationism *within* queer communities is, and always has been, rife. Throughout recent history, trans people have been very forthcoming with their own ideas about the 'right' and 'wrong' ways to be trans, with the more 'respectable' groups often writing to national newspapers to attack other trans people for being too scandalous and too politically radical.[57] Out of the kaleidoscopic mix of mutually exclusive truths comes the resolute conviction that certain trans subgroups are deplorable; inimical, even expendable. Non-binary and genderfluid people, for instance, are often targeted by binary trans people for supposedly 'cheapening' cultural understandings of gender diversity.[58] Meanwhile, Black trans and trans of colour people have been rendered invisible by the White LGBTQI+ movement's often highly dismissive and sometimes deliberately erasive attitude towards the intersections of transphobia and racism. Labour councillor and trans activist Rachael Webb reported a 'generally racist reaction' from fellow activists when she raised the possibility of collaborating with anti-racism causes in the early 1990s, leading her to describe the White trans community of the time as 'a reactionary backwater'.[59] In *Black on Both Sides: A Racial History of Trans Identity* (2017), Black historian C. Riley Snorton explores how White trans culture has 'symptomatically disavowed coarticulations of antiblack and antitrans violence', as exemplified by the erasure of Black disabled man Phillip DeVine's death from popular memories of the 1993 Humboldt murders, in which DeVine was killed alongside White trans man Brandon Teena and White cis woman Lisa Lambert. In the 1999 film based on the murders, *Boys Don't Cry*, only Teena and Lambert are commemorated.[60]

If you look hard enough, then, you stand a good chance at finding just about any imaginable transphobic (or racist, or ableist, or sexist, or xenophobic, or Islamophobic ...) idea circulating in some sector of the trans population. This is not an excuse – bigotry is damaging and unworthy no matter from where it originates – but it does help explain *why* the likes of Davies and Rowling see it as advantageous to disguise their vitriol as a form of solidarity with a silent trans majority. At a glance, their imputation is *believable* because there is no shortage of trans people who are willing to lend their voices to Davies's and Rowling's absurd conspiracy theories, and this aura of plausibility helps to alleviate the intellectual pressure on Britain's leading transphobes by creating the false impression that they are only signal-boosting downtrodden ordinaries. When taken together with the memetic appeal to freedom of speech discussed earlier in this chapter, authentocratic imputation is a highly effective masking strategy in that it successfully redirects the general population's gaze away from the obvious tensions inherent in Britain's anti-trans coalitions, and helps in the process maintain the wobbly pretence of common cause. Ideological precision is thus sacrificed for the sake of political efficacy. In the end, goes the logic, it changes little if trans people's rights are eroded in the name of God, women's safety, common sense, or scientific fact. It's the *outcome* that really matters; so long as the alliance wins on this issue, all else is sophistry.

PART IV

The future

9

A coming storm?

The anti-trans movement's progressive strengthening of bonds is a troubling thing to observe as a trans person. It's one thing to go up against a hodgepodge mess of competing ideologies, and quite another to go up against an integrated machinery of weaponised hatred. Even as public opinion continues, albeit with some periodic reversals, to shift in a more hospitable direction, it will be quite some time before we can say that we are out of the densest woods. As deeply as transphobia has taken root in our society, it might well be that we have not yet witnessed the worst of the effects that could conceivably arise from the anti-trans informational echo-chamber. Extremist and conspiratorial movements are often most dangerous in the final years before their decline into irrelevance, as participants recognise that the clock is ticking and their ability to command media coverage and public interest is fading away; as they see law and media and society move on and cease to care about yesterday's battle in the culture wars. It may yet get worse before it gets better.

We can recognise some of the most troubling portents in the United States, where a concerted effort is already under way in the right-wing media to stir up a wave of righteous anti-trans violence. Shortly before noon on Tuesday, 24 May 2022, a gunman entered Robb Elementary School in Uvalde, Texas and opened fire, killing 21 people. Within hours, users of the far-right imageboard 4chan began circulating the lie that the shooter was a trans woman.[1] Forty-one days later, in Highland Park, Illinois, another shooter opened fire on an Independence Day parade, taking seven lives, before being seen in women's clothing during his attempted escape, prompting far-right theorists to say that he, too, was a trans woman. In fact, the clothing was simply a disguise.[2] A further 57 days later, on 30 August, a hoax bomb threat was called in to the Boston Children's Hospital by a woman who falsely believed that the hospital was performing hysterectomies on trans minors and pressuring them to undergo surgical transition,[3] an idea promoted by the popular reactionary Twitter account @LibsofTik-Tok. Although this account is operated by a Jewish woman named Chaya Raichik, the idea that hospitals are 'sexualising' children for ideological and financial gain is linked by other theorists to the hybrid transphobic/antisemitic notion that the 'sudden' growth in the availability of gender-affirming medical care is part of a nefarious, child-grooming, reality-subverting plot by Jews, principally the Pritzker family.[4]

By the time of the Colorado Springs LGBTQI+ club shooting on 19–20 November 2022, the idea that the LGBTQI+ community was engaged in the mass grooming of children was so ubiquitous that right-wing coverage of the atrocity focused almost exclusively on alleged trans wrongdoings, including 'sexualised' drag performances in the presence of children (the performers at such events are usually clad head-to-toe in over-the-top pantomime costume, exposing very little skin), and the supposed capture of paediatric care by the dogmatists of gender ideology. Little attention was paid to the lives lost in the shooting, or the broader problem of queerphobia in the media leading to violent acts of retribution. Right-wing YouTube influencers like Tim Pool and Matt Walsh, conspiracy mills like Libs of TikTok, and even popular television hosts like Fox's Tucker Carlson spread the callous lie that the shooting was simply a natural response to the LGBTQI+ community's imagined misconduct towards children.[5] At the 2023 Conservative Political Action Conference, Catholic far-right media personality Michael Knowles went so far as to demand that 'transgenderism must be eradicated from public life entirely',[6] and such language will no doubt become more commonplace in the aftermath of the Nashville school shooting on 27 March 2023. The shooter, who killed three children and three adults at a Christian school, was a trans man. The Metropolitan Nashville Police is currently speculating that 'resentment' at having had to attend the school as a child may be a component in the shooter's motives.[7] Given the far-right's hunger for a clear-cut case of a trans mass-murderer whose wrongs can be generalised to reflect on all trans people, it is no surprise that this event is already becoming a key point of reference for anti-trans politicians and social media personalities.[8] 'TransTerrorism' is their hashtag of choice.

Accusations of widespread child murder and grooming carried out by trans people are also endemic to QAnon. An Information Age 'conspiracy of everything', QAnon is a multi-layered network of conspiracy theories strongly aligned with the extreme right-wing segments of the US's evangelical movement,[9] structured around the belief that there exists a Satanic 'cabal' of child-murdering liberal globalists that only a promised 'Storm' of mass arrests and executions, to be carried out by Donald Trump, will halt.[10] Although QAnon's symbolic leaders, an imaginary network of high-level US civil and military figures known as Q, never once mentioned trans people in any of the thousands of 'Drops' (coded intelligence releases) posted to the imageboards 4chan, 8chan and 8kun,[11] Q's target audiences were already primed by popular narratives of trans predation and contagion to see trans people as part of an insidious plot to destroy their noble, traditional lifestyles.[12] We are witnessing in real time the abandonment of all subtlety, and the ready-made proliferation of anti-trans beliefs in both religious and feminist contexts enables such wanton bloodthirst to spread still further.

The phrases *plumbing the depths* and *reaching new lows* occur frequently in conversations about the far-right, but where transphobia is concerned, the truly remarkable thing is not the depths to which believers sink, but rather that the movement has struggled, for all its malicious creativity, to produce anything more depraved than the material that is already available in respected newspapers, on surface-web social media platforms, and in the Gender Studies sections of high street bookshops. Just think of all the absurd fabrications we have encountered in these pages – children are being corrupted and cajoled by a manufactured 'social contagion' so as to expand the trans population; trans people are trying to silence their critics – most of all, women – because they are really patriarchal shock-troopers sent in to break feminist resistance; trans women perform 'total rape' by simply existing in women's spaces; trans women are forcing cis lesbians to sleep with them; trans people are trying to destroy the very concepts of reality and truth;

trans identity is a disguised form of ancient mysticism, and on we go, deeper down the dank rabbit hole.

Leading trans historian Jules Gill-Peterson has described what she calls the 'laundering' of transphobic conspiracy theories for mainstream consumption,[13] but I would note that, very often, transphobic lies do not begin life in the far-right or similar alcoves of hate and then find their way outwards, but rather originate in mainstream discourses and *then* find their most violent expression in the far-right. Case in point: by the time QAnon's morbid fascination with trans people began to pick up in 2019, the bottom of the barrel had been well and truly scraped clean by well-connected anti-trans feminist and Christian commentators in Britain and the United States, and the Uvalde and Highland Park lies were not far removed from the lies put forth by the likes of Janice Raymond and the Christian Institute. The characterisation of trans women as 'total' rapists, to use Raymond's words, is but one particularly ugly example. As Shon Faye writes:

> This image of the trans woman as a living, breathing act of rape is a potent and persistent trope in the transphobic discourses of both right-wing men and anti-trans feminists: both groups are capable of providing cover for the other to perpetuate it. If transition itself is a rape, so this argument goes, then the trans woman is already guilty by the mere fact of her existence and can expect to be punished.[14]

The casual association of trans people with abhorrent crimes that carry hefty sentences under the law does not stop there. J. K. Rowling's 2020 novel *Troubled Blood* features a male murderer who wears women's clothing in order to lure his female victims – a classic example of the 'trans predator' archetype, very popular in Britain's tabloids at present. This was, she insists, based on real cases and not a deliberate attempt to smear trans people, although even were this true, the implications carried by such a narrative in the current discursive climate cannot possibly be lost on Rowling, who chose to write it anyway.[15] In the 2022 follow-up, *Ink Black Heart*, a woman is harassed by trans activists and then murdered after she expresses transphobic opinions online, thus actualising, in the most inelegantly on-the-nose fashion imaginable, trans people's supposed fantasies of an Orwellian suppression of wrong-think.[16] If this agonisingly implicatory train of thought – the narrative that there exists an unpopular, insular minority that possesses a counter-intuitive and wholly disproportionate vice-grip on the levers of media and state power, which it uses to attack, murder and imprison nay-sayers – gives you *déjà vu*, there's a good reason: Transphobic imaginations never stray far from standard antisemitic models for conspiratorial hypothesis.[17] What's new is old.

Much as these parties might protest that all they are doing is voicing legitimate concerns about rapid societal change, there are only so many logical conclusions to be drawn from their portrayal of trans people as paedophilic, raping, murdering, child-indoctrinating, grooming, anti-democratic, self-obsessed, God-killing, truth-bending, science-denying heretics – and none of those conclusions are conducive to peaceful coexistence. With so abhorrent a statement of faith, political transphobia habitually teeters on the edges of stochastic terrorism: mass character assassination with the (sometimes subconscious) intent to encourage others – those with less to lose than established politicians, authors, journalists, academics and pundits – to resort to violence. The messaging is underhanded enough to preserve *some* plausible deniability, but specific enough to impart a clear call to action that runs something like this: 'Look around and see what's happening. Women are in danger. Children are in danger. Traditions are being destroyed. Western [White / Christian] civilisation is being weakened [feminised / secularised / postmodernised] from within. Now, *what are you going to do about it*?'

While one arm of political transphobia reaches for physical violence, the other works to enact purposeful harm through the channels of officialdom. State executive, legislative and judicial branches across the US have attempted, in some cases successfully, to implement stringent anti-trans policies that seek no less than to make trans life untenable. These measures include bans on trans people using the public bathrooms that accord most closely with their gender identities (the infamous 'bathroom bills'),[18] bans on trans women athletes competing in both professional and non-professional women's sporting categories,[19] and bans on medical practitioners providing gender-affirming healthcare and counselling to minors.[20] Senate Bill 129 in Oklahoma proposes to ban such care for anyone *up to the age of 25*, well beyond the medical age of majority of 16 in the state, and the sudden removal of this care from young trans people could force some to undergo the unnecessary mental pain of involuntary detransition.[21] All the while, some of the country's ultra-conservative governors, including Ron DeSantis of Florida, are transparently using anti-trans rhetoric and the promise of executive crackdowns on 'woke' culture to increase their popularity in the ever-rightward-lurching Republican Party.[22] Nor is this a uniquely American problem. On the other side of the Atlantic, UK Prime Minister Rishi Sunak announced in March 2023 the launch of a review into relationships, sex, and health education in England in response to spurious concerns raised by evangelical Tory MP Miriam Cates that children were being exposed to 'age-inappropriate, extreme, sexualising and inaccurate' information, including LGBTQI+ inclusive content – a move that teaching unions have described as 'politically motivated'.[23] The capacity for statutory power to tear apart trans life and to leave in its wake irreparable personal and communal wounds far outstrips anything that individual terrorists can inflict. In the final analysis, anti-trans legislation is simply the centralised dispensation of programmatic malice, and transphobic figureheads like Rowling, as humorously incompetent and cartoonishly untactful as they can be, are actively boosting the cultural momentum behind these acts of legalised anthropo-vandalism.

Trans-affirming readers, or anyone to whom open defamation and violence – whether terroristic or statutory – is an unconscionable method of resisting change, arrive with some urgency, then, at the most difficult question: what can *we* do about it? Well, which *we*? Trans activists and trans-affirming feminists (the overlap between the two is fairly large, though not complete) are in a difficult position, because experience tells us that no amount of reasoned argumentation will ever convince anti-trans feminists to distance themselves from the more reactionary schisms of evangelicals and others on the Christian Right. I would not be so presumptuous as to dispute that observation – after all, the 2022 British anti-trans feminist film *Adult Human Female* ends with the unintentionally insightful words 'We will not fucking move' – but I would like to suggest that intersectional feminists have been guilty of overlooking the 'other' half of the picture.

One of the culturally intriguing consequences of secularisation has been the rapid concentration of biblical knowledge in increasingly niche communities, making the inner workings of those communities ever more impenetrable to anyone looking in. Certainly, to the average secular trans-affirming feminist, evangelicals and our systems of biblical signification just seem *weird*. The dearth of people who are capable of mixing a fluency in transfeminist vernaculars with a fluency in evangelical vernaculars makes the gap seem even wider. From such a vantage point, it is easy to conclude that evangelical Christianity is a swamp from which one either escapes, in the way one escapes any 'cult', or else remains ensnared within forever, being bigoted and theocratic to the end. There is no middle ground, and therefore no point venturing into that vast, opaque fog. Better to leave the swamp creatures to their own affairs and build a better world around them.

Even were we to accept this as truth, we simply cannot afford as trans people to leave so powerful a current of transphobic thought as that which exists in some pockets of the evangelical movement so drastically underexamined and so dangerously underchallenged. This, I believe, is where parallel lines of dialogue between secular trans-affirming feminists and trans-affirming evangelicals (yes, they exist) must come into play; presenting models for moral, theoretical, theological and organisational conjunction that take as their starting point the innate value of human diversity – whether it be divinely instituted, naturally created, anthropogenically synthesised, or a mixture of all three – rather than ideological anti-dualism, and offering spaces in which to build strategies for mutual deradicalisation that address the anti-trans coalition from within *both* of its main biomes. As odd as it might appear, there will always be LGBTQI+ churchgoers in evangelical spaces, and it is in all of our interests to ensure that evangelical leaders are equipped to understand sexual and gender diversity and, if needed, help LGBTQI+ congregants to appropriate support.

For this to be possible, however, we so desperately need a sufficiently educated and organised, or at the very least *eager*, group of evangelicals in positions of communal influence with whom trans-feminists might coordinate. Currently, while it is easy enough to find individual evangelicals who fit the bill, particularly among younger evangelicals, it is difficult to identify any such group that is organised, contactable, visible, connected and willing to publicly question conventional wisdom in the movement. A simple Google search for the words 'trans evangelical' or some variation on that theme usually makes for depressing reading. What of evangelicals, then? What role can *we* play in creating a less transphobic future?

10

Getting Christianity right

Friday, 17 February 2023 – One year and a handful of days after Kellie-Jay Keen's pitiable anti-trans protest in Nottingham city centre, I returned to Speaker's Corner under a wholly different set of circumstances. Darkness had fallen; the winds brushed through a much larger crowd of some hundred-or-so trans people and allies; the heavens withheld their waters, for the most part, as candles breathed in the great sadness of huddled souls. On 11 February, Brianna Ghey, a 16-year-old trans girl, had been murdered in Warrington, a large post-industrial town nestled between Manchester and Liverpool. In cities across the UK, including Nottingham, vigils were held to celebrate the life of this young woman and to mourn the hateful tragedy of her loss. As tears fell and hearts pained, the horrible *realness* of transphobia crashed through the flimsy dissociative barriers I had hurriedly fabricated to protect my composure. When a trans Methodist minister emotionally lamented the role that churches have played in spreading anti-trans hate, I cracked. It was too much.

I am today no closer to resolving the contradictions in my being than I was when I embarked on this journey. In bringing this book to completion, few things struck me as an evangelical Christian more than the fact that we are (very deservedly, in many cases) regarded as a group with whom it is shameful for any forward-thinking person, most of all a feminist, to associate. This is, of course, a bit of a problem for me, as I am politically a socialist feminist, and yet theologically I would fall somewhere into conservative evangelicalism. In large part, the nucleus of the problem is that the adjective *conservative*, usually taken in a political rather than doctrinal or theological sense, is popularly regarded as superfluous, because the evangelical movement in its entirety is thought by many to be comprised of hopeless reactionaries – hypocritical moralists and foul confidence tricksters of the American televangelist variety – with little to no capacity for compassion, reason, or moderation. This is an understandable conclusion. Totalising, yes, but not groundless from an experiential perspective. These very failings – inflexibility, unreason, intemperance, and not least, facile moralism – have been on powerful display throughout the history of evangelical interactions with LGBTQI+ communities. What's more, the obsessive queerphobia of a powerful but relatively minute number of evangelicals has poisoned the movement's image to such an extent that knowledge of our callous, inveterate bigotry is now a matter of 'common sense'. Water is wet. The sun is hot. Evangelicals hate trans people.

In the year 2000, as the subject of trans people's legal rights was inching its way into mainstream consciousness, a journalist at *The Times* casually informed her readers that, so far as religious perspectives were concerned, trans identities were 'opposed the most strongly in evangelical churches'.[1] Concordantly, trans campaigner Christine Burns has written in her memoirs that evangelical Christians can 'generally be relied upon to fulminate on demand' whenever LGBTQI+ rights are in contention.[2] There usually seems no need for commentators to add nuance to such statements, since contrary voices that might challenge this stark impression have been few and far-between. In the 2000s and 2010s, a trans evangelical named Elaine Sommers, working as part of the group Accepting Evangelicals, campaigned for the movement to adopt 'a more conciliatory and accepting stance' on gender issues,[3] but little visible progress seems to have been made, and Accepting Evangelicals has since been absorbed by a larger ecumenical inclusive Christian organisation named OneBodyOneFaith.[4]

The Evangelical Fellowship for Lesbian & Gay Christians (EFLGC) is another now-defunct organisation that momentarily served as a space for trans evangelical organising in Britain. Trans issues were discussed at the Fellowship's 2004 annual meeting,[5] and in 2009 the ecumenical trans group Sibyls was invited to lead a workshop for the Fellowship on the relationship between Christian faith and gender identity. The leaders of Sibyls later recalled of the 2009 event that 'trans-friendly EFLGC members were keen for the group's name to be changed to reflect its readiness to welcome trans people (one member present identified as trans)',[6] although this change of name does not seem to have happened, and the group's website went offline in 2021. In general, trans evangelical organising in Britain has been both low-key and intermittent, in part because those trans-affirming evangelical networks that do exist are often forced to adopt an 'underground' or subaltern character due to the dominance and charisma of conservative leaders in the movement – a trend explored in Deborah Jian Lee's ground-breaking and still highly relevant book on progressive evangelicalism in the United States, *Rescuing Jesus: How People of Color, Women & Queer Christians are Reclaiming Evangelicalism* (2015).[7]

More tangible outcomes have been secured by individual churches and church families. Oasis Trust, a Christian charity founded by Steve Chalke in 1985 with a focus on youth homelessness and other issues of social and economic justice, was a member of the Evangelical Alliance until 2014, when the Alliance discontinued Oasis's membership over a page on the Trust's website that included a reference to Chalke's support for same-sex marriage, announced in 2013.[8] Oasis, having declined the Alliance's request to 'equally profile the traditional Christian view' on its online platforms, re-stated in the aftermath of its expulsion a 'profound belief that the ethos, values, and mission of Oasis sit firmly within the Evangelical tradition'.[9] With Oasis having been loosed from the traditionalist oversight of the Alliance, but remaining rooted in an evangelical spiritual identity, Chalke went on to hold a renaming ceremony for a trans intersex man at Oasis Church Waterloo in 2016.[10] Oasis has also become something of a safe haven for other churches leaving anti-trans evangelicalism – churches like Oasis Hub Hull, previously Hull Community Church, which underwent a journey towards inclusivity in the 2010s under the leadership of Anne Dannerolle, and is now, as Oasis Hub, an LGBTQI+ affirming member of Inclusive Church.[11] Oasis Hull has carried over some of the worship practices from its prior identity, although it does not publicise itself in alignment with evangelicalism and is not affiliated with mainline evangelical institutions.

As these stories show, progress very often means leaving the formal trappings of the evangelical world behind, even if doing so can sadly reduce the internal pressures for attitudinal change in those churches that remain in the fold. Christian ethicist David P. Gushee, who made waves by calling for full acceptance of gay Christians in his 2014 book *Changing our Mind: A Call from America's Leading Evangelical Ethics Scholar for Full Acceptance of LGBT Christians in the Church*,[12] narrated his journey *out of* American evangelicalism in another book just three years later.[13] Sharing a similar trajectory, Ken Wilson founded an evangelical church in Ann Arbor, Michigan, in 1975, and in the following decades became a prominent thought leader in the Vineyard family of neo-charismatic evangelical churches, but he left the church in 2014 because Vineyard's hard-line anti-LGBTQI+ stance was increasingly incompatible with his own calls for greater acceptance.[14] With the only options for queer Christians and their allies so often being limited to hiding, staying quiet, or fleeing, fundamental change is delayed still further. As Deborah Lee notes in *Rescuing Jesus*, these acts of self-preservation, flowing from the completely natural desire to find more agreeable church communities, can accidentally militate to ensure that ultra-conservative, pseudo-biblical views, though often not shared by the majority of ordinary believers, nonetheless 'go unchallenged by fellow evangelicals'.[15] Most of those who might be able to pull the movement back to its senses have already jumped ship.

All the while, no small number of church leaders in out-and-proud evangelical churches have actively participated in the institutionalised spiritual abuse of trans people. In November 1997, a trans churchgoer named Janine told the *Daily Express* of her traumatic experience of coming out as trans at St Hugh's, a charismatic evangelical Anglican church in Luton:

> The crunch came last Sunday when I went to receive Holy Communion and was refused by a church member. The vicar was standing by his side but did nothing. I felt humiliated and worthless. Afterwards when I spoke to the vicar he said he didn't hear anything and later refused to speak to me. I expected to experience hate from some corners of our society but I never expected it to come from Christians in my own church. It is the hypocrisy of their views and values which really upsets me. In my hour of greatest need my church failed me.[16]

On a broader level, the Parakaleo Ministry, founded in London in the 1990s by self-professed former cross-dresser Keith Tiller as a centre for prayer-based trans-to-cis conversion 'therapy', was supplied with a steady flow of victims by evangelical church leaders who, in Tiller's words, were 'concerned for someone they know who is either cross-dressing or calling themselves transsexual'. These individuals were, Tiller admits, 'invariably under some form of duress to make contact with me'.[17] One of those 'helped' by Tiller, a trans woman named Marissa Dainton, spoke to *The Guardian* about her experiences in 2004.[18] 'Soon after her first sex change' in 1993, recounts *Guardian* journalist David Batty, Dainton

joined an evangelical church and became convinced her operation was sinful. She stopped taking oestrogen and was prescribed testosterone. Her beard and body hair began to grow back, and her sex drive soared. Before getting married to another member of the congregation six years ago, she had her artificial vagina removed. This left her with smooth skin where her genitals once were.

Through her church, Dainton found Keith Tiller and Parakaleo. She grew close to Tiller and in 1996 they co-authored a pamphlet titled 'Male and Female He Created Them', in which Dainton wrote that she repented from her trans identity after feeling that God had revealed to her that it was an aberration 'born of sin'. Her strong desire to present as feminine and wear feminine clothing continued, but because her church 'had made such a big hoo-ha' about her identity, she says she 'didn't feel [she] had anywhere to go'. Dainton eventually found her way out of this destructive bubble and into a supportive community of trans people, but Tiller continued to insist that it was possible to simply pray the trans away. He told *The Guardian*: 'I personally know people in the US and Australia who have resumed living in their original biological gender role. Nearly all claim to have done so as a result of Christian conviction.'

Instead of distancing itself from Tiller, the Evangelical Alliance invited him to assume joint (though unstated) authorship of its 2000 report on *Transsexuality*,[19] and it later posted a list of Tiller's prejudicial and medically unsound recommendations for 'church leaders who encounter transsexual people' on its website.[20] Another Evangelical Alliance report published in 2006, *Gender Recognition: A Guide for Churches to the Gender Recognition Act*, was also the bitter fruit of a collaboration with Parakaleo.[21] Despite the Evangelical Alliance tentatively seeking to modernise its approach in recent years, with Peter Lynas, the Alliance's UK Director, making a point of talking to groups of trans people prior to writing *Transformed*,[22] the organisation has yet to apologise for enabling and amplifying the Parakaleo Ministry's coercive malpractice. Not that an apology alone would achieve much. At this stage, tepid and gradual change is painfully inadequate. Only a root-and-branch overhaul of evangelical thought and practice on the subjects of sexuality and gender (by which I mean a *return* to the Bible with an inquisitive mind, not an *abandonment* of the Bible), coupled with a *sustained and heartfelt* repentance, can hope to recover the movement from its potentially fatal superannuation. Should we choose that path, the questions to which we must make ourselves accountable are fundamental and uncomfortable.

Trans people are most accustomed to asking how radical feminists – *any* feminists – can justify cooperating with evangelicals, but I want to turn that on its head. How can evangelical Christians – *any* Christians – justify working hand-in-hand with the anti-trans feminist movement; a movement that has no other purpose than to spread transphobic disinformation and fear, a movement that specialises in punching down, a movement founded upon harassment and intimidation, and that calls for the cessation of trans people's very existence? Are these the friends kept by a community whose God is 'near to the broken-hearted' (Psalm 34:18) and promises to 'wipe away every tear' (Revelation 21:4)? More immediately, and more specifically, we must ponder: does the evangelical Church actually *desire* for trans people to join the family of God, or has it given up on them? Does it love them not as repressed, depressed, fragmented, truncated, synthetic versions of themselves, but simply *as themselves*? If so, can the Church humble itself, admit wrongdoing, and lay the groundwork for reconciliation?

All of these prompts for introspection can be summed up in a single question asked by Letha Scanzoni and Nancy Hardesty, two of the founders of evangelical feminism, in the concluding passages of their seminal book *All We're Meant To Be: A Biblical Approach to Women's Liberation* (1974): 'Will the church repeat its past errors or learn from them?'[23] This simple but punchy arrangement of eleven words presents an either-or scenario, conjuring the image of a forking path. One way – the same old way – is well-trodden and well-lit, and would be very easy to traverse; the other, lightly trodden and unilluminated, looks uninviting. It is frightening in its unfamiliarity. However, as Jesus taught, these considerations are morally irrelevant to the godly appraisal of our options, for 'the road is easy that leads to destruction ... [and] the road is hard that leads to life' (Matthew 7:13–14). Let's take the hard path.

Whatever conceptual tools and scriptural foundations we use to visualise our options, the answers to the above questions *should* be easy to discern; at least, a glance at our source material would suggest so. As trans Anglican priest Rachel Mann reminds us: 'The way of Christ is an invitation to love our enemies, to bring an end to oppositions of mistrust, fear and sometimes hate.'[24] There is nothing integral about Christianity, nor even the evangelical movement, that condemns it to being eternally behind the curve of social justice. Evangelical Christians affirm that the divine call to emulate God's steadfast love, communicated to us through the Bible, supersedes cultural trends or passing political concerns that arise in the face of new challenges. This may sound rather basic and even a little saccharine, but the God of love has no regard for humanity's nonsensical hierarchies. Even those considered morally unclean by the upper crust of society are invited to carry forth the gospel. The apostle Matthew was a tax collector, a despised representative of the Roman imperial order (Matthew 9:9–13), and the first Gentile to be baptised into the covenant community of Christ was a eunuch, an individual who would likely have been barred from entering the Temple in Jerusalem (Deuteronomy 23:1; Acts 8:26–40).

While Christians have failed more often than we have succeeded in reflecting the universality of God's love, Jesus left no room in his teachings for us to doubt that we must, as a religious calling, *keep trying*. In fact, to do otherwise is to do nothing less than turn away from him. But if our convictions are to have any meaning at all, they must entail rising above, as Jesus did and does, the urge to

pillory those maligned in any given societal context, be they transgressors of normative moral standards (Luke 7:36–50, 18:9–14;
John 8:1–11) or those who are socially ostracised, lonely, and inad-
equately cared-for (Mark 5:1–20; John 5:1–8). Every effort to take
away the rights and erode the dignity of a minoritised group must
surely prompt a deep unease in our souls. The realisation that we
have been complicit in such an effort should tear at the very fabric
of who we are.

When Jesus spoke the Beatitudes from atop the mount ('Blessed
are the poor in spirit ... those who mourn ... the meek ... those
who are persecuted', Matthew 5:3–12), the profundity of the
message was not solely in the minutiae – who is blessed and what
they will receive – but also in the absolute inversion of worldly
(meaning primarily Greek and Roman, more than Jewish) social
orders.[25] This is one of the key themes of Jesus's entire ministry:
those you revile, I love. Those you have given up on, I encourage. Those deemed unworthy, I treasure. Those who feel lost, I will
move heaven and earth to find, even if I must leave the ninety-nine
to rescue the hundredth (Matthew 18:10–14). The early evangelists
carried this counter-cultural impulse in their hearts. By the time
the Jesus movement reached the city of Thessalonica in northern
Greece in the mid-first century, the standard plea that opponents
of the movement would make to the Roman authorities (at least
according to the author of the Acts of the Apostles, to whom this
was no doubt a wryly satisfying piece of inadvertent flattery) was
that '[t]hese people ... have been turning the world upside down'
(Acts 17:6). As the world changes, so the implications of a world
turned 'upside down' change with it. And so these words from trans
Christian poet Jay Hulme, though they might ring unacceptably
subversive to a scriptural purist, are no more than a rearticulation
of Christ's wholesale embrace for a different context:

> Blessed are those who try; those who transform, who transition.
> Blessed are the queers; who love creation enough to live the
> truth of it,
> despite a world that tells them they cannot.[26]

The Church is meant to act as a conduit for God's love, not an intermediary. It does not get to decide by diktat who is in and who is out, however much it seems to think it can. Almost every church has been guilty to a greater or lesser degree of behaving like an overzealous lawmaker, adding voluminous exception clauses to the Beatitudes in order to avoid responsibility for translating them into works. In its dealings with those oppressed because they are women, Black, Jewish, gay, trans, non-binary, disabled, and working-class, the Christian Church has done nothing less than blaspheme the gentleness of Christ's heart.[27] Black gay Anglican priest Jared Robinson-Brown calls this incredible deficiency of tenderness a 'famine of Grace',[28] and given this appalling reality, it is, in the words of another gay Anglican priest, Charlie Bell, 'no small miracle' that *any* LGBTQI+ people go to church.[29] Churches can feel downright *dangerous*, as one Black trans man from the United States relates:

> Churches make me anxious. Being in a room with that many Christians is dangerous for me because of who I am. As an LGBTQ person, I have to be ready to defend myself at all times, whether it's verbal or physical attacks. Being a Black man means walking out of the house and wondering if you'll live long enough to see it again. Being chronically ill means having the constant pressure to prove you deserve to live, even if you're not seen as a 'productive member of society.' If I walk into a packed church, the chances of running into someone who thinks I'm a sin, a mistake, inferior, or all of the above are extremely high. Whether they say something or not depends on their personality and how comfortable they feel in that environment, but I don't know that until it happens. By then, it's too late.[30]

Even were it our *openly expressed desire* to turn away those who belong to minoritised groups, we could hardly have designed a more assuredly hostile environment than that which we have cultivated through a mixture of sheer absent-mindedness and wanton stubbornness.

As hopeless as the situation looks, I believe evangelical Christians *can* recapture our Spirit-guided instinct for radical justice, as other church communities have done and are doing. Non-evangel-ical readers might scoff. *What a ridiculous hallucination.* Indeed, it is difficult to explain to anyone who does not personally know any evangelicals that there *are* reasons to hope for a better evangel-icalism in the not-too-distant future. The first justification for my believing that we can do better is the fact that, in the past, some of us *have* done better. Shortly after the first 'sex-change' operation at Johns Hopkins Hospital in Maryland in 1966, Roy D. Gresham, general secretary of the Baptist Convention of Maryland, a regional arm of the evangelical Southern Baptist Convention, told the local newspaper: 'This is an area of medical science and not morally prohibitive. It would be more wrong morally to leave these people [in modern parlance, those experiencing gender dysphoria] in their unfortunate situation.'[31] In 1977/8, another Southern Baptist minister from Missouri named David Edens wrote a short piece for a collection of religious viewpoints on gender-nonconform-ity compiled by the Erickson Educational Foundation. Edens's comments concerning surgical interventions in cases of gender dysphoria are, like Gresham's, remarkable precisely because they are free of that condemnatory overtone that so defines more recent evangelical expositions:

As a counselor I have worked with only one transsexual and have seen in his behavior modification a transformation akin to the Christian phenomenon called conversion or being 'born again.' Answers to life's complicated problems are not easily found, but abundant life and wholeness seem to be what the gospel is all about. Jesus was not a stone caster. He was always eager to restore health to those who were blind or deaf, or palsied, or taken in the act of adultery. The helping professions today must strive for a compassion born of understanding and coupled with an intelligence of what we can and cannot do for people. God loves the transsexual as much as anyone else. And He wants us to act responsibly in giving of skills which can aid the transsex-ual to a more abundant life in this world.[32]

Edens's statement was not wholly representative of Southern Baptist opinion at the time, but neither was the strictly anti-trans view. In

1977, the Board of Directors of the Baptist General Convention of Oklahoma voted to ban 'sex-change' operations at the Baptist Medical Center in Oklahoma City – however, this was only after it had been revealed that the Center had been a major hub for this type of surgery over the previous four years, performing on over 50 trans patients in that time. Joe Ingram, executive director of the Convention, declared that there would be no 'ifs, ands or question marks' on this subject after the vote, but two doctors at the Medical Center, David William Foerstler and Charles Reynolds, publicly dissented. They were insistent that the operations were 'consistent with their religious beliefs', and declared (in dated language): 'If Jesus Christ were alive today, undoubtedly He would render help and comfort to the transsexual as He did the leper, the blind and the lame.'[33] It seems the dominant traditionalist faction on the Board of Directors came down so heavily against 'sex-change' procedures precisely because they were aware that, left to their own religious judgements, ordinary Southern Baptists would not automatically become transphobic.

The second justification for my optimism is more anecdotal. Imprinted on my mind is a reel of images; wincing faces; the shocked, disheartened, troubled reactions of loving and gentlehearted siblings in Christ whenever I have mentioned what some of our movement's leaders have been saying about trans people; utter disbelief that manifests as a scrunched brow and a slow sigh; the emotional tremors that precede a tectonic doctrinal shift. The door is unlocked. Set ajar. It's time to push.

First and foremost, we must deal urgently with the spectre of Gnosticism, a category of thought invented in the eighteenth century and now mentioned in countless evangelical books and reports that touch on trans identity, despite the fact that most trans people probably have no idea what it is, still less see themselves as its modern standard-bearers. The Gnostic charge – the assertion that trans people are perpetuating the same body/mind dualist philosophy as the ancient Gnostics – is intellectually, theologically and morally lazy. It draws on a superficial similarity between an artificially defined 'Gnosticism' and *one* mode of understanding trans embodiment (the 'wrong body' narrative), while ignoring the inconvenient truths that many trans people think of their bodies in entirely different ways, and that, anyway, 'the Gnostics' as traditionally understood aimed for universal androgyny in a post-material sense, not free expression of gender diversity *in the material world*. All that is to say: evangelical purists are aiming at an imaginary target.

To any trans person who enters the wrong evangelical church, however, it will immediately become apparent that the effects of this phantom battle are very real. I am thinking, for example, of the pastor who repeatedly and pointedly told me, presumably because I look quite obviously trans, that I should attend their 'sexual sanity' course on my first-ever visit to his church (I am asexual, so I am not sure what I could have gained from this), and then proceeded to ask me for my name multiple times throughout our conversation, as if he simply could not process the concept that someone with a deep-ish voice could be called Rebecca. I think also of the congregant in another evangelical church who would not cease asking for my 'real name', and who, unsolicited, took it upon herself to run me through the absolute basics of the Christian theology of gender and creation (as she perceived it), seemingly being convinced that doing so would force an epiphany upon me. These are just some of the more comical of my experiences.

Most others in the trans and non-binary communities steer clear of the oddly modern-looking, unnervingly clean buildings occupied by we evangelicals, living their lives with nary a thought given to this peculiar movement of outwardly irritable religionists. Their cis allies – parents, siblings, friends and compassionate strangers alike – give evangelical churches an equally wide berth. If progress is to be made, we must realise that it is not they, but the Church, that faces cultural oblivion if this situation continues, and so noxious is our reputation that few outside our ranks will mourn should that come to pass. That is the status to which we have fallen. Instead of turning the world upside down, we have resolved to chain it in place, giving divine authority – not ours to apportion – to entirely anthropogenic, temporary and circumstantial social precedents out of a choleric fear of social change. Because of this, we are considered a base obstacle to a better future. A hope vacuum.

The challenge for evangelical churches is therefore to leave hang-ups about Gnosticism in the past, along with other tempting oversimplifications that impinge upon one's compassion, and to resist the temptation to carry on the sordid, indefensible cohabitation with anti-trans feminists. My plea to church leaders is this: push yourselves to talk or write about gender identity without ever using the words *Gnostic, dualism,* or *gender ideology* (except to outline the deficiencies of past precedent), and without insinuating that trans identity is counter-factual, an unprecedented invention of (post)modernity, a departure from the real, or somehow anti-God. Give due respect to the scriptures in their wholeness by trying to form a biblical opinion on the matter that does not rely exclusively on a myopic, uncharitable and decontextualised reading of sturdy old 'clobber passages' like Genesis 1:27, Deuteronomy 22:5, or Matthew 19:4. Remember the wisdom of Paul:

> [D]o not pronounce judgment before the time, before the Lord comes, who will bring to light the things now hidden in darkness and will disclose the purposes of the heart. Then each one will receive commendation from God. (1 Corinthians 4:5)

It is not for us to know the purposes of the hearts of others. Still less is it our role as Christians in the world to weaponise the powers of terrestrial law to resolve doctrinal controversies (1 Corinthians 5:1–8), as has seemingly been the objective of so much conservative evangelical political advocacy on matters of sexuality and gender. Yes, it is no doubt rewarding when governments can be manipulated in such a way as to delay the evangelical movement's inevitable reckoning with the observable realities of trans life, particularly through the necromantic preservation of the legal gender binary and through special pleading for the continued legal immunity of prayer-based conversion 'therapy'. But neither Herod nor Caesar is your friend in the final analysis. Remember also the wisdom of James concerning the duplicity of the mighty and the wealthy in their dealings with communities of faith:

> Is it not the rich who oppress you? Is it not they who drag you into the courts? Is it not they who blaspheme the excellent

name that was invoked over you? If you really fulfill the royal law according to the scripture, 'You shall love your neighbour as yourself,' you do well. But if you show partiality, you commit sin and are convicted by the law as transgressors. For judgment will be without mercy to anyone who has shown no mercy; mercy triumphs over judgement. (James 2:6–13)

The most merciful thing you can do in the first instance is read and listen. If you feel lost in the terminology of trans identity (as many trans people do at times!), Juno Dawson's *What's the T?: The Guide to All Things Trans and/or Non-Binary* (2021), aimed primarily at a teen audience but no less useful to any beginner, is a beautifully accessible and succinct introduction to the subject of trans identity, including its various expressions and practical considerations.[34] Once you are comfortable with the basics, you may want to move on to books by LGBTQI+ Christians. Some recommendations to get you started might include *This is My Body: Hearing the Theology of Transgender Christians* (2016)[35] and *The Book of Queer Prophets* (2020),[36] both edited collections of trans and queer Christian perspectives. There is also a helpful chapter titled 'Trans and Christian?' by Jack Woodruff in Victoria Turner's *Young, Woke and Christian: Words from a Missing Generation* (2022).[37] In a similar vein, Alex Clare-Young's *Transgender. Christian. Human.* (2019) is a radically honest autobiography of a transmasculine United Reformed Church priest.[38] On the scholarly front, Austen Hartke's *Transforming: The Bible and the Lives of Transgender Christians* (2018) is a trans Christian's in-depth examination of what the Bible has to say about gender diversity – invaluable in a genre dominated by cis people.[39] And on the practical front, guidance for making a church environment safe, affirming and enriching for trans people can be found in *Trans Affirming Churches: How to Celebrate Gender-Variant People and their Loved Ones* (2020) by Anglican priest Christina Beardsley and United Reformed Church minister Chris Dowd.[40] Although this will not be the easiest or most invigorating advice to hear, I would strongly discourage any preaching by non-LGBTQI+ preachers on issues relating to gender diversity, whether as a one-off or part of a series, that has not taken into consideration at least *some* trans stories and trans theologies.

Churches are liable otherwise to entrench past conceptual errors and further alienate any church-searching LGBTQI+ people who might happen to be in attendance.

You may come out the other side of this process with your views unchanged, your ministry unaffected, and your determination renewed to stay the course, firm and forthright in the undying confusion of righteous ignorance, towards steady annihilation. I pray otherwise. I pray for a future in which evangelical bodies – some of them, at least – will *show up* at the next major juncture in the 'trans debate' with a zeal to make trans people's lives better, not worse; that they will respond to the next policy consultation on gender recognition or conversion therapy or trans healthcare with the same immovable drive to chase the Kingdom of God that burns so brightly when many other matters of social and economic justice, like hunger and poverty, are on the table. Through it all, I maintain some modicum of hope that the movement will soon return to the place to which all peoples of God are unrelentingly assigned by scripture: at the bleeding edge of justice in all its forms. When we arrive there – that is, when we return *home* from our long misadventure – perhaps God will meet us with words not dissimilar to those imagined by lesbian Lutheran pastor Emmy Kegler in her commentary on the parables of the Prodigal Son and the Lost Coin:

> No matter why you left or where you went, you are mine ... No matter how you rolled away or what corner you were dropped in, you are mine ... I am so sorry you had to go, and I am eternally glad to have you back again.[41]

Let's go home. Let's start over. Let's get this right.

Notes

INTRODUCTION

1. Wellcome Collection, PP/KIN/C/14/3, 'A prayer for transsexuals', *SHAFT Newsletter*, no. 1, February 1980.
2. K. Keen, 'Nottingham #womenscorner', *YouTube*, 13 February 2022. https://youtu.be/1Hq3_9tyB24?t=485 (accessed 13 September 2022).
3. S. Stryker, *Transgender history: the roots of today's revolution*, Second Edition (New York: Seal Press, 2017), pp. 226–7.
4. A. Zanghellini, 'Philosophical problems with the gender-critical feminist argument against trans inclusion', *SAGE Open*, vol. 10, no. 2, 2020, p. 1. https://doi.org/10.1177%2F2158244020927029
5. M. Murphy, '"TERF" isn't just a slur, it's hate speech', *Feminist Current*, 21 September 2017. www.feministcurrent.com/2017/09/21/terf-isnt-slur-hate-speech/ (accessed 11 August 2021).
6. J. Saul, 'Why the words we use matter when describing anti-trans activists', *The Conversation*, 5 March 2020. https://theconversation.com/why-the-words-we-use-matter-when-describing-anti-trans-activists-130990 (accessed 17 September 2022).
7. V. Smythe, 'I'm credited with having coined the word "Terf". Here's how it happened', *The Guardian*, 28 November 2018. www.theguardian.com/commentisfree/2018/nov/29/im-credited-with-having-coined-the-acronym-terf-heres-how-it-happened (accessed 13 September 2022).
8. C. Williams, 'You might be a TERF if …', *The Trans Advocate*, 2017. www.transadvocate.com/you-might-be-a-terf-if_n_10226.htm (accessed 13 September 2022).
9. S. Hines, 'Sex wars and (trans) gender panics: identity and body politics in contemporary UK feminism', *The Sociological Review Monographs*, vol. 68, no. 4, 2020, p. 705. https://doi.org/10.1177%2F0038026120934684
10. E. Horbury and C. Yao, 'Empire and eugenics: trans studies in the United Kingdom', *TSQ: Transgender Studies Quarterly*, vol. 7, no. 3, 2020, p. 450. https://doi.org/10.1215/23289252-8553104
11. E. Willis, 'Radical feminism and feminist radicalism', *Social Text*, nos. 9–10, Spring/Summer 1984, p. 93. https://doi.org/10.2307/466537
12. R. Rowland and R. Klein, 'Radical feminism: history, politics, action' in D. Bell and R. Klein (eds), *Radically speaking: feminism reclaimed* (North Geelong: Spinifex, 1996), p. 10.
13. B. Caine, *English feminism, 1780–1980* (Oxford: Oxford University Press, 1997), pp. 222–7, 239–40 and 255–71.

14. R. Lee, 'Judith Butler's scientific revolution: foundations for a transsexual Marxism' in J. J. Gleeson and E. O'Rourke (eds.), *Transgender Marxism* (London: Pluto Press, 2021), p. 64.

15. C. Romero, 'Praying for torture: why the United Kingdom should ban conversion therapy', *The George Washington International Law Review*, vol. 51, no. 1, 2019, pp. 201–30. https://gwilr.org/?page_id=2557

16. M. Howarth, 'Backlash over SNP's threat to free speech; religious groups and women's right campaign join outcry', *Daily Mail Scotland*, 25 July 2020. www.pressreader.com/uk/scottish-daily-mail/20200725/281689732134295 (accessed 12 August 2022).

17. Scottish Government, 'Gender Recognition Reform (Scotland) Bill: analysis of responses to the public consultation exercise', September 2021, p. ii. www.gov.scot/publications/gender-recognition-reform-scotland-bill-analysis-responses-public-consultation-exercise/documents/

18. D. W. Bebbington, *Evangelicalism in modern Britain: a history from the 1730s to the 1980s* (London: Unwin Hyman, 1989), pp. 2–17.

19. W. Martin, *With God on our side: the rise of the religious right in America* (New York: Broadway Books, 2005), pp. 191–220.

20. Bebbington, *Evangelicalism in modern Britain*, pp. 57–60.

21. J. Ashworth et al., *Churchgoing in the UK: a research report from Tearfund on church attendance in the UK* (London: Tearfund, 2007), p. 16.

22. M. Dinic, 'How religious are British people', *YouGov*, 29 December 2020. https://yougov.co.uk/topics/society/articles-reports/2020/12/29/how-religious-are-british-people (accessed 16 November 2022).

23. K. L. Nadal, T. Erazo and J. Schulman, 'Caught at the intersections: microaggressions toward lesbian, gay, bisexual, transgender, and queer people of color' in R. Ruth and E. Santacruz (eds), *LGBT psychology and mental health: emerging research and advances* (Santa Barbara, CA: ABC-CLIO, 2017), pp. 133–52.

24. J. Serano, *Whipping girl: a transsexual woman on sexism and the scapegoating of femininity*, Second Edition (New York: Seal Press, 2016), p. 12.

25. 'Transphobia', *Merriam-Webster.com Dictionary*. www.merriam-webster.com/dictionary/transphobia (accessed 18 August 2022); 'Transphobia', *Oxford Lexico Dictionary*. https://www.lexico.com/definition/transphobia (accessed 18 August 2022).

26. T. M. Bettcher, 'Transphobia', *TSQ: Transgender Studies Quarterly*, vol. 1, nos. 1–2, 2014, p. 249. https://doi.org/10.1215/23289252-2400181

27. Ibid., p. 251.

28. G. J. Holyoake, *John Stuart Mill: as some of the working classes knew him* (London: Trübner & Co., 1873), pp. 8–9.

29. E. H. H. Green, *Ideologies of conservatism: conservative political ideas in the twentieth century* (Oxford: Oxford University Press, 2004), pp. 2–3.

30. M. Smith, 'Where does the British public stand on transgender rights in 2022?', results of YouGov study, 20 July 2022. https://yougov.co.uk/topics/lifestyle/articles-reports/2022/07/20/where-does-british-public-stand-transgender-rights (accessed 26 August 2022).

CHAPTER 1. WARZONE

1. Z. Playdon, *The hidden case of Ewan Forbes: the transgender trial that threatened to upend the British establishment* (London: Bloomsbury Publishing, 2021), ch. 3.
2. C. Hutton, *The tyranny of ordinary meaning: Corbett v Corbett and the invention of legal sex* (Basingstoke: Palgrave Macmillan, 2019), pp. 83–121.
3. The National Archives, BN 80/143, N. T. Brown to the British Railways Controller for Corporate Pensions, 12 December 1978.
4. Wellcome Collection, PP/KIN/C/14/3, 'A letter from a member to an MP', *SHAFT Newsletter*, no. 13, February 1982, pp. 7–8.
5. S. Hines, *Gender diversity, recognition and citizenship: towards a politics of difference* (Basingstoke: Palgrave Macmillan, 2013), p. 21.
6. L. Avery, 'The legal labyrinth that faces the transsexual', *The Guardian*, 4 October 1982.
7. Wellcome Collection, PP/KIN/C/2/8/1/7, C. Scott, 'Self-Help Association for Transsexuals: a newly formed group', *Beaumont Bulletin*, vol. 11, no. 6, January/February 1980, pp. 18–19.
8. Wellcome Collection, PP/KIN/C/15, Tara and Hazel, Editorial, *Transsexual Action Group Newsletter*, vol. 3, no. 6, 1982, pp. 1–2.
9. S. Whittle, 'Transgender rights: the European Court of Human Rights and new identity politics for a new age' in A. Hegarty and S. Leonard (eds), *A human rights: an agenda for the 21st century* (London: Cavendish Publishing, 1999), pp. 201–16.
10. M. Rees, *Dear sir or madam: a journey from female to male* (London: Cassell, 1996), ch. 26.
11. Press for Change, 'Recognising the identity and rights of transsexual and transgender people in the United Kingdom: a report for the Interdepartmental Working Group On Transsexual Issues', June 1999. https://web.archive.org/web/20000816213815/http:/www.pfc.org.uk/workgrp/pfcrpt1.htm (archived from the original, accessed 22 February 2022).
12. E. Griffiths, 'The Sex Discrimination (Gender Reassignment) Regulations 1999', *Journal of Civil Liberties*, vol. 4, no. 1, pp. 230–36.
13. A. N. Sharpe, 'A critique of the Gender Recognition Act 2004', *Journal of Bioethical Inquiry*, vol. 4, no. 1, pp. 33–42. https://doi.org/10.1007/s11673-007-9032-y
14. R. Karim, 'Protected characteristics' in J. Wadham et al. (eds), *Blackstone's guide to the Equality Act 2010*, Fourth Edition (Oxford: Oxford University Press, 2021), pp. 23–4.
15. K. Gupta, Why the Marriage (Same Sex) Act 2013 does not bring marriage equality: the case of trans* people', *Inherently Human*, 13 July 2013. https://inherentlyhuman.wordpress.com/2013/07/31/why-the-marriagesame-sex-act-2013-does-not-bring-marriage-equality-the-case-of-trans-people/ (accessed 29 November 2022).
16. 'UK government to block Scottish gender bill', *BBC News*, 16 January 2023. www.bbc.co.uk/news/uk-politics-64288757 (accessed 16 January 2023).

17. K. Steinmetz, 'The transgender tipping point', *Time Magazine*, 29 May 2014. https://time.com/135480/transgender-tipping-point/ (accessed 26 July 2022).

18. R. Pearce, S. Erikainen and B. Vincent, 'TERF wars: an introduction', *The Sociological Review Monographs*, vol. 68, no. 4, 2020, pp. 677–98. https://doi.org/10.1177/0038026120934713

19. Evangelical Alliance, 'Basis of faith', as of 2022. www.eauk.org/about-us/how-we-work/basis-of-faith (accessed 7 September 2022).

20. D. W. Bebbington, *The dominance of evangelicalism: the age of Spurgeon and Moody* (Leicester: Inter-Varsity Press, 2005), pp. 155–7.

21. Ibid., pp. 159–60.

22. P. Lynas, *Transformed: a brief biblical and pastoral introduction to understanding transgender in a changing culture* (London: Evangelical Alliance, 2018), p. 15.

23. Ibid., p. 25.

24. Ibid., p. 28.

25. S. Ahmed, 'An affinity of hammers', *TSQ: Transgender Studies Quarterly*, vol. 3, nos. 1–2, 2016, pp. 22–34. https://doi.org/10.1215/23289252-3334151; C. Adair and A. Z. Aizura, '"The transgender craze seducing our [sons]"; or, all the trans guys are just dating each other', *TSQ: Transgender Studies Quarterly*, vol. 9, no. 1, 2022, pp. 44–64. https://doi.org/10.1215/23289252-9475509

26. S. Hines, 'The feminist frontier: on trans and feminism', *Journal of Gender Studies*, vol. 28, no. 2, 2019, p. 152. https://doi.org/10.1080/09589236.2017.1411791 ; C. McLean, 'The growth of the anti-transgender movement in the United Kingdom. The silent radicalization of the British electorate', *International Journal of Sociology*, vol. 51, no. 6, 2021, pp. 475–6. https://doi.org/10.1080/00207659.2021.1939946

27. Lynas, *Transformed*, p. 23.

28. M. V. Carrera-Fernández and R. DePalma, 'Feminism will be trans-inclusive or it will not be: why do two cis-hetero woman educators support transfeminism?', *The Sociological Review*, vol. 68, no. 4, 2020, pp. 745–62. https://doi.org/10.1177/0038026120934686

29. Lynas, *Transformed*, p. 25.

30. Transgender Trend, *Supporting gender diverse and trans-identified students in schools* (Lewes: Transgender Trend, 2018), pp. 9, 25.

31. S. Hines, 'Sex wars', p. 707.

32. S. Faye, *The transgender issue: an argument for justice* (London: Allen Lane, 2021), pp. 220–21.

33. S. Lister, 'Tory and Labour MPs dramatically unite to stand up for women in toxic gender rights debate', *The Express*, 20 April 2023. www.express.co.uk/news/politics/1760269/womens-rights-miriam-cates-rosie-duffield-trans (accessed 30 April 2023).

34. V. Parsons, 'Activist instrumental in the launch of the LGB Alliance linked to anti-abortion and anti-LGBT+ hate groups', *PinkNews*, 3 June 2020. www.pinknews.co.uk/2020/06/03/lgb-alliance-gary-powell-center-bioethics-culture-alliance-defending-freedom-anti-lgbt/ (accessed 26 July 2022).

35. N. Place, 'Kathleen Stock: professor accused of transphobia takes job at "anti-woke" University of Austin', *The Independent*, 9 November 2021. www.

independent.co.uk/news/world/americas/kathleen-stock-transphobia-university-austin-b1954486.html (accessed 26 September 2022).

36. N. Reimann, 'The University of Austin – the self-proclaimed anti-censorship institution', *Forbes*, 8 November 2021. www.forbes.com/sites/nicholas reimann/2021/11/08/heres-what-we-know-about-the-university-of-austin-the-self-proclaimed-anti-censorship-institution/?sh=26f029aa51a8 (accessed 26 September 2022).

37. P. Califia, *Sex changes: the politics of transgenderism* (San Francisco, CA: Cleis Press, 1997), p. 89.

38. S. Clarke and M. Moore, 'ALERT: transphobic feminism and far right activism rapidly converging', Trans Safety Network, 18 March 2021. https://transsafety. network/posts/gcs-and-the-right/ (accessed 22 July 2022).

39. D. Paternotte and R. Kuhar, 'Disentangling and locating the "global right": anti-gender campaigns in Europe', *Politics and Governance*, vol. 6, no. 3, 2018, pp. 6–19. https://doi.org/10.17645/pag.v6i3.1557

40. S. Bassi and G. LaFleur, 'Introduction: TERFs, gender-critical movements, and postfascist feminisms', *TSQ: Transgender Studies Quarterly*, vol. 9, no. 3, 2022, pp. 313, 322. https://doi.org/10.1215/23289252-9836008

41. A. Lavizzari and M. Prearo, 'The anti-gender movement in Italy: Catholic participation between electoral and protest politics', *European Societies*, vol. 21, no. 3, 2019, pp. 422–42. https://doi.org/10.1080/14616696.2018.1536801; P. Żuk and P. Żuk, '"Murderers of the unborn" and "sexual degenerates": analysis of the "anti-gender" discourse of the Catholic Church and the nationalist right in Poland', *Critical Discourse Studies*, vol. 17, no. 5, 2020, pp. 566–88. https://doi.org/10.1080/17405904.2019.1676808

42. Transgender Archives, Victoria, University of Ulster TGA collection, 2014-020, 9.63, Janus Information Facility, *Religious aspects of transsexualism* (Galveston, TX: University of Texas Medical Branch, 1978), p. 7.

43. T. McGirk, 'Sexual dilemma for the Vatican', *The Independent*, 18 February 1989.

44. 'Vatican moves to ban all sex-change priests, nuns', *Sydney Morning Herald*, 2 February 2003. www.smh.com.au/world/vatican-moves-to-ban-all-sex-change-priests-nuns-20030202-gdg7cx.html (accessed 3 March 2023).

45. L. Fullam, '"Gender theory," nuclear war, and the Nazis', *Commonweal Magazine*, 23 February 2015. www.commonwealmagazine.org/gender-theory-nuclear-war-and-nazis-0 (accessed 11 September 2022).

46. R. Kuhar and D. Paternotte (eds), *Anti-gender campaigns in Europe: mobilizing against equality* (London: Rowman & Littlefield, 2017), pp. 8–15, 262.

47. GATE, *Mapping anti-gender movements in the UK* (New York: GATE, 2022), p. 17.

48. J. Fae, 'The press' in C. Burns (ed.), *Trans Britain: our journey from the shadows* (London: Unbound, 2018), p. 203; J. Fae, 'The tribes of anti-trans', *Medium*, 8 August 2021. https://jane-67706.medium.com/the-tribes-of-anti-trans-84d6b908005f (accessed 22 June 2022).

49. J. Robinson-Brown, *Black, gay, British, Christian, queer: the church and the famine of grace* (London: SCM Press, 2021), p. 102.

50. J. Wolffe, *The expansion of evangelicalism: the age of Wilberforce, More, Chalmers and Finney* (Nottingham: Inter-Varsity Press, 2006), pp. 122–50.

51. P. D. H. Cochran, *Evangelical feminism: a history* (London: New York University Press, 2005), pp. 1–2; S. K. Gallagher, 'The marginalization of evangelical feminism', *Sociology of Religion*, vol. 65, no. 3, 2004, pp. 215–37. https://doi.org/10.2307/3712250

52. A. Wilson, 'Beautiful difference: the (whole-Bible) complementarity of male and female', *The Gospel Coalition*, 20 May 2021. www.thegospelcoalition.org/article/beautiful-complementarity-male-female/ (accessed 8 February 2023).

53. S. Allen, 'What is complementarianism?', Fellowship of Independent Evangelical Churches, 14 December 2016. https://fiec.org.uk/resources/what-is-complementarianism (accessed 26 July 2022).

54. E. Miller, 'Why is British media so transphobic?', *The Outline*, 5 November 2018. https://theoutline.com/post/6536/british-feminists-media-transphobic (accessed 30 March 2021).

55. A. Phipps, *Me, not you: the trouble with mainstream feminism* (Manchester: Manchester University Press, 2020), p. 107.

56. M. Gevisser, *The pink line: the world's queer frontiers* (London: Profile Books, 2020), ch. 4.

57. R. Dawkins, *The god delusion* (London: Bantam Press, 2006), pp. 327–8.

58. D. C. Bradley, 'Transsexualism – ideology, legal policy and political culture' in Council of Europe, *Transsexualism, medicine and law: proceedings of the XXIIIrd colloquy on European law* (Strasbourg: Council of Europe Publishing, 1993), p. 61.

59. C. Provost and N. Archer, 'Christian right and some UK feminists "unlikely allies" against trans rights', *Open Democracy*, 18 October 2018. www.opendemocracy.net/en/5050/christian-right-feminists-uk-trans-rights/ (accessed 30 March 2021).

60. Family Policy Alliance, 'Unlikely allies for privacy and safety: a radical feminist group & Christian pro-family group', 9 January 2017. https://familypolicyalliance.com/issues/2017/01/09/unlikely-allies-for-privacy-and-safety-a-radical-feminist-group-christian-pro-family-group/ (accessed 19 November 2022).

61. S. Schmidt, 'Conservatives find unlikely ally in fighting transgender rights: radical feminists', 7 February 2020. www.washingtonpost.com/dc-md-va/2020/02/07/radical-feminists-conservatives-transgender-rights/ (accessed 19 November 2022).

62. R. A. Williams, *Trans-gressive: a trans woman on gender, feminism, and politics* (London: Jessica Kingsley Publishers, 2019), p. 159.

63. A. Phipps, *The politics of the body* (Cambridge: Polity, 2014), p. 42.

64. Cochran, *Evangelical feminism*, p. 1.

65. H. Joyce, *Trans: when ideology meets reality* (London: Oneworld, 2021), pp. 247–52.

66. J. Bindel, 'Feminism's dangerous new allies', *UnHerd*, 31 January 2021. https://unherd.com/2020/10/feminisms-dangerous-new-allies/ (accessed 30 March 2022).

67. J. Bindel, *Feminism for women: the real route to liberation* (London: Constable, 2021), p. 22.
68. L. Olufemi, *Feminism, interrupted: disrupting power* (London: Pluto Press, 2020), p. 60.
69. H. Barthélemy, 'Christian right tips to fight transgender rights: separate the T from the LGB', *Southern Poverty Law Center*, 23 October 2017. www.splcenter.org/hatewatch/2017/10/23/christian-right-tips-fight-transgender-rights-separate-t-lgb (accessed 12 August 2022).
70. @CaseyExplosion, 'Whatever TERF ideology was, whatever TERFs themselves think they are, they have become entirely co-opted by the anti-LGBT evangelical movement', *Twitter*, 8 July 2018. https://twitter.com/caseyexplosion/status/1015978441886306305 (accessed 12 August 2022); B. Tannehill, 'JK Rowling is an unwitting tool of the religious right', *Los Angeles Blade*, 10 July 2020. www.losangelesblade.com/2020/07/10/jk-rowling-is-an-unwitting-tool-of-the-religious-right/ (accessed 12 August 2022).
71. J. Vile, 'A TERF-far right alliance has launched a new transphobic onslaught', *Left Voice*, 7 December 2021. www.leftvoice.org/a-terf-far-right-alliance-has-launched-a-new-transphobic-onslaught/ (accessed 12 August 2022).
72. H. Greensmith, 'A room of their own: how anti-trans feminists are complicit in Christian Right anti-trans advocacy', *Political Research Associates*, 14 July 2020. https://politicalresearch.org/2020/07/14/room-their-own (accessed 24 November 2022); Political Research Associates, 'Disrupting anti-trans feminist advocacy: an interactive training', *Vimeo*, timestamps 18:05, 21:35. https://vimeo.com/443535988?fbclid=IwAR1lpQTWCw-hMFiSOwq7shn0Tr7d4tyS14X9INDXWdsGgmX02DcfJeFW4i8 (accessed 13 January 2023).
73. Shaun, 'J. K. Rowling's new friends', *YouTube*, 14 October 2022, timestamp 28:00. https://youtu.be/Ou_xvXJJk7k?t=1680 (accessed 24 February 2023.
74. ContraPoints, 'The witch trial of J. K. Rowling', *YouTube*, 17 April 2023, timestamp 1:47:55. https://youtu.be/EmToioxG6zg?t=6475 (accessed 19 April 2023).
75. A. Ferber, 'Judith Butler on the culture wars, JK Rowling and living in "anti-intellectual times"', *The New Statesmen*, 22 September 2020. www.newstatesman.com/international/2020/09/judith-butler-culture-wars-jk-rowling-and-living-anti-intellectual-times (accessed 12 August 2022).
76. R. Wallbank, 'Contemporary human rights issues for people with transsexualism', conference paper, *GENDYS 2004, The Eighth International Gender Dysphoria Conference*, Manchester, 2004. www.gender.org.uk/conf/2004/wbk.htm
77. C. Libby, 'Sympathy, fear, hate: trans-exclusionary radical feminism and evangelical Christianity', *TSQ: Transgender Studies Quarterly*, vol. 9, no. 3, 2022, pp. 425–42. https://doi.org/10.1215/23289252-9836078
78. Ibid., pp. 436–8.
79. L. Stahl, 'The latest form of transphobia: saying lesbians are going extinct', *Washington Post*, 19 March 2021. www.washingtonpost.com/outlook/the-latest-form-of-transphobia-saying-lesbians-are-going-extinct/2021/03/18/072a95fc-8786-11eb-82bc-e58213caa38e_story.html (accessed 24 November 2022).

80. C. H. Schotten, 'TERFism, Zionism, and right-wing annihilationism: toward an internationalist genealogy of extinction phobia', *TSQ: Transgender Studies Quarterly*, vol. 9, no. 3, 2022, p. 344. https://doi.org/10.1215/23289252-9836022

81. Ibid., p. 336.

82. Ibid., pp. 336–42.

83. Ibid., pp. 352–3.

84. Ibid., p. 356.

85. D. M. Lewis, *The origins of Christian Zionism: Lord Shaftesbury and evangelical support for a Jewish homeland* (Cambridge: Cambridge University Press).

86. C. Binfield, 'Jews in evangelical dissent: the British Society, the Herschell connection and the pre-millenarian threat', *Studies in Church History. Subsidia*, vol. 10, 1994, pp. 225–70. https://doi.org/10.1017/S0143045900000247

87. P. D. Miller, 'Evangelicals, Israel and US foreign policy', *Survival: Global Politics and Strategy*, vol. 56, no. 1, 2014, pp. 7–26. https://doi.org/10.1080/0 0396338.2014.882149

88. T. Laqueur, *Making sex: body and gender from the Greeks to Freud* (London: Harvard University Press, 1990), p. 149.

89. Ibid., p. 198.

90. H. Chiang, *After eunuchs: science, medicine, and the transformation of sex in modern China* (Chichester: Columbia University Press, 2018), pp. 179–3.

91. F. Dabhoiwala, *The origins of sex: a history of the first sexual revolution* (London: Allen Lane, 2012), pp. 143–4.

92. J. Gill-Peterson, *Histories of the transgender child* (London: University of Minnesota Press, 2018), ch. 3.

93. V. Pricopi, 'From ancient Gnostics to modern scholars – issues in defining the concept of "Gnosticism"', *Revista Romaneasca pentru Educatie Multidimensionala*, vol. 5, no. 2, 2013, pp. 41–56. http://dx.doi.org/10.18662/ rrem/2013.0502.04

94. M. A. Williams, *Rethinking "Gnosticism": an argument for dismantling a dubious category* (Oxford: Princeton University Press, 1996), pp. 116–38; A. Marjanen, 'Gnosticism' in S. A. Harvey and D. G. Hunter (eds), *The Oxford handbook of early Christian studies* (Oxford: Oxford University Press), pp. 203–20.

95. D. Brakke, 'Self-differentiation among Christian groups: the Gnostics and their opponents' in M. M. Mitchell and F. M. Young (eds), *The Cambridge history of Christianity, volume 1: origins to Constantine* (Cambridge: Cambridge University Press, 2008), pp. 245–60.

96. D. MacCulloch, *A history of Christianity* (London: Allen Lane, 2009), p. 124.

97. G. Filoramo, *A history of Gnosticism*. Translated by A. Alcock. (Oxford: Basil Blackwell, 1990), pp. xiii-xviii.

98. J. Gray, *Seven types of atheism* (New York: Farrar, Straus and Giroux, 2018), p. 75.

99. I. Hassan, 'The new Gnosticism: speculations on an aspect of the postmodern mind', *Boundary*, vol. 2, no. 3, 1973, pp. 546–70. https://doi.org/10.2307/302297; R. Lundin, *The culture of interpretation: Christian faith and the postmodern world* (Grand Rapids, MI: William B. Eerdmans Publishing, 1993), pp. 76–103.

100. J. Sacks, *Not in God's name: confronting religious violence* (London: Hodder, 2016), pp. 53–65.

101. P. D. Scalia, 'Mary, destroyer of all heresies', *The Catholic Thing*, 14 August 2016. www.thecatholicthing.org/2016/08/14/mary-destroyer-of-all-heresies/ (accessed 13 August 2022).

102. D. Dormor, 'Religious perspectives on intersexual and transgender identity and relationships', conference paper, *Challenging Gender, Gender Challenges*, University of Hong Kong, 1 December 2010. www.academia.edu/4561356/ Religious_perspectives_on_intersexual_and_transgender_identity_and_ relationships (accessed 13 August 2022).

103. J. Prosser, *Second skins: the body narratives of transsexuality* (New York: Columbia University Press, 1998), p. 69; M. Lovelock, 'Call me Caitlyn: making and making over the "authentic" transgender body in Anglo-American popular culture', *Journal of Gender Studies*, vol. 26, no. 6, 2017, pp. 675–87. https://doi.org/10.1080/09589236.2016.1155978

104. S. Stone, 'The *Empire* strikes back: a posttranssexual manifesto' in J. Epstein and K. Straub (eds), *Body guard: the cultural politics of gender ambiguity* (London: Routledge, 1991), pp. 280–304.

105. J. Jacques, *Trans: a memoir*, second edition (London: Verso, 2016), p. 305.

106. E. Clare, *Brilliant imperfection: grappling with cure* (London: Duke University Press, 2017), p. xvi.

107. T. M. Bettcher, 'Trapped in the wrong theory: rethinking trans oppression and resistance', *Signs*, vol. 39, no. 2, 2014, p. 399. http://dx.doi.org/10.1086/673088

108. Ibid., pp. 400–401.

109. J. Gill-Peterson, 'The technical capacities of the body: assembling race, technology, and transgender', *TSQ: Transgender Studies Quarterly*, vol. 1, no. 3, 2014, p. 407. https://doi.org/10.1215/23289252-2685660

110. D. Valentine, *Imagining transgender: an ethnography of a category* (London: Duke University Press, 2007), p. 219.

111. H. Savage, *Changing sex?: transsexuality and Christian theology*, Doctoral thesis (PhD), Durham University, 2006, pp. 211–12.

112. P. O. Bischoff, *Evangelicalism is dead* (Eugene, OR: Resource Publications, 2020), pp. 26–32.

113. A. R. Favale, 'Evangelical Gnosticism', *First Things*, May 2018. www.firstthings.com/article/2018/05/evangelical-gnosticism (accessed 18 September 2022).

114. T. Rice, *Evangelicals, the Gnostic impulse, and the natural world*, Master's thesis, Milligan University, December 2021. http://hdl.handle.net/11558/6011

115. D. E. Cowan, 'Exposing Gnosticism' in D. W. Trompf, G. B. Mikkelsen and J. Johnston (eds), *The Gnostic world* (London: Routledge, 2018), ch. 63.

116. P. Jones, *The gnostic empire strikes back: an old heresy for the new age* (Phillipsburg: P&R Publishing, 1992), p. 72.

CHAPTER 2. OF FEMINISTS AND MYSTICS

1. J. G. Raymond, *A passion for friends: toward a philosophy of female affection* (North Geelong: Spinifex, 2001), pp. xi, 79.

2. J. G. Raymond, 'About', personal website. https://janiceraymond.com/about/ (accessed 9 September 2022).

3. J. Bindel, 'Janice Raymond: the original Terf', *UnHerd*, 26 November 2021. https://unherd.com/2021/11/meet-the-original-terf/ (accessed 9 September 2022).

4. K. O'Donnell, 'The theological basis for trans-exclusionary radical feminist positions' in N. Banerjea et al. (eds.), *Lesbian feminism: essays opposing global heteropatriarchies* (London: Zed Books, 2019), pp. 135–62.

5. S. Stryker and S. Whittle, preface to J. G. Raymond, 'Sappho by surgery: the transsexually constructed lesbian-feminist' in S. Stryker and S. Whittle (eds.) *The transgender studies reader* (London: Routledge, 2006), p. 131.

6. Wellcome Collection, PP/KIN/2/8/1/10, 'Transsexual Action Group', *Beaumont Bulletin*, vol. 14, no. 4, September/October 1982, pp. 18–19.

7. R. Carroll, *Transgender and the literary imagination: changing gender in twentieth-century writing* (Cambridge: Cambridge University Press, 2018), pp. 67–72.

8. B. Reay, *Trans America: a counter-history* (Cambridge: Polity, 2020), pp. 140–79.

9. S. Nanda, *Gender diversity: crosscultural variations* (Long Grove: Waveland Press, 1999), pp. 96–7.

10. Wellcome Collection, PP/KIN/C/2/8/1/7, Hazel, 'Letters to the editor', *Beaumont Bulletin*, vol. 11, no. 3, July/August 1979, pp. 41–4; PP/KIN/C/15, Tara and Hazel, 'Editorial', *Transsexual Action Group Newsletter*, vol. 3, no. 6, 1982, pp. 1–2.

11. C. Hannabach, 'Sandy Stone, the trans woman who struck back at TERF-y art', *Dismantle Magazine*, 1 August 2022. https://dismantlemag.com/2022/08/01/sandy-stone-terf-art-trans-woman/ (accessed 6 October 2022).

12. Independent Voices (via Digital Transgender Archive), ft848q88b, 'An open letter to Olivia Records', *Lesbian Connection*, November 1977. www.digitaltransgenderarchive.net/files/ft848q88b

13. E. R. Green, 'Debating trans inclusion in the feminist movement: a trans-positive analysis', *Journal of Lesbian Studies*, vol. 10, nos. 1–2, 2006, pp. 234–9. https://doi.org/10.1300/j155v10n01_12

14. F. Mackay, *Radical feminism: feminist activism in movement* (Basingstoke: Palgrave Macmillan, 2015), pp. 233–5.

15. C. Williams, 'The ontological woman: a history of deauthentication, dehumanization, and violence', *The Sociological Review*, vol. 68, no. 4, 2020, p. 723. https://doi.org/10.1177/0038026120938292

16. J. J. Gleeson and E. O'Rourke, 'Introduction' in Gleeson and O'Rourke, *Transgender Marxism*, p. 12.

17. J. G. Raymond, *The transsexual empire: the making of the she-male* (London: Beacon Press, 1979), p. 112.

18. M. Daly, *The church and the second sex* (London: Beacon Press, 1968), pp. 178–81.

19. Raymond, *Transsexual empire*, p. 169.

20. N. D. Lewis, 'Women in Gnosticism' in J. E. Taylor and I. L. E. Ramelli (eds.), *Patterns of women's leadership in early Christianity* (Oxford: Oxford University Press, 2021), pp. 109–29.

21. C. Partridge, '"Scotch-taped together": anti-"androgyny" rhetoric, transmisogyny, and the transing of religious studies', *Journal of Feminist Studies in Religion*, vol. 34, no. 1, 2018, pp. 68–75. https://doi.org/10.2979/jfemistudreli.34.1.09

22. J. Cahana, 'Androgyne or undrogyne?: queering the Gnostic myth', *Numen*, vol. 61, nos. 5–6, 2014, pp. 509–24. https://doi.org/10.1163/15685276-12341340

23. E. M. Yamauchi, 'The Nag Hammadi library', *The Journal of Library History (1974–1987)*, vol. 22, no. 4, 1987, pp. 427–8. www.jstor.org/stable/25541847

24. M. Meyer (ed.), *The Nag Hammadi scriptures* (London: HarperOne, 2007), p. 291.

25. J. Barton, *A history of the Bible: the book and its faiths* (London: Allen Lane, 2019), pp. 272–4.

26. Keith Sharpe, *The gay gospels: good news for lesbian, gay, bisexual, and transgendered people* (Winchester: O-Books, 2011), pp. 189–90.

27. Meyer, *Nag Hammadi*, p. 153, emphasis added.

28. J. Raymond, 'The illusion of androgyny', *Quest: A Feminist Quarterly*, vol. 2, 1977, pp. 57–66.

29. Raymond, *Transsexual empire*, p. 157.

30. Ibid., p. 158.

31. Ibid., p. 162.

32. M. Reeves, *The good God: enjoying Father, Son and Spirit* (Milton Keynes: Paternoster, 2012), p. 37.

33. Raymond, *Transsexual empire*, pp. 169–70.

34. J. Raymond, *Doublethink: a feminist challenge to transgenderism* (North Geelong: Spinifex, 2021), p. 23.

35. Quoted in J. Manion, *Female husbands: a trans history* (Cambridge: Cambridge University Press, 2020), pp. 58–60.

36. S. de Beauvoir, *The second sex*. Translated by H. M. Parshley. (London: Jonathan Cape, 1953), p. 273.

37. E. V. Spelman, 'Woman as body: ancient and contemporary views', *Feminist Studies*, vol. 8, no. 1, 1982, p. 127. https://doi.org/10.2307/3177582

38. de Beauvoir, *Second sex*, p. 195.

39. R. R. Ruether, *Sexism and god-talk: toward a feminist theology* (Boston, MA: Beacon Press, 1983), p. 54.

40. G. Greer, 'The habit of a lifetime', *The Guardian*, 27 November 2003. www.theguardian.com/world/2003/nov/27/gender.religion (accessed 11 September 2022).

41. G. Greer, *The whole woman*, Twenty-First Anniversary Edition (London: Doubleday, 2012), pp. 70–72.

42. G. Greer, *The madwoman's underclothes: essays & occasional writings 1968–85* (London: Picador, 1986), p. 190.

43. J. Morris, *Conundrum* (London: Faber and Faber, 1974), p. 3.

44. B. Hausman, *Changing sex: transsexualism, technology, and the idea of gender* (London: Duke University Press, 1995), p. 164.

45. M. Eichler, *The double standard* (London: Croom Helm, 1980), pp. 72–88; L. M. Lothstein, *Female-to-male transsexualism: historical, clinical, and theoretical issues* (London: Routledge & Kegan Paul, 1983), pp. 233–44.

46. M. Daly, *Pure lust: elemental feminist philosophy* (London: The Women's Press, 1984), p. 12.

47. Ibid., pp. 50–52.

48. J. Raymond, *The transsexual empire: the making of the she-male*, Second Edition (London: Teachers College Press, 1994), pp. xi–xxxv.

49. W. J. Blumenfeld and M. S. Breen (eds.), *Butler matters: Judith Butler's impact on feminist and queer studies* (London: Routledge, 2005).

50. C. Garner, 'Fellows divided over don who breached last bastion', *The Independent*, 25 June 1997.

51. G. Greer, *The whole woman* (London: Doubleday, 1999), p. 3.

52. Ibid., pp. 80–93.

53. J. Roughgarden, *Evolution's rainbow: diversity, gender, and sexuality in nature and people* (Berkeley: University of California Press, 2013), p. 23.

54. J. C. Jones, *The annals of the TERF wars and other writings* (Willingdon: Radical Notion Books, 2022), p. 130.

55. K. Stock, *Material girls: why reality matters for feminism* (London: fleet, 2021), p. 153.

56. S. Jeffreys, *Gender hurts: a feminist analysis of the politics of transgenderism* (London: Routledge, 2014), pp. 41–4.

57. J. K. Rowling, 'J. K. Rowling writes about her reasons for speaking out on sex and gender issues', blog post, 10 June 2020. www.jkrowling.com/opinions/j-k-rowling-writes-about-her-reasons-for-speaking-out-on-sex-and-gender-issues/ (accessed 13 August 2022).

58. F. de Waal, *Different: what apes can teach us about gender* (London: Granta Books, 2022), p. 315.

59. R. Rooney, *My body is me!* (Lewes: Transgender Trend, 2015).

CHAPTER 3. TRANS AS HERESY IN EVANGELICAL THOUGHT

1. 'Can a person be born with the wrong gender', *Got Questions*, 4 January 2022. www.gotquestions.org/born-wrong-gender.html (accessed 2 December 2022).

2. J. Milbank, 'What liberal intellectuals get wrong about transgenderism', *Catholic Herald*, 13 January 2017. https://catholicherald.co.uk/long-read-what-liberal-intellectuals-get-wrong-about-transgenderism/ (accessed 2 December 2022).

3. M. M. Miller, 'Transgenderism and the end of the sacramental order', *Crisis Magazine*, 27 May 2021. www.crisismagazine.com/2021/transgenderism-and-the-end-of-the-sacramental-order (accessed 13 August 2022).

4. D. Cloutier and L. T. Johnson, 'The church and transgender identity: some cautions, some possibilities', *Commonweal Magazine*, 10 March 2017. www. commonwealmagazine.org/church-transgender-identity (accessed 2 December 2022).

5. Congregation for the Doctrine of the Faith, 'Letter Placuit Deo to the bishops of the Catholic Church on certain aspects of Christian salvation', The Vatican. www.vatican.va/roman_curia/congregations/cfaith/documents/rc_con_ cfaith_doc_20180222_placuit-deo_en.html (accessed 30 June 2022).

6. F. Watts, 'Transsexualism and the church', *Theology & Sexuality*, vol. 9, no. 1, 2002, p. 80. https://doi.org/10.1177%2F135583580200900105 ; C. Beardsley, 'Taking issue: the transsexual hiatus in *Some issues in human sexuality*', *Theology*, vol. 108, no. 845, 2005, pp. 342–3. https://doi.org/10.1177%2F004 0571X0510800504

7. 'O'Donovan, Rev. Canon Oliver Michael Timothy', *Who's Who & Who Was Who*, 1 December 2019. https://doi.org/10.1093/ww/9780199540884.013. U28763

8. O. O'Donovan, *Transsexualism and Christian marriage* (Cambridge: Grove Books, 1982).

9. O. O'Donovan, 'Transsexualism and Christian marriage', *Journal of Religious Ethics*, vol. 11, no. 1, 1983, p. 147.

10. Ibid., p. 158.

11. R. Scruton, 'Dead? I demand a second opinion', *The Times*, 29 March 1983.

12. R. Scruton, *Sexual desire: a philosophical investigation* (London: Weidenfeld and Nicholson, 1986), pp. 276–7.

13. O'Donovan, 'Transsexualism', p. 146.

14. W. Grudem, *Countering the claims of evangelical feminism: biblical responses to the key questions* (New York: Crown Publishing Group, 2010), pp. 165, 188.

15. D. G. Bloesch, 'Reply to Randy Maddox', *Christian Scholar's Review*, no. 17, 1987–88, pp. 281–4.

16. Evangelical Alliance Policy Commission, *Transsexuality* (Milton Keynes: Paternoster, 2000), p. 82.

17. D. Horton, *Changing channels? A Christian response to the transvestite and transsexual* (Cambridge: Grove Books, 1994).

18. D. Horton, 'Evangelical Alliance press release of 14th May about transsexual people. Response from Revd. David Horton', *Gendys Journal*, no. 11, 2000. www.gender.org.uk/gendys/2000/11hrton.htm

19. D. Horton, 'The transsexual as witness', conference paper, *GENDYS 2K, The Sixth International Gender Dysphoria Conference*, Manchester, 2000. www. gender.org.uk/conf/2000/horton20.htm

20. House of Bishops, *Some issues in human sexuality: a guide to the debate* (London: Church House Publishing, 2003), p. 249.

21. R. Song, *Human genetics: fabricating the future* (Cleveland, OH: Pilgrim Press, 2002), pp. 67–9.

22. C. Burns, *Pressing matters: a trans activism memoir volume 2 (1998–2007)* (London: Amazon Kindle Publishing, 2014), loc. 4000.

23. House of Lords debate (HL deb), 14 January 2004, vol. 657, c. GC 73.

24. O. O'Donovan, *Transsexualism: issues and argument* (Cambridge: Grove Books, 2007).

25. A. T. Walker, *God and the transgender debate: what does the Bible actually say about gender identity?* (Epsom: The Good Book Company, 2017), pp. 14–15.

26. S. James, *Gender ideology: what do Christians need to know?* (Fearn: Christian Focus, 2019), p. 76.

27. N. T. Wright, 'Gender-fluid world', Letters to the editor, *The Times*, 3 August 2017.

28. Lynas, *Transformed*, pp. 12, 27.

29. P. Sprinkle, *Embodied: transgender identities, the church & what the Bible has to say* (Colorado Springs, CO: David C Cook, 2021), p. 88. Sprinkle renders the word 'trans' with an asterisk (trans*), which is sometimes done to include related identities, like non-binary and a-gender, which generally come under the trans umbrella but are not interchangeable.

30. Ibid., pp. 92, 95.

31. Ibid., ch. 9.

32. Ibid., p. 88.

33. S. Allberry, *What God has to say about our bodies: how the gospel is good news for our physical selves* (Wheaton, IL: Crossway, 2021), p. 21.

34. Ibid., p. 23.

35. Ibid., p. 59.

36. Ibid., p. 40.

37. T. Keller, *Making sense of God: an invitation to the skeptical* (New York: Viking, 2016), pp. 118–32.

38. J. Sabia-Tanis, *Trans-gender: theology, ministry, and communities of faith*, Second Edition (Eugene, OR: Wipf and Stock, 2018), pp. 90–91.

39. D. Horton, 'Transgendered Christians', *Gendys Journal*, no. 9, 2000. www.gender.org.uk/gendys/2000/09hrton.htm ; B. Hazlehurst and E. Sommers, 'Accepting Evangelicals: listening to T', *Church of England Newspaper*, 5 June 2014. www.churchnewspaper.com/38174/archives (accessed 13 August 2022).

40. K. Pope, 'I'm a parent of a transgender teen and I disagree with the advice of the Christian Institute', *Premier Christianity*, 4 November 2019. www.premierchristianity.com/home/im-a-parent-of-a-transgender-teen-and-i-disagree-with-the-advice-of-the-christian-institute/3146.article (accessed 13 August 2022).

41. M. Guyton, 'Why is NT Wright calling transgender people Gnostics?', *Patheos*, 4 August 2017. www.patheos.com/blogs/mercynotsacrifice/2017/08/04/nt-wright-calling-transgender-people-gnostics/ (accessed 14 September 2022).

42. D. P. Gushee, 'Reconciling evangelical Christianity with our sexual minorities: reframing the biblical discussion', *Journal of the Society of Christian Ethics*, vol. 35, no. 2, 2015, p. 141. https://doi.org/10.1353/sce.2015.0041

43. Horton, 'Evangelical Alliance press release', www.gender.org.uk/gendys/2000/11hrton.htm

44. S. James, '8 ways your church should respond to the transgender agenda', *Evangelical Times*, 20 February 2019. www.evangelical-times.org/articles/

cultural-and-ethical/8-ways-your-church-should-respond-to-the-transgender-agenda/ (accessed 12 August 2022).

45. M. R. Michelson and B. F. Harrison (eds.), *Transforming prejudice: identity, fear, and transgender rights* (Oxford: Oxford University Press, 2020), p. 153.

46. Y. Kanamori et al., 'A comparison between self-identified evangelical Christians' and nonreligious persons' attituddes toward transgender persons', *Psychology of Sexual Orientation and Gender Diversity*, vol. 4, no. 1, 2017, pp. 80, 83. doi/10.1037/sgd0000166

47. C. G. Lynch, 'Speaking to the LGBT community with grace and truth', *Decision Magazine*, 1 February 2019. https://decisionmagazine.com/speaking-to-the-lgbt-community-with-grace-and-truth/ (accessed 13 August 2022).

CHAPTER 4. THE ALLIANCE GOES TO WAR

1. C. R. Trueman, *The rise and triumph of the modern self: cultural amnesia, expressive individualism, and the road to sexual revolution* (Wheaton, IL: Crossway, 2020), pp. 339–78.

2. S. James, 'Are we all "omnigender" now?', *Affinity Social Issues Bulletin*, no. 32, 2016, pp. 2–13.

3. Lynas, *Transformed*, pp. 23–5.

4. New Social Covenant Unit, 'What is being taught in Relationships and Sex Education in our schools? A call for a government review', March 2023, pp. 3, 28. www.newsocialcovenant.co.uk/RSE%20BRIEFING%20FINAL%20 1631%20(IS)_small.pdf (accessed 13 March 2023); M. Lothian-McLean, 'The Tories want you to panic about sex education', *Novara Media*, 10 March 2023. https://novaramedia.com/2023/03/10/the-tories-want-you-to-panic-about-sex-education/ (accessed 13 March 2023).

5. Libby, 'Sympathy, fear, hate', p. 426.

6. Christian Medical Fellowship, 'Written evidence submitted by the Christian Medical Fellowship (GRA1857)', Women and Equalities Committee, 2020, p. 7. https://committees.parliament.uk/writtenevidence/18043/pdf/ (accessed 30 June 2022); Christian Institute, 'Written evidence from the Christian Institute [GRA1621]', Women and Equalities Committee, 2020, p. 3. https:// committees.parliament.uk/writtenevidence/17798/pdf/ (accessed 30 June 2022).

7. 'UK woman wins discrimination case over transgender tweets', *Decision Magazine*, 8 July 2022. https://decisionmagazine.com/uk-woman-wins-discrimination-case-over-transgender-tweets/ (accessed 13 August 2022).

8. R. Brubaker, *Trans: gender and race in an age of unsettled identities* (Oxford: Princeton University Press, 2016), pp. 24–8.

9. L. Littman, 'Parent reports of adolescents and young adults perceived to show signs of a rapid onset of gender dysphoria', *PLoS ONE*, vol. 14, no. 3, 2018. https://doi.org/10.1371/journal.pone.0214157

10. G. R. Bauer et al., 'Do clinical data from transgender adolescents support the phenomenon of "rapid onset gender dysphoria"?', *The Journal of Pediatrics*, vol. 243, 2022, pp. 224–7. https://doi.org/10.1016/j.jpeds.2021.11.020

11. A. J. Restar, 'Methodological critique of Littman's (2018) parental-respondents account of "rapid-onset gender dysphoria"', *Archives of Sexual Behavior*, vol. 49, 2020, pp. 61–6. https://doi.org/10.1007/s10508-019-1453-2

12. A. Shrier, *Irreversible damage: the transgender craze seducing our daughters* (Washington, DC: Regnery Publishing, 2020), chs. 2–3.

13. Sprinkle, *Embodied*, ch. 10.

14. L. Littman, 'Rapid onset of gender dysphoria in adolescents and young adults: a descriptive study', *Journal of Adolescent Health*, vol. 60, no. 2, supp. 1, 2017. https://doi.org/10.1016/j.jadohealth.2016.10.369

15. Lynas, *Transformed*, p. 20.

16. E. Flournoy, 'No, it's not a joke: the Christian Right's appropriation of feminism', *Rethinking Marxism*, vol. 25, no. 3, 2013, pp. 350–66. https://doi.org/10.1080/08935696.2013.798970

17. G. Elliison, 'Who needs evidence? Radical feminism, the Christian Right and sex work research in Northern Ireland' in S. Armstrong, J. Blaustein, and H. Alistair (eds.), *Reflexivity and criminal justice: intersections of policy, practice and research* (Basingstoke: Palgrave Macmillan, 2017), pp. 289–314; S. Dhaliwal, 'Christian fundamentalism in the UK: moral sword of justice or moral crusaders?', *Feminist Dissent*, no. 2, 2017, pp. 118–47. https://doi.org/10.31273/fd.n2.2017.66

18. V. S. Wells, 'British media is increasingly transphobic. Here's why', *Xtra Magazine*, 20 January 2021. https://xtramagazine.com/power/transphobia-britain-terf-uk-media-193828 (accessed 17 August 2022).

19. S. Whittle and F. Simkiss, 'A perfect storm: the UK Government's failed consultation on the Gender Recognition Act, 2004' in C. Ashford and A. Maine (eds.), *Research handbook on gender, sexuality and the law* (Cheltenham: Edward Elgar Publishing, 2020), pp. 228–9.

20. H. H. Williams, 'From family values to religious freedom: conservative discourse and the politics of gay rights', *New Political Science*, vol. 40, no. 2, 2018, pp. 246–62. https://doi.org/10.1080/07393148.2018.1449064

21. Scottish Government, 'Gender Recognition Reform (Scotland) Bill: analysis of responses to the public consultation exercise', September 2021, p. 56. www.gov.scot/publications/gender-recognition-reform-scotland-bill-analysis-responses-public-consultation-exercise/documents/ (accessed 17 January 2023).

22. Christian Concern, 'Written evidence submitted by Christian Concern (GHA1325)', Women and Equalities Committee, 2020, p. 3. https://committees.parliament.uk/writtenevidence/17424/pdf/ (accessed 30 June 2022).

23. F. Renz, '(De)regulating trans identities' in Ashford and Maine, *Research handbook*, pp. 248–9.

24. R. Sandland, 'Feminism and the Gender Recognition Act 2004', *Feminist Legal Studies*, vol. 13, no. 1, 2005, pp. 55–7. https://doi.org/10.1007/s10691-005-1456-3

25. Z. Kirk-Robinson, 'Report to the consultation on the spousal veto', LGBTory, 2014, p. 11. www.lgbtconservatives.org.uk/sites/www.lgbtconservatives.org.

uk/files/report_to_the_consultation_on_the_spousal_veto.pdf (accessed 28 November 2022).

26. Authentic Equity Alliance, 'Written evidence submitted by Authentic Equity Alliance [GRA2019]', Women and Equalities Committee, 2020, p. 2. https://committees.parliament.uk/writtenevidence/18623/pdf/ (accessed 30 June 2022).

27. M. Yardley, 'Written evidence submitted by Miranda Yardley [1840]', Women and Equalities Committee, 2020 p. 1. https://committees.parliament.uk/writtenevidence/18025/pdf/ (accessed 30 June 2022).

28. Sex Matters, 'Written evidence submitted by Sex Matters (GRA1876)', Women and Equalities Committee, 2020, pp. 1–2. https://committees.parliament.uk/writtenevidence/18062/pdf/ (accessed 30 June 2022).

29. A. Sharpe, R. Freedman and R. Auchmuty, 'What would changes to the Gender Recognition Act mean? Two legal views', *The Conversation*, 5 October 2018. https://theconversation.com/what-would-changes-to-the-gender-recognition-act-mean-two-legal-views-103204 (accessed 13 August 2022).

30. Women and Equalities Committee, 'Oral evidence: reform of the Gender Recognition Act, HC 884', House of Commons, 9 December 2020. https://committees.parliament.uk/oralevidence/1393/pdf/ (accessed 30 June 2022).

31. Transgender Trend, *Children's rights impact assessment: Allsorts trans inclusion schools toolkit* (Lewes: Transgender Trend, 2019), p. 11.

32. V. Madrigal-Borloz, 'Practices of so-called "conversion therapy"', report to the Human Rights Council, United Nations General Assembly, 2020. http://arc-international.net/wp-content/uploads/conversion-therapy-IESOGI-A_HRC_44_53_E.pdf (accessed 3 March 2023).

33. Raymond, *Transsexual empire*, p. 178.

34. P. Kelleher, '"Gender critical" author Helen Joyce says she wants to "reduce" number of trans people: "chilling"', *PinkNews*, 3 June 2022. www.pinknews.co.uk/2022/06/03/helen-joyce-transgender-lgbtq/ (accessed 17 September 2022).

35. Christian Institute, *The transgender craze* (Newcastle: Christian Institute, 2020), p. 6. www.christian.org.uk/resource/the-transgender-craze/

36. LGB Alliance, 'Our letter to MPs on conversion therapy', 30 March 2021. https://lgballiance.org.uk/2021/03/31/letter-to-mps/ (accessed 13 August 2022).

37. Sex Matters, 'Response to the government consultation: banning conversion therapy', 2022, pp. 1–2. https://sex-matters.org/wp-content/uploads/2022/02/Response-to-conversion-therapy-consultation.pdf (accessed 13 August 2022).

38. Merched Cymru, 'Conversion therapy consultation response', 2021, p. 1. https://merchedcymru.wales/wp-content/uploads/2021/12/Conversion-Therapy-consultation-response-December-2021.pdf (accessed 13 August 2022); For Women Scotland, 'UK Government: banning conversion therapy', 2022, p. 1. https://forwomen.scot/wp-content/uploads/2022/02/UKGov-Conversion-Therapy-FWS-submission-04Feb2022.pdf (accessed 13 August 2022).

39. LGB Alliance, 'LGB Alliance's response to the Government consultation on banning conversion therapy', 2021. https://lgballiance.org.uk/2021/11/30/lgb-alliances-response-to-the-government-consultation-on-banning-conversion-therapy/ (accessed 13 August 2022).

40. Women's Human Rights Campaign, 'WHRC response to conversion therapy consultation', 2021. www.womensdeclaration.com/documents/255/WHRC_UK_conversion_therapy_submission_2021.pdf (accessed 13 August 2022); Bayswater Support Group, 'Banning conversion therapy: a response from the Bayswater Support Group', 2022. https://bayswatersupport.org.uk/wp-content/uploads/2022/01/Conversion-Therapy-Submission-Final.pdf (accessed 13 August 2022).

41. F. Ashley, *Banning transgender conversion practices: a legal and policy analysis* (Vancouver: UBC Press, 2022), pp. 93–100.

42. Government Equalities Office, 'Banning conversion therapy', UK Government website, 2021. www.gov.uk/government/consultations/banning-conversion-therapy/banning-conversion-therapy (accessed 13 August 2022).

43. Ministers, 'Ministers' consultation response', 2021. https://ministers consultationresponse.com/ (accessed 13 August 2022).

44. S. Clarke, 'Evangelical conference brings together ultraconservative and gender critical figures', Trans Safety Network, 23 May 2022. https://transsafety.network/posts/fet-conference-may-2022/ (accessed 13 August 2022).

45. Family Education Trust, 'Family Education Trust response to the Government's consultation on banning conversion therapy', 2021, p. 6. https://familyeducationtrust.org.uk/wp-content/uploads/2021/12/DWE-Banning-Conversion-Therapy-FET-Response.pdf (accessed 13 August 2022).

46. J. Stevens, 'Conversion therapy: a biblical response', Fellowship of Independent Evangelical Churches, 25 May 2021. https://fiec.org.uk/resources/conversion-therapy-a-biblical-response (accessed 13 August 2022).

47. Let Us Pray, 'What does the Government mean by "conversion therapy"?', 2021. https://letuspray.uk/conversion (accessed 13 August 2022).

48. Evangelical Alliance, 'Have your say on the government's consultation to ban conversion therapy', 2021. www.eauk.org/what-we-do/public-policy/ending-conversion-therapy/have-your-say-on-the-governments-conversion-therapy-ban-consultation (accessed 13 August 2022).

49. A. Cowburn, 'Boris Johnson accused of creating "loophole" in proposed conversion therapy ban', *The Independent*, 14 April 2021. www.independent.co.uk/news/uk/politics/boris-johnson-conversion-therapy-lgbt-b1831141.html (accessed 20 August 2022).

50. C. Dyer, 'Gender conversion therapy: why is banning it so divisive?', *The British Medical Journal*, vol. 377, 2022. https://doi.org/10.1136/bmj.0943

51. L. Patel, 'UK's ban on conversion therapy should include transgender people', *The British Medical Journal*, vol. 377, 2022. http://dx.doi.org/10.1136/bmj.01453

52. L. Truss, 'Written ministerial statement: response to Gender Recognition Act (2004) consultation', Government Equalities Office, 22 September 2020. www.gov.uk/government/speeches/response-to-gender-recognition-act-2004-consultation (accessed 13 August 2022).

53. D. King et al., 'Reform of the Gender Recognition Act: analysis of consultation responses', Government Equalities Office, 2020. https://assets.publishing. service.gov.uk/government/uploads/system/uploads/attachment_data/ file/919890/Analysis_of_responses_Gender_Recognition_Act.pdf (accessed 13 August 2022).

54. M. Donelan, 'Online safety update', UK Government, 17 January 2023. https:// questions-statements.parliament.uk/written-statements/detail/2023-01-17/ hcws500 (accessed 17 January 2023).

55. 'Nicola Sturgeon says gender reform row will go to court', *BBC News*, 17 January 2023. www.bbc.co.uk/news/uk-scotland-scotland-politics-64264063 (accessed 17 January 2023).

56. UK Government, 'Policy statement of reasons on the decision to use section 35 with respect to the Gender Recognition Reform (Scotland) Bill', 17 January 2023, pp. 3–5. https://assets.publishing.service.gov.uk/government/uploads/ system/uploads/attachment_data/file/1129495/policy-statement-section-35-powers-Gender-Recognition-Reform-_Scotland_-Bill.pdf (accessed 17 January 2023).

57. Ibid., pp. 5–7.

58. Ibid., pp. 7–13.

59. Future of Legal Gender Project, 'Abolishing legal sex status: the challenge and consequences of gender-related law reform', May 2022, p. 37. www.kcl.ac.uk/ law/research/future-of-legal-gender-abolishing-legal-sex-status-full-report. pdf

60. Dhaliwal, 'Christian fundamentalism in the UK', p. 141.

61. W. Grzebalska, E. Kováts and A. Pető, 'Gender as symbolic glue: how "gender" became an umbrella term for the rejection of the (neo)liberal order', *Political Critique*, 13 January 2017. http://politicalcritique.org/long-read/2017/gender-as-symbolic-glue-how-gender-became-an-umbrella-term-for-the-rejection-of-the-neoliberal-order/ (accessed 21 August 2022).

62. S. Mayer and B. Sauer, '"Gender ideology" in Austria: coalitions around an empty signifier' in Kuhar and Paternotte, *Anti-gender campaigns*, p. 33.

CHAPTER 5. GENDER ORTHODOXY

1. Council on Biblical Manhood and Womanhood, 'The Nashville Statement', 2014. https://cbmw.org/nashville-statement/#articles (accessed 3 March 2023).

2. W. Grudem, *Systematic theology: an introduction to biblical doctrine*, Second Edition (London: Inter-Varsity Press, 2020), p. 1.

3. W. Grudem, *Christian ethics: an introduction to biblical moral reasoning* (Wheaton, IL: Crossway, 2018), p. 37.

4. Ibid., p. 874.

5. G. G. Bolich, *Crossdressing in context: dress, gender, transgender, and crossdressing*, vol. 4: *Transgender & religion* (Raleigh, NC: Psyche's Press, 2008), pp. 140–41.

6. J. DeRouchie, 'Confronting the transgender storm: new covenant reflections on Deuteronomy 22:5', *Journal for Biblical Manhood and Womanhood*, vol. 21, no. 1, 2016. https://cbmw.org/2016/05/25/jbmw-21-1-confronting-the-transgender-storm-new-covenant-reflections-from-deuteronomy-225/

7. J. Hübner, 'The Nashville Statement: a critical review', *CBE International*, 30 January 2019. www.cbeinternational.org/resource/nashville-statement-critical-review/ (accessed 3 March 2023).

8. Grudem, *Systematic theology*, p. 21.

9. Ibid., p. 411.

10. Ibid., p. 86.

11. Ibid., p. 143.

12. Ibid., p. 75.

13. Ibid., p. 144.

14. M. Foucault, *The order of things: an archaeology of the human sciences* (New York: Pantheon Books, 1971), p. xv.

15. Grudem, *Systematic theology*, p. 395.

16. Ibid., p. 412.

17. Grudem, *Christian ethics*, p. 119.

18. Ibid., p. 157.

19. Ibid., p. 50.

20. Ibid., p. 120.

21. Grudem, *Systematic theology*, p. 159.

22. Ibid., p. 160.

23. Grudem, *Christian ethics*, p. 251.

24. Ibid., p. 875.

25. N. T. Wright, 'Historical Paul and "systematic theology": to start a discussion' in C. Walsh and M. W. Elliott (eds.), *Biblical theology: past, present, and future* (Eugene, OR: Cascade Books, 2016), p. 160.

CHAPTER 6. REBELLION

1. L. Salazar, *Roots of rejection, roots of injustice: digging deeper into society's negative response to transgenderism and gender nonconformity and how it intersects with dogma*, Master's paper, Vancouver School of Theology, 2013, pp. 10–14.

2. V. Roberts, *Transgender: Christian compassion, convictions and wisdom for today's big questions* (Epsom: The Good Book Company, 2016), p. 52; emphasis added.

3. O. Strachan, *Reenchanting humanity: a theology of mankind* (Fearn, UK: Mentor, 2019), pp. 173–4.

4. Evangelical Alliance and Christian Research, *21st century evangelicals: a snapshot of the beliefs and habits of evangelical Christians in the UK* (London: Evangelical Alliance, 2011), p. 23.

5. N. Guthrie, *Even better than Eden: nine ways the Bible's story changes everything about your story* (Wheaton, IL: Crossway, 2018), p. 49.

6. V. Kolakowski, 'Towards a Christian ethical response to transsexual persons', *Theology and Sexuality*, vol. 1997, no. 6, pp. 16–20. https://doi.org/10.1177/135583589700300602

7. Southern Baptist Convention, 'On transgender identity', 1 June 2014. https://www.sbc.net/resource-library/resolutions/on-transgender-identity/ (accessed 6 December 2022).

8. S. Greenblatt, *The rise and fall of Adam and Eve: the story that created us* (London: Vintage, 2018), p. 6.

9. R. A. Mohler, 'The transgender challenge: an evangelical response', *Decision Magazine*, 1 January 2017. https://decisionmagazine.com/transgender-challenge-evangelical-response-2/ (accessed 6 December 2022).

10. A. Hartke, *Transforming: the Bible & the lives of transgender Christians* (Louisville: Westminster John Knox Press, 2018), pp. 143–53.

11. M. Carden, 'Genesis/Bereshit' in D. Guest, R. E. Goss, M. West and T. Bohache (eds.), *The queer Bible commentary* (London: SCM Press, 2006), pp. 27–8.

12. J. Ladin, *The soul of the stranger: reading God and Torah from a transgender perspective* (Waltham, UK: Brandeis University Press, 2018), p. 27.

13. Ibid., p. 30.

14. Ibid., p. 32.

15. M. W. Bychowski, 'On Genesis: transgender and subcreation', *TSQ: Transgender Studies Quarterly*, vol. 6, no. 3, 2019, p. 444. https://doi.org/10.1215/23289252-7549598

16. Ibid., pp. 444–6.

17. F. P. Retief, 'Eunuchs in the Bible', *Acta Theologica*, vol. 26, no. 2, 2006 (Supplementum 7), pp. 247–58. https://doi.org/10.4314/actat.v26i2.52578

18. J. D. Hester, 'Eunuchs and the postgender Jesus: Matthew 19.12 and transgressive sexualities', *Journal for the Study of the New Testament*, vol. 28, no.1, 2005, pp. 13–40. https://doi.org/10.1177/0142064X05057772

19. C. Greenough, *Queer theologies: the basics* (Abingdon-on-Thames: Taylor & Francis, 2019), pp. 100–103.

20. K. Apostolacus, 'The Bible and the transgender Christian: mapping transgender hermeneutics in the 21st century', *Journal of the Bible and its Reception*, vol. 5, no. 1, 2018, pp. 7–8, 18–20. https://doi.org/10.1515/jbr-2016-0027

21. M. Davie, *Transgender liturgies: should the Church of England develop liturgical materials to mark gender transition?* (London: Latimer Trust, 2017), p. 56.

22. Strachan, *Reenchanting humanity*, pp. 22–3.

23. Ibid., p. 41.

24. J. Milton, 'Paradise Lost' in G. Campbell (ed.), *John Milton: the complete English poems* (London: Everyman's Library, 1992), p. 363.

25. M. Yarhouse, *Understanding gender dysphoria: navigating transgender issues in a changing culture* (London: IVP Academic, 2015), pp. 35–9.

26. S. McQuoid, *In his image: a biblical introduction to social ethics* (London: Wilberforce Publications, 2020), p. 92.

27. O. Strachan and G. Peacock, *The grand design: male and female he made them* (Fearn, UK: Christian Focus, 2016), p. 92.

28. Wellcome Collection, PP/KIN/C/14/3, 'Divine guidance', *SHAFT Newsletter*, no. 9, June 1981, p. 8.
29. This point is addressed at greater length in K. E. Stuart, *The uninvited dilemma: a question of gender* (Lake Oswegeo, NY: Metamorphous Press, 1983), pp. 96–7.
30. K. Armstrong, *Paul: the apostle we love to hate* (Boston, MA: New Harvest, 2015), p. 12.
31. J. M. G. Barclay, 'What makes Paul challenging today?' in B. W. Longenecker, *The new Cambridge companion to St. Paul* (Cambridge: Cambridge University Press, 2020), p. 311.
32. K. F. Kroll, 'Transsexuality and religion: a personal journey' in B. Bullough, V. L. Bullough and J. Elias (eds.), *Gender blending* (New York: Prometheus Books, 1997), pp. 492–4.
33. M. E. Lowe, 'From the same spirit: receiving the theological gifts of transgender Christians', *Dialog: A Journal of Theology*, vol. 56, no. 1, 2017, p. 33. https://doi.org/10.1111/dial.12293
34. S. Bader-Saye, 'The transgender body's grace', *Journal of the Society of Christian Ethics*, vol. 39, no. 1, 2019, p. 90. https://doi.org/10.5840/jsce2019445
35. Lynas, *Transformed*, p. 5.

CHAPTER 7. 'GOD IS BULLSHIT, AND SO IS GENDER.'

1. W. Kaufman, 'New atheism and its critics', *Philosophy Compass*, vol. 14, no. 1, 2019. https://doi.org/10.1111/phc3.12560
2. V. J. Stenger, *The new atheism: taking a stand for science and reason* (New York: Prometheus Books, 2009); S. Kettell, 'Faithless: the politics of new atheism', *Secularism & Nonreligion*, vol. 2, 2103, pp. 61–72. http://doi.org/10.5334/snr.al
3. C. Hitchens, *God is not great: how religion poisons everything* (New York: Twelve Books, 2007), p. 5.
4. E. Miller, 'Why is British media so transphobic?', *The Outline*, 5 November 2018. https://theoutline.com/post/6536/british-feminists-media-transphobic?zd=1&zi=iv74xdyn (accessed 8 August 2021).
5. H. Lewis, 'The battle over gender: what makes you a man or a woman, anyway?', *The New Statesman*, 13 September 2013. www.newstatesman.com/politics/2013/09/battle-over-gender-what-makes-you-man-or-woman-anyway (accessed 10 August 2022).
6. A. Flood, 'Richard Dawkins loses 'humanist of the year' title over trans comments', *The Guardian*, 20 April 2021. www.theguardian.com/books/2021/apr/20/richard-dawkins-loses-humanist-of-the-year-trans-comments (accessed 10 August 2022).
7. H. Greensmith, 'Atheist Richard Dawkins swings to anti-trans right in grasp at broader intellectual relevance', *Religion Dispatches*, 30 November 2021. https://religiondispatches.org/atheist-richard-dawkins-swings-to-anti-trans-right-in-grasp-at-broader-intellectual-relevance/ (accessed 30 July 2022).

8. N. Duffy, 'Richard Dawkins tells students upset by Germaine Greer to "go home and hug a teddy"', *PinkNews*, 26 October 2015. www.pinknews.co.uk/2015/10/26/richard-dawkins-tells-students-upset-by-germaine-greer-to-go-home-and-hug-a-teddy/ (accessed 1 August 2021).

9. K. Lofton, 'Pulpit of performative reason', *TSQ: Transgender Studies Quarterly*, vol. 9, no. 3, 2022, p. 444. https://doi.org/10.1215/23289252-9836092

10. E. Mohammed-Smith, 'I never thought "New Atheism" would become a tool of the Christian Right', *Flux*, 4 February 2022. https://flux.community/eiynah-mohammed-smith/2022/02/i-never-thought-new-atheism-would-become-tool-christian-right (accessed 10 August 2022).

11. Z. Jones, 'Atheist transphobia: superstition over science', *The Orbit*, 15 May 2014. https://the-orbit.net/zinniajones/2014/05/atheist-transphobia-superstition-over-science/ (accessed 10 August 2022); original emphasis.

12. Women's Liberation Radio News, 'Emiliann Lorenzen interviews Exulansic', 16 December 2021. https://womensliberationradionews.com/2021/12/16/emiliann-lorenzen-interviews-exulansic/ (accessed 10 August 2022).

13. F. Tremblay, 'Gender atheism is the next misunderstood idea', blog post, 5 June 2014. https://francoistremblay.wordpress.com/2014/06/05/gender-atheism-is-the-next-misunderstood-idea/ (accessed 14 September 2022).

14. E. Zerofsky, 'How the Claremont Institute became a nerve center for the American right', *The New York Times Magazine*, 3 August 2022. www.nytimes.com/2022/08/03/magazine/claremont-institute-conservative.html (accessed 22 November 2022).

15. S. Weir, 'How gender atheism saved my body', *The American Mind*, 4 August 2021. https://americanmind.org/salvo/how-gender-atheism-saved-my-body/ (accessed 10 August 2022).

16. D. A. Westbrook and J. R. Lewis, 'Scientology and Gnosticism: L. Ron Hubbard's "The factors" (1953)' in Trompf, Mikkelsen and Johnston, *The Gnostic world*, ch. 59.

17. M. Osborne, 'Gender Atheism: a critical manifesto', *Wrong Speak*, 25 February 2022. https://wrongspeak.net/gender-atheism-a-critical-manifesto/ (accessed 10 August 2022).

18. S. Weir, 'Gender Jesuits', *The American Mind*, 1 November 2022. https://americanmind.org/salvo/gender-jesuits/ (accessed 22 November 2022).

19. D. Fisher, 'The Butlerian jihad', *Uncommon Ground*, 7 October 2017. https://uncommongroundmedia.com/countering-postmodernism-relativism/?utm_content=cmp-true (accessed 17 March 2023).

20. M. Yardley, 'Suffer the children: how young people became the collateral damage of transgender ideology', blog post, 15 November 2017. https://mirandayardley.com/en/suffer-the-children-how-children-became-the-collateral-damage-of-transgender-ideology/ (accessed 8 August 2021).

21. M. Yardley, 'The colonisation of the boyhood of pre-gay children by heterosexual transgender activists: interview with @BlanchardPhD', blog post, 13 October 2017. https://mirandayardley.com/en/the-colonisation-of-the-boyhood-of-pre-gay-children-by-heterosexual-transgender-activists-interview-with-blanchardphd/ (accessed 8 August 2021).

22. K. Burns, 'The rise of anti-trans "radical" feminists, explained', *Vox*, 5 September 2020. https://www.vox.com/identities/2019/9/5/20840101/terfs-radical-feminists-gender-critical (accessed 10 August 2022); S. Pederson, *The politicization of Mumsnet* (Bingley: Emerald Publishing Limited, 2020).

23. K. J. M. Baker, 'Mumsnet and the fostering of anti-trans radicalization', *Lux Magazine*, no. 1, January 2021. https://lux-magazine.com/article/the-road-to-terfdom/ (accessed 23 August 2022).

24. Dervel, response to 'Transgender kids article in today's Guardian', *Mumsnet*, 5 April 2015, p. 3. www.mumsnet.com/Talk/womens_rights/2348226-Transgender-kids-article-in-todays-Guardian?pg=3 (accessed 30 April 2021).

25. OTheHugeManatee, response to 'Universities, free speech and the transgender lobby', *Mumsnet*, 14 March 2016, p. 1. www.mumsnet.com/Talk/womens_rights/2591930-Universities-free-speech-and-the-transgender-lobby (accessed 30 April 2022).

26. Cwenthryth, response to 'How can we work towards a constructive debate about all things transgender?', *Mumsnet*, 24 January 2018, p. 3. www.mumsnet.com/Talk/womens_rights/3149293-how-can-we-work-towards-a-constructive-debate-about-all-things-transgender?pg=3 (accessed 15 March 2021).

27. L. Blade and B. Kay, *Unsporting: how trans activism and science denial are destroying sport* (Toronto: Rebel News, 2020), p. 13.

28. D. Soh, *The end of gender: debunking the myths about sex and identity in our society* (New York: Threshold Editions, 2020), pp. 1–11.

29. I. Sanger, *Born in the right body: gender identity ideology from a medical and feminist perspective* (London: Amazon Publishing, 2022), pp. 71, 168.

30. Joyce, *Trans*, p. 300.

31. S. LeDrew, *The evolution of atheism: the politics of a modern movement* (Oxford: Oxford University Press, 2015), pp. 178–212.

32. Rationality Rules, 'Richard Dawkins STRIPPED of Humanist of the Year Award', *YouTube*, 29 April 2021. https://www.youtube.com/watch?v=sAy2GOv9fd8 (accessed 15 February 2022).

33. R. Isomaa, 'YouTube drama in an atheist public: a case study', *Secularism & Nonreligion*, vol. 11, no. 1, 2022, pp. 1–13. https://doi.org/10.5334/snr.146

34. M. Salter, 'From geek masculinity to Gamergate: the technological rationality of online abuse', *Crime, Media, Culture*, vol. 14, no. 2, 2018, pp. 247–64. https://doi.org/10.1177%2F1741659017690893

35. 'American Atheists VP on Richard Dawkins' comments about trans people', *American Atheists*, 12 April 2021. https://www.atheists.org/2021/04/american-atheists-richard-dawkins-trans-people/ (accessed 30 July 2022).

36. É. P. Torres, 'From the enlightenment to the dark ages: how "new atheism" slid into the alt-right', *Salon*, 29 July 2017. www.salon.com/2017/07/29/from-the-enlightenment-to-the-dark-ages-how-new-atheism-slid-into-the-alt-right/ (accessed 30 July 2022).

37. A. Bidmead, *The politics of new atheism: an examination of the aims, impact and validity of the movement within a British context*, PhD thesis, Swansea University, 2015, p. 6; original emphasis.

CHAPTER 8. MASKING STRATEGIES

1. C. Payne, 'Transphobia and the left: bogus science and bogus Marxism', *Socialist Alternative*, 12 May 2020. www.socialistalternative.org/2020/05/12/transphobia-and-the-left-bogus-science-and-bogus-marxism/ (accessed 17 August 2022).

2. A. Zottola, *Transgender identities in the press: a corpus-based discourse analysis* (London: Bloomsbury, 2021), pp. 130–32.

3. C. Burns, 'Transsexual people and the press: collected opinions from transsexual people themselves', Press for Change report, November 2004, § b.3.c.

4. A. Pearson, 'Why taking offence is the new national sport', *The Daily Telegraph*, 17 January 2013. www.telegraph.co.uk/comment/columnists/allison-pearson/9806112/Why-taking-offence-is-Britains-new-national-sport.html (accessed 14 August 2022).

5. A. Pierce, 'I've had it up to here with these gender fascists!', *The Daily Mail*, 1 March 2017. www.dailymail.co.uk/debate/article-4269792/ANDREW-PIERCE-powerful-transgender-lobby.html (accessed 14 August 2022).

6. D. Sandbrook, 'March of the thought police', *The Daily Mail*, 17 June 2017. www.dailymail.co.uk/news/article-4612720/Tim-Farron-s-ousting-Lib-Dem-leader-left-victory.html (accessed 14 August 2022).

7. R. Clark, 'Free speech is at risk from the easily-offended', *The Express*, 9 November 2018. www.express.co.uk/comment/expresscomment/1043047/free-speech-risk-easily-offended-woman-hour-radio-4 (accessed 14 August 2022).

8. A. Pearson, 'I am sick of being silenced by social-justice warriors whose self-assurance is only matched by their ignorance', *The Daily Telegraph*, 26 March 2019. www.telegraph.co.uk/women/life/sick-silenced-social-justice-warriors-whose-self-assurance-matched/ (accessed 17 August 2022).

9. J. Bindel, 'Lesbians are being erased by transgender activists', *The Spectator*, 29 June 2021. www.spectator.co.uk/article/lesbians-are-being-erased-by-transgender-activists (accessed 17 August 2022).

10. T. Young, 'The enemies of liberty are hunting in packs. That is why we must band together and fight for free speech', *The Mail on Sunday*, 23 February 2020. www.dailymail.co.uk/debate/article-8032877/TOBY-YOUNG-enemies-liberty-hunt-packs-band-fight-free-speech.html (accessed 14 August 2022).

11. 'The Times view on the risks of gender self-identification', *The Times*, 10 December 2019. www.thetimes.co.uk/article/the-times-view-on-the-risks-of-gender-self-identification-the-gender-trap-bmb3roovn (accessed 14 August 2022).

12. N. Lawson, 'Sex change operations don't work', *The Times*, 6 February 1996.

13. H. Spencer, 'Nigella Lawson apologises for 1993 comments on person's choice to have gender surgery', *The Independent*, 9 September 2020. www.independent.co.uk/life-style/nigella-lawson-apology-christie-elan-cane-non-

gendered-1993-evening-standard-column-b421049.html (accessed 6 August 2022).

14. R. Littlejohn, 'He's not only in the wrong body ... He's in the wrong job', *The Daily Mail*, 21 December 2012. [The article was removed from the *Daily Mail*'s website shortly after its publication].

15. H. Pidd, 'Lucy Meadows coroner tells press: "shame on you"', *The Guardian*, 28 May 2013. www.theguardian.com/uk/2013/may/28/lucy-meadows-coroner-press-shame (accessed 14 August 2022).

16. R. Greenslade, 'Daily Mail urged to fire Richard Littlejohn after death of Lucy Meadows', *The Guardian*, 22 March 2013. www.theguardian.com/media/greenslade/2013/mar/22/richard-littlejohn-transgender (accessed 15 August 2022).

17. L. Purves, 'Even foaming dinosaurs deserve free speech', *The Times*, 25 March 2013. www.thetimes.co.uk/article/even-foaming-dinosaurs-deserve-free-speech-7x97kjsvxzn (accessed 15 August 2022).

18. S. Moore, 'Seeing red: the power of female anger', *The New Statesman*, 8 January 2013. www.newstatesman.com/politics/2013/01/seeing-red-power-female-anger (accessed 14 August 2022).

19. 'Moore apologises for "Brazilian transsexual" remark', *PinkNews*, 14 January 2013. www.pinknews.co.uk/2013/01/14/guardian-columnist-suzanne-moore-apologises-for-brazilian-transsexual-remark/ (accessed 15 August 2022).

20. S. Moore, 'Why I had to leave The Guardian', *UnHerd*, 25 November 2019. https://unherd.com/2020/11/why-i-had-to-leave-the-guardian/ (accessed 15 August 2022).

21. J. Burchill, 'Hey trans people, cut it out', *Spiked*, 15 January 2013. www.spiked-online.com/2013/01/15/hey-trans-people-cut-it-out/ (accessed 15 August 2022).

22. H. Lewis, 'What the row over banning Germaine Greer is really about', *The New Statesman*, 27 October 2015. www.newstatesman.com/politics/2015/10/what-row-over-banning-germaine-greer-really-about (accessed 17 August 2022).

23. M. Reisz, 'The corrosion of conformity', *The Times Higher Education Supplement*, 7 January 2016. www.timeshighereducation.com/features/interview-joanna-williams-university-of-kent (accessed 17 August 2022).

24. J. Williams, 'Apparently I am too dangerous to be let loose on innocent students', *The Sunday Telegraph*, 18 November 2018. www.telegraph.co.uk/news/2018/11/17/apparently-dangerous-let-loose-innocent-students-news/ (accessed 17 August 2022).

25. G. Linehan, 'Speaking out against transgender extremists has made me the most hated man on the Internet', *The Mail on Sunday*, 9 February 2020. www.dailymail.co.uk/news/article-7982837/How-hated-man-internet-writes-Graham-Linehan.html (accessed 17 August 2022); J. Burchill, 'The envious woke are finally being defeated on campus', *The Telegraph*, 7 March 2021. www.telegraph.co.uk/news/2021/03/07/envious-woke-finally-defeated-campus/ (accessed 17 August 2022).

26. H. Brunskell-Evans, *Transgender body politics* (North Geelong: Spinifex, 2020), pp. 60–66.

27. H. Barnes, *Time to think: the inside story of the collapse of the Tavistock's gender service for children* (London: Swift, 2023), p. 223.

28. P. Morgan, 'Let's wake up and wipe out wokery!', *The Mail on Sunday*, 11 October 2020. www.dailymail.co.uk/news/article-8826969/Lets-wake-wipe-wokery-PIERS-MORGAN-hoped-kinder-snarling-world-Covid.html (accessed 17 August 2022).

29. N. Ferrari, 'Let's hear it for Germaine Greer ... now that's something I thought I'd never say', *The Express*, 1 November 2015. www.express.co.uk/comment/columnists/nick-ferrari/616139/Germaine-Greer-2018-World-Cup-Sunday-Church (accessed 17 August 2022).

30. C. Hutchison, 'Church leaders claim hate crime laws could ban criticism of trans issues', *The Herald*, 12 February 2021. www.heraldscotland.com/news/19086774.church-leaders-claim-hate-crime-laws-ban-criticism-trans-issues/ (accessed 24 August 2022).

31. K. Falkner, 'The freedom to hold a belief is something we all need to protect', *Equality and Human Rights Commission*, 17 June 2021. www.equalityhumanrights.com/en/our-work/blogs/freedom-hold-belief-something-we-all-need-protect (accessed 13 August 2022).

32. S. Cowan and S. Morris, 'Should "gender critical" views about trans people be protected as philosophical beliefs in the workplace? Lessons for the future from Forstater, Mackereth and Higgs', *Industrial Law Journal*, vol. 51, no. 1, 2022, pp. 1–37. https://doi.org/10.1093/indlaw/dwac002

33. R. Cooke, 'Interview: "Now other women are free to say what they believe": researcher who lost her job over transgender tweets', *The Guardian*, 10 July 2022. www.theguardian.com/society/2022/jul/10/maya-forstater-transgender-tweets-tribunal-ruling (accessed 13 August 2022).

34. Christian Institute, *Free to disagree* (Newcastle: Christian Institute, 2020), p. 3.

35. Trans Safety Network, 'Religious right linked law firm receives £314k from "gender critical" causes', 16 January 2021. https://transsafety.network/posts/christian-right-linked-law-firm/ (accessed 13 August 2022).

36. N. Kennedy, 'Anti-trans activists are using "mirror propaganda". Here's how to spot it', *Open Democracy*, 5 December 2022. www.opendemocracy.net/en/5050/anti-trans-transphobia-gender-critical-mirror-propaganda/ (accessed 7 December 2022).

37. C. Lowbridge, 'The lesbians who feel pressured to have sex and relationships with trans women', *BBC News*, 26 October 2021. www.bbc.co.uk/news/uk-england-57853385 (accessed 12 September 2022).

38. BBC Executive Complaints Unit, 'We're being pressured into sex by some trans women, bbc.co.uk', 31 May 2022. www.bbc.co.uk/contact/ecu/newsonlineoctober2021 (accessed 12 September 2022).

39. 'Open letter signed by 16,000 calls for BBC apology over trans article', *BBC News*, 28 October 2021. www.bbc.co.uk/news/entertainment-arts-59074096 (accessed 12 September 2022).

40. House of Lords debate (HL deb), 26 November 2015, vol. 767, c. 852.

41. House of Commons debate (HC deb), 17 May 2018, vol. 641, cc. 226WH–227WH.
42. Department for Education, 'Higher education: free speech and academic freedom', UK Government, February 2021, p. 5. www.gov.uk/government/publications/higher-education-free-speech-and-academic-freedom (Accessed 17 August 2022).
43. R. Bennett, 'Students told not to ban speakers for "transphobia"', *The Times*, 2 February 2019. www.thetimes.co.uk/article/students-told-not-to-ban-speakers-for-transphobia-vq3vctl8j (accessed 17 August 2022).
44. E. Smith, *No platform: a history of anti-fascism, universities and the limits of free speech* (London: Routledge, 2020).
45. Quoted in H. Ewens, 'Inside the Great British TERF war', *Vice*, 16 June 2020. www.vice.com/en/article/889qe5/trans-rights-uk-debate-terfs (accessed 10 August 2022).
46. J. Kennedy, *Authentocrats: culture, politics and the new seriousness* (London: Repeated, 2018), p. 8.
47. Ibid., 28.
48. HC deb, 21 November 2018, vol. 649, c. 340WH.
49. J. Glass, 'Anti-trans activists hit out at "parasitic" trans people at event in Parliament', *PinkNews*, 15 March 2018. www.pinknews.co.uk/2018/03/15/anti-trans-activists-hit-out-at-parasitic-trans-people-at-event-in-parliament/ (accessed 17 September 2022).
50. HC deb, 11 October 2017, vol. 629, c. 327.
51. HC deb, 13 November 2018, vol. 649, c. 176.
52. HC deb, 21 November 2018, vol. 649, c. 324WH.
53. Ibid., c. 328WH.
54. Company numbers 12273984 (Fair Play for Women), 13308625 (Woman's Place UK), 12035713 (Transgender Trend).
55. HC deb, 21 November 2018, vol. 649, c. 324WH.
56. Rowling, 'J. K. Rowling writes about her reasons for speaking out'.
57. 'Letters: standing up for transsexual rights', *The Guardian*, 4 May 2018. www.theguardian.com/society/2018/may/04/standing-up-for-transsexual-rights (accessed 9 August 2022).
58. S. B. Bergman and M. Barker, 'Non-binary activism' in C. Richards, W. P. Bouman and M. Barker (eds.), *Genderqueer and non-binary genders* (Basingstoke: Palgrave Macmillan, 2017), p. 41.
59. Bishopsgate Institute, Purnell/47, R. Webb, 'Delusions and definitions', *Rogue*, April–June 1991.
60. C. R. Snorton, *Black on both sides* (London: University of Minnesota Press, 2017), p. 181.

CHAPTER 9. A COMING STORM?

1. S. Sardarizadeh and K. Devlin, 'Texas shooting: how false rumours spread that gunman was trans', *BBC News*, 28 May 2022. www.bbc.co.uk/news/61607042 (accessed 25 August 2022).

2. M. Thalen, 'Why the far-right is desperate to push false claims that recent mass shooters were trans', *Daily Dot*, 6 July 2022. www.dailydot.com/debug/far-right-claims-highland-park-shooter-transgender/?amp (accessed 31 August 2022).

3. A. Woodward, 'Suspect arrested for bomb threat against Boston Children's Hospital amid waves of anti-trans harassment', *The Independent*, 15 September 2022. www.independent.co.uk/news/world/americas/crime/boston-children-hospital-bomb-threat-suspect-b2168386.html (accessed 19 September 2022).

4. J. Bilek, 'The billionaire family pushing synthetic sex identities (SSI)', *Tablet*, 14 June 2022. www.tabletmag.com/sections/news/articles/billionaire-family-pushing-synthetic-sex-identities-ssi-pritzkers (accessed 31 August 2022).

5. B. Goggin and K. Tenbarge, 'Right-wing influencers and media double down on anti-LGBTQ rhetoric in the wake of the Colorado shooting', *MSNBC News*, 23 November 2022. www.nbcnews.com/tech/internet/right-wing-influencers-media-double-anti-lgbtq-rhetoric-wake-colorado-rcna58371 (accessed 25 November 2022).

6. G. Kilander, 'CPAC speaker sparks alarm with call for transgenderism to be "eradicated"', *The Independent*, 5 March 2023. www.independent.co.uk/news/world/americas/us-politics/cpac-transgenderism-daily-wire-michael-knowles-b2294252.html (accessed 7 March 2023).

7. D. K. Li, E. Ortiz and M. Lenthang, 'Police chief tells NBC News a sense of "resentment" may have fueled Nashville shooter's attack at former school', *NBC News*, 28 March 2023. www.nbcnews.com/news/us-news/nashville-christian-school-shooter-appears-former-student-police-chief-rcna76876 (accessed 28 March 2023).

8. M. Walsh, 'Ep. 1138 – Christian children murdered by trans mass shooter', *The Daily Wire*, 28 March 2023. www.dailywire.com/episode/ep-1138-christian-children-murdered-by-trans-mass-shooter (accessed 29 March 2023); J. Marcus, 'Twitter restricts Marjorie Taylor Greene after tweets about trans people and Nashville shooting', *The Independent*, 29 March 2023. www.independent.co.uk/news/world/americas/us-politics/twitter-ban-marjorie-taylor-greene-b2309784.html (accessed 29 March 2023).

9. S. L. MacMillen, 'QAnon – religious roots, religious responses', *Critical Sociology*, vol. 48, no. 6, 2022, 989-1004. https://doi.org/10.1177/08969205211063565

10. M. Rothschild, *The storm is upon us: how QAnon became a movement, cult, and conspiracy theory of everything* (London: Monoray, 2021), pp. 150–53.

11. Drops 2682, 3613, and 3295, among others, do mention gender divisions in passing.

12. M. Bloom and S. Moskalenko, *Pastels and pedophiles: inside the mind of QAnon* (Stanford, CA: Stanford University Press, 2021), p. 100.

13. J. Gill-Peterson, 'From gender critical to QAnon: anti-trans politics and the laundering of conspiracy', *The New Inquiry*, 13 September 2021. https://thenewinquiry.com/from-gender-critical-to-qanon-anti-trans-politics-and-the-laundering-of-conspiracy/ (accessed 31 August 2022).

14. Faye, *The transgender issue*, p. 244.

15. C. Grady, 'J.K. Rowling's transphobic new novel sees her at the mercy of all her worst impulses', *Vox*, 23 September 2020. www.vox.com/culture/21449215/ troubled-blood-review-jk-rowling-transphobia-controversy (accessed 13 October 2022).

16. E. Harrison, 'JK Rowling's new book features woman who is killed after being accused of transphobia', *The Independent*, 31 August 2022. www.independent. co.uk/arts-entertainment/books/news/jk-rowling-new-book-transphobe-ink-black-heart-b2156272.html (accessed 13 October 2022).

17. J. A. Cohen, 'The eradication of "Talmudic abstractions": anti-Semitism, transmisogyny and the National Socialist project', *Verso*, 19 December 2018. www.versobooks.com/blogs/4188-the-eradication-of-talmudic-abstractions-anti-semitism-transmisogyny-and-the-national-socialist-project (accessed 28 March 2023).

18. Z. Murib, 'Administering biology: how "bathroom bills" criminalize and stigmatize trans and gender nonconforming people in public space', *Administrative Theory & Praxis*, vol. 42, no. 2, 2020, pp. 153–71. https://doi. org/10.1080/10841806.2019.1659048

19. T. Ermyas, 'Wave of bills to block trans athletes has no basis in science, researcher says', *NPR*, 18 March 2021. www.npr.org/2021/03/18/978716732/ wave-of-new-bills-say-trans-athletes-have-an-unfair-edge-what-does-the-science-s (accessed 11 January 2023).

20. A. Izaguirre, 'Florida to ban transgender health care treatment for minors', *Associated Press*, 4 November 2022. https://apnews.com/article/ron-desantis-health-business-florida-government-and-politics-78e417a184718de8b9e71f f32efbc77f (accessed 11 January 2023).

21. B. Levin, 'Oklahoma bill would ban gender-affirming care for people under 26, could force some to detransition', *Vanity Fair*, 5 January 2023. www. vanityfair.com/news/2023/01/oklahoma-gender-affirming-care-ban-bill (accessed 11 January 2023).

22. C. Stroop, 'Florida Republican governor is attacking trans rights to gain power', *Open Democracy*, 4 August 2022. www.opendemocracy.net/en/5050/ florida-republican-governor-desantis-attack-trans-rights/ (accessed 11 January 2023).

23. A. Adu and R. Adams, 'Sex education review is "politically motivated", say teaching unions', *The Guardian*, 8 March 2023. www.theguardian.com/ education/2023/mar/08/sex-education-review-is-politically-motivated-say-teaching-unions (accessed 13 March 2023).

CHAPTER 10. GETTING CHRISTIANITY RIGHT

1. R. Gledhill, 'Clergymen who cross the line, *The Times*, 20 June 2000.

2. C. Burns, 'First to do harm', blog post, 10 July 2012. http://blog.plain-sense. co.uk/2012/07/first-do-no-harm.html (accessed 1 October 2022).

3. E. Sommers, 'Faith, gender and me: interview with a Christian crossdresser', Accepting Evangelicals, https://web.archive.org/web/20170712083052/http:// www.acceptingevangelicals.org/transgender/fgm1/ (archived from the original, accessed 18 August 2022).

4. OneBodyOneFaith, 'OneBodyOneFaith welcomes Accepting Evangelicals', 2021. www.onebodyonefaith.org.uk/news/1b1f-ae/ (accessed 18 August 2022).

5. M. Dark, 'Something to celebrate', The Evangelical Fellowship for Lesbian and Gay Christians, 26 April 2004. https://web.archive.org/web/20160302104000/ http://www.eflgc.org.uk/something-to-celebrate/ (archived from the original, accessed 10 January 2023).

6. C. Beardsley, M. O'Brien and J. Woolley, 'Exploring the interplay: the Sibyls' "Gender, Sexuality and Spirituality" workshop', *Theology & Sexuality*, vol. 16, no. 3, 2010, p. 264. https://doi.org/10.1558/tse.v16i3.259

7. D. J. Lee, *Rescuing Jesus: how people of colour, women & queer Christians are reclaiming evangelicalism* (Boston, MA: Beacon Press, 2015), pp. 131–69.

8. E. Thornton, 'Steve Chalke backs gay relationships', *Church Times*, 18 January 2013. www.churchtimes.co.uk/articles/2013/18-january/news/uk/steve-chalke-backs-gay-relationships (accessed 10 January 2023).

9. S. E. Zylstra, 'Major ministry kicked out of Evangelical Alliance UK over homosexuality stance', *Christianity Today*, 5 May 2014. www.christianitytoday. com/news/2014/may/major-ministry-kicked-out-evangelical-alliance-chalke-oasis.html (accessed 10 January 2023).

10. 'Steve Chalke to host church "renaming ceremony" for transgender man', *Premier Christian News*, 30 October 2016. https://premierchristian.news/en/ news/article/steve-chalke-to-host-church-renaming-ceremony-for-transgender-man (accessed 10 January 2023).

11. J. Ozanne, 'LGBT stories – can conservative evangelical churches ever change?', *ViaMedia*, 7 July 2021. https://viamedia.news/2021/07/07/lgbt-stories-can-conservative-evangelical-churches-ever-change/?amp (accessed 2 September 2022).

12. D. P. Gushee, *Changing our mind: a call from America's leading evangelical ethics scholar for full acceptance of LGBT Christians in the church* (Ann Arbor, MI: Read The Spirit Books, 2014).

13. D. P. Gushee, *Still Christian: following Jesus out of American evangelicalism* (Louisville, KY: Westminster John Knox Press, 2017).

14. J. Leonard, 'Leaving the Vineyard: an evangelical congregation splits over gay rights', *Ann Arbor Observer*, 31 December 2015. https://annarborobserver. com/leaving-the-vineyard/ (accessed 10 January 2023).

15. Lee, *Rescuing Jesus*, p. 263.

16. S. Rayment, 'The vicar wears a dress in church so why can't I?', *Daily Express*, 23 November 1997.

17. K. Tiller, 'Ministry update', Parakaleo Ministry, 2001. https://web.archive.org/ web/20010309183508fw_/http:/www.parakaleo.co.uk/keitht.html (archived from the original, accessed 18 August 2022).

18. D. Batty, 'Mistaken identity', *The Guardian*, 31 July 2004. www.theguardian. com/society/2004/jul/31/health.socialcare (accessed 12 August 2022).

19. Burns, *Pressing matters*, loc. 3949.

20. K. Tiller, 'Transsexualism: some considerations to assist church leaders who encounter transsexual people', Evangelical Alliance, 2003. https://web.archive. org/web/20030422234653/http://www.eauk.org/CONTENTMANAGER/

Content/PoliticsandSociety/currentissues/Transexual2.cfm (archived from the original, accessed 18 August 2022).

21. S. Cornwall, '"State of mind" versus "concrete set of facts": the contrasting of transgender and intersex in church documents on sexuality', *Theology and Sexuality*, vol. 15, no. 1, 2009, pp. 19–20. https://doi.org/10.1558/tse.v15i1.7

22. P. Lynas, 'Why I wrote Transformed', Evangelical Alliance, 29 November 2018. www.eauk.org/news-and-views/why-i-wrote-transformed (accessed 18 August 2022).

23. L Scanzoni and N. Hardesty, *All we're meant to be: a biblical approach to women's liberation* (Waco, TX: Word Books, 1974), p. 204.

24. R. Mann, *Dazzling darkness: gender, sexuality, illness & God* (Glasgow: Wild Goose Publications, 2012), p. 124.

25. R. T. Kendall, *The sermon on the mount* (Oxford: Monarch Books, 2011), p. 24.

26. J. Hulme, *The backwater sermons* (London: Canterbury Press, 2021), p. 90.

27. D. Ortlund, *Gentle and lowly: the heart of Christ for sinners and sufferers* (Wheaton, IL: Crossway, 2020), pp. 51–8.

28. Robinson-Brown, *Black, gay, British, Christian, queer*, pp. 1–12.

29. C. Bell, *Queer holiness: the gift of LGBTQI people to the church* (London: Darton, Longman and Todd, 2022), p. 32.

30. BFoundAPen, 'As a Black trans man, walking into church can cause me harm', *LEVEL*, 14 August 2019. https://level.medium.com/facing-christianity-as-a-black-trans-man-de333061ddbf (accessed 24 March 2023).

31. W. Wallace, 'Clerics approve of sex-change operation', *Baltimore Sun*, 23 November 1966.

32. Transgender Archives, Victoria, University of Ulster TGA collection, 2014-020, 9.63, Janus Information Facility, *Religious aspects of transsexualism* (Galveston, TX: University of Texas Medical Branch, 1978), p. 14.

33. J. Scarborough, 'Sex-change surgery banned at Southern Baptist hospital', *Independent Press-Telegram*, 15 October 1977.

34. J. Dawson, *What the T? The no-nonsense guide to all things trans and/or non-binary for teens* (London: Wren & Rook, 2021).

35. C. Beardsley and M. O'Brien (eds.), *This is my body: hearing the theology of transgender Christians* (London: Darton, Longman and Todd, 2016).

36. R. Hunt (ed.), *The book of queer prophets: 24 writers on sexuality and religion* (London: HarperCollins UK, 2020).

37. V. Turner, *Young, woke and Christian: words from a missing generation* (London: SCM Press, 2022), ch. 7.

38. A. Clare-Young, *Transgender. Christian. Human.* (Glasgow: Wild Goose Publications, 2019).

39. A. Hartke, *Transforming: the Bible and the lives of transgender Christians* (Louisville, KY: Westminster John Knox Press, 2018).

40. C. Beardsley and C. Dowd, *Trans affirming churches: how to celebrate gender-variant people and their loved ones* (London: Jessica Kingsley Publishers, 2020).

41. E. Kegler, *One coin found: how God's love stretches to the margins* (Minneapolis, MN: Fortress Press, 2019), pp. 8–9.

Index